Neylan McBaine, author of *Pioneering*
The Untold Story of Suffrage in Utah

This collection is, first and foremost, a trove of insight and inspiration from some of the Church's greatest scholars of our day. The illustrious gathering of global thinkers with impressive degrees demonstrates that faithful disciples of Christ can be multidimensional and that wrestling with complexity can lead to stronger testimonies. That the contributors happen to all be women marks a new frontier in our communal education: men can now be expected to gain as much from our greatest female voices as women have been expected to gain from male voices.

Jonathan A. Stapley, author of *The Power of Godliness: Mormon Liturgy and Cosmology*

Our lives are complicated—every one. What is planted as simple often grows in unexpected ways. *Every Needful Thing* demonstrates that growth can be variously inspiring, beautiful, and heartbreaking. It also demonstrates how growth can be deeply faithful. This collection of essays is for everyone, but the burgeoning student will find a particular value: generous and diverse examples of women constructively navigating scholarship, faith, and profession. Take note and learn from the best of our worldwide community.

Renata Forste, International Vice President, Brigham Young University-Provo

Each essay is unique in how it integrates faith and academic practice—just as the life experiences of each individual is unique. I think that is one of the strengths of the book. Some focus more on their personal life journey to the gospel and to their discipline. Others focus on what they have learned as an academic and how it informs their faith or helps them integrate faith and intellect as they grapple with hard questions. They draw on their faith both in terms of spiritual strength and intellectual success.

Laurel Thatcher Ulrich, 300th Anniversary University Professor emerita, Harvard University

Thoughtful and educated readers will enjoy these essays. The emphases on career choice, navigating religious and secular learning, and living comfortably in a plural environment may be especially appealing to young adults, but they should also be helpful to anyone interested in what it means to be part of a global church.

Adam S. Miller, author of *Original Grace: An Experiment in Restoration Thinking*

The voices gathered here—smart, strong, honest, charitable—prove that every voice is needed. They demonstrate our ongoing need to keep enrolling new students in the Restoration's ever-expanding "school of the prophets," fostering a global cadre of alumni who can speak from diverse perspectives and embody a deep cross section of faith. Hearing these voices is inseparable from the work of searching for God.

Katherine Kitterman, author of *Thinking Women: A Timeline of Suffrage in Utah*

This collection feels rich and welcoming, bringing the reader into a vibrant community of disciples who feel and think deeply. I think many young adult readers will feel as I did—that the contributors are a much-needed virtual circle of mentors, role models, friends, and sisters in the gospel. Their dedication to their disciplines and to the gospel encourages me to pursue truth and excellence as well.

Patrick Q. Mason, author of *Restoration: God's Call to the 21st-Century World*

This book is full of profound witnesses by Latter-day Saint women who have dedicated their lives to expanding their capacities both "by study and also by faith." These are serious people worth paying serious attention to. If you're looking to have a little more faith—in God, in humanity, in the gospel, in the ability to live meaningfully with complexity—here are words of wisdom for you.

Every Needful Thing

A
Living Faith
Book

Living Faith books are for readers who cherish the life of the mind and the things of the Spirit. Each title offers an example of faith in search of understanding, the unique voice of a practicing scholar who has cultivated a believing heart.

OTHER LIVING FAITH BOOKS INCLUDE:

Samuel M. Brown, *First Principles and Ordinances: The Fourth Article of Faith in Light of the Temple*

Samuel M. Brown, *Where the Soul Hungers: One Doctor's Journey from Atheism to Faith*

James E. Faulconer, *Thinking Otherwise: Theological Explorations of Joseph Smith's Revelations*

Terryl L. Givens, *The Doors of Faith*

George B. Handley, *The Hope of Nature: Our Care for God's Creation*

George B. Handley, *If Truth Were a Child*

Ashley Mae Hoiland, *One Hundred Birds Taught Me to Fly: The Art of Seeking God*

Melissa Wei-Tsing Inouye, *Crossings: A Bald Asian American Latter-day Saint Woman Scholar's Ventures through Life, Death, Cancer & Motherhood (Not Necessarily in That Order)*

Charles Shirō Inouye, *Zion Earth Zen Sky*

Patrick Q. Mason, *Planted: Belief and Belonging in an Age of Doubt*

Patrick Q. Mason and J. David Pulsipher, *Proclaim Peace: The Restoration's Answer to an Age of Conflict*

Adam S. Miller, *Letters to a Young Mormon* (2nd ed.)

Steven L. Peck, *Evolving Faith: Wanderings of a Mormon Biologist*

Thomas F. Rogers, *Let Your Hearts and Minds Expand: Reflections on Faith, Reason, Charity, and Beauty*

Matthew Wickman, *Life to the Whole Being: The Spiritual Memoir of a Literature Professor*

Every Needful Thing

ESSAYS

ON THE LIFE OF THE MIND

AND THE HEART

Edited by

Melissa Wei-Tsing Inouye

&

Kate Holbrook

BYU
Maxwell
Institute

This book is the result of a joint publishing effort by the
Neal A. Maxwell Institute for Religious Scholarship and
Deseret Book Company.

The paper used in this publication meets the minimum
requirements of the American National Standards for Information
Sciences—Permanence of Paper for Printed Library Materials.
ANSI Z39.48-19

ISBN: 978-1-63993-126-2

Library of Congress Control Number: 2022943901

(CIP data on file)

Cover Design: Heather Ward

Cover Art: Melissa Tshikamba

Book Design: Kachergis Book Design

Printed in the United States of America

Organize yourselves;
prepare every needful thing;
and establish a house,
even a house of prayer,
a house of fasting,
a house of faith,
a house of learning,
a house of glory,
a house of order,
a house of God.

DOCTRINE AND COVENANTS 88:119

To our children,
and to the rising
generation.

TABLE OF CONTENTS

PART TWO

In theory, in principle, in doctrine, in the law of the gospel, . . . of things both in heaven and in the earth, and under the earth

PART THREE

Things which have been, things which are, things which must shortly come to pass; things which are at home, things which are abroad

PART FOUR

The wars and the perplexities of the nations, and the judgments which are on the land

PART FIVE

A knowledge also of countries and of kingdoms—
that ye may be prepared in all things when
I shall send you again to magnify the calling
whereunto I have called you

ACKNOWLEDGMENTS

The coeditors would like to acknowledge the many people who worked to bring this book into being. Spencer Fluhman, executive director of the Maxwell Institute, supported the project from the beginning. Miranda Wilcox and Morgan Davis, coeditors of the Living Faith series, also championed the book. They tirelessly read, commented, and made suggestions for improvement. Editors Lori Forsyth and Jessica Mitton lovingly worked through the prose, clarifying and correcting. Peer reviewers generously contributed time and insight to detailed reports, making suggestions that immeasurably improved the book's framing and content. We express gratitude to Anne Kachergis and Rebecca Schreiber for designing the interior of the book, to Tessa Hauglid for indexing, to Heather Ward for designing the book cover, and to Melissa Tshikampabo Kamba for creating the lovely artwork on the cover. Morgan Davis, Lori Forsyth, Lorena Ortiz, and Jorge Morales helped with Spanish language translation and communication. Gabriel Saez reached out through the network of Latter-day Saint professionals in South America to help us find contributors. In this process, we also relied on work already done by Ryan Saltzgiver and the Global Histories team at the Church History Department to identify and capture the stories of extraordinary Latter-day Saints around the world. We are grateful to colleagues at the Church History Department of The Church of Jesus Christ of Latter-day Saints for their support of our work. Finally, but most of all, we would like to thank our families for their loving support and persistent vitality.

CONTRIBUTORS

LANEY MCCLAIN ARMSTRONG

DMA, University of Washington (2013); Director of Choral Studies, San Francisco Girls Chorus

EMILY BATES

PhD, Harvard Medical School (2005); Associate Professor, Department of Pediatrics, University of Colorado Anschutz Medical Campus

MARION BISHOP

MD, University of Utah (2004); PhD, New York University (1998); Private Practice Emergency Medicine Physician

CARRIEANNE SIMONINI DELOACH

PhD, Rice University (2021); Veteran Medical Service Corps Officer, 101st Airborne (AIR ASSAULT) Division, United States Army; CEO, Cheeky Muse Vintage

LISA GROW

JD, Harvard Law School (1997); Howard W. Hunter Professor of Law, J. Reuben Clark Law School, Brigham Young University

ELIZABETH HAMMOND

MD, University of Utah (1967); Professor of Pathology and Adjunct Professor of Internal Medicine (Cardiology), University of Utah School of Medicine

TONA HANGEN

PhD, Brandeis University (1999); Professor of History at Worcester State University

KEAKAOKAWAI VARNER HEMI

PhD, Te Piringa–Faculty of Law, University of Waikato (2016); Lecturer and Assistant Vice Chancellor Pacific, University of Waikato

KATE HOLBROOK

PhD, Boston University (2014); Academic Outreach Director, Church History Department of The Church of Jesus Christ of Latter-day Saints

VALERIE M. HUDSON

PhD, Ohio State University (1983); University Distinguished Professor and Holder of the George H.W. Bush Chair, Department of International Affairs, Texas A&M University

ESOHE FRANCES IKPONMWEN

LL.B (HONS), University of Nigeria (1974/1978); Fellow of the Commonwealth Judicial Education Institute; Emeritus Chief Judge, Edo State

MELISSA WEI-TSING INOUYE

PhD, Harvard University (2011); Senior Lecturer in Asian Studies, University of Auckland; Historian, Church History Department of The Church of Jesus Christ of Latter-day Saints

FARINA KING

PhD, Arizona State University (2016); Horizon Chair in Native American Ecology and Culture and Associate Professor of Native American Studies, University of Oklahoma

KYRA N. KRAKOS

PhD, Washington University in St. Louis (2011); Professor of Biology, Maryville University; Research Associate, Missouri Botanical Garden

NOEMÍ LUBOMIRSKY

PhD, University of La Plata (2017); Adjunct Professor, University of La Plata

JENNY HALE PULSIPHER

PhD, Brandeis University (1999); Professor of History, Brigham Young University

TANYA WENDT SAMU

PhD, University of Canterbury (2013); Senior Lecturer in Education, University of Auckland

ARIEL CLARK SILVER

PhD, Claremont Graduate University (2011); President-Elect, Nathaniel Hawthorne Society; Independent Scholar

MICHALYN STEELE

JD, Georgetown University Law Center (2001); Marion G. Romney Professor of Law, J. Reuben Clark Law School, Brigham Young University

KIMBERLY APPLEWHITE TEITTER

PsyD, Yeshiva University (2015); Postdoctoral Fellow, Boston Children's Hospital Division of Adolescent Medicine/Harvard Medical School; Licensed Psychologist and Adjunct Instructor, University of Utah

ASTRID S. TUMINEZ

PhD, Massachusetts Institute of Technology (1996); President, Utah Valley University

ANA MARÍA GUTIÉRREZ VALDIVIA

MD, PhD, Universidad Nacional de San Agustín (2013); Former Academic Vice Chancellor, Universidad Nacional de San Agustín

ROSALYNDE FRANDSEN WELCH

PhD, University of California at San Diego (2004); Senior Research Fellow, Neal A. Maxwell Institute for Religious Scholarship, Brigham Young University

JULIE BARROTT WILLIS

PhD, University of Utah (2010); Professor of Geology and Associate Dean, Brigham Young University–Idaho

CONNIE XIAOHUA ZHANG

MBA, Harvard Business School (2002); CEO, Riley River Consultants

Every Needful Thing

Introduction

MELISSA WEI-TSING INOUYE

& KATE HOLBROOK

Melissa Wei-Tsing Inouye is the fourth-generation descendant of immigrants to the United States from Kaiping, China, and Fukuoka, Japan. She was raised in Southern California and received AB and PhD degrees from Harvard University. She is a senior lecturer in Asian studies at the University of Auckland and a historian at the Church History Department of The Church of Jesus Christ of Latter-day Saints. She is the author of China and the True Jesus: Charisma and Organization in a Chinese Christian Church *(Oxford 2019) and* Crossings: A Bald Asian American Latter-day Saint Woman Scholar's Ventures through Life, Death, Cancer & Motherhood (Not Necessarily in That Order) *(Deseret Book 2019). She enjoys hiking and digging in the dirt with her husband, four children, and Labrador-cattle dog cross, Bertie.*

Kate Holbrook has a BA from Brigham Young University, an MTS from Harvard Divinity School, and a PhD from Boston University. She is the Academic Outreach Director at the Church History Department of The Church of Jesus Christ of Latter-day Saints, where she focuses on women's history.

Kate's books include The First Fifty Years of Relief Society: Key Documents in Latter-day Saint Women's History, Women and Mormonism: Historical and Contemporary Perspectives, *and* At the Pulpit: 185 Years of Discourses by Latter-day Saint Women. *She enjoys reading, cooking, gardening, and taking walks with her husband and three children.*

IN DECEMBER 1832, only two years into the institutional life of the fledgling "Church of Christ," Joseph Smith Jr. received a revelation.[1] The Lord wanted him to establish a school. As we read in Doctrine and Covenants 88:78–80, this school was not to be a place for religious learning only but a place for seeking a wide range of secular knowledge: science, history, current events, domestic and foreign affairs, geopolitics, culture, geography.

> Teach ye diligently and my grace shall attend you, that you may be instructed more perfectly in theory, in principle, in doctrine, in the law of the gospel, in all things that pertain unto the kingdom of God, that are expedient for you to understand;
>
> Of things both in heaven and in the earth, and under the earth; things which have been, things which are, things which must shortly come to pass; things which are at home, things which are abroad; the wars and the perplexities of the nations, and the judgments which are on the land; and a knowledge also of countries and of kingdoms—
>
> That ye may be prepared in all things when I shall send you again to magnify the calling whereunto I have called you, and the mission with which I have commissioned you.

Once the "School of the Prophets" was underway, students also learned languages, including Hebrew but also English. Joseph Smith and most of the other Church elders who attended the school had

1. Doctrine and Covenants 88.

grown up in poor families and had little education—as Joseph put it, "mearly instructtid in reading and writing and the ground rules of Arithmatic." On several occasions, Joseph went home to his family in the evenings and taught them the same grammar lesson he had learned that day in the School of the Prophets.[2]

The homely image of the Prophet Joseph earnestly rehearsing his English grammar lesson with family members suggests he felt learning was something to be cherished and shared. Joseph Smith's theological teachings and practical sensibilities expanded into each other. He taught that mortal beings and the Creator of the universe exist on the same continuum and that human beings are both eternally existent intelligences and children of a divine Heavenly Mother and Heavenly Father.[3] The all-powerful Creator Gods did not originate matter but merely organized it and prepared it to bring forth dynamic life, including human beings created in their image. These Gods were not completely impervious to human actions but could even be moved to weep by their children's wickedness.[4] Smith introduced Hebrew Bible institutions into antebellum North America and founded a sacred community at the edge of the frontier that was multiracial and multinational in character.[5]

2. Nathan Waite, "A School and an Endowment," in *Revelations in Context*, ed. Matthew McBride and James Goldberg (Salt Lake City, UT: The Church of Jesus Christ of Latter-day Saints, 2016), https://www.churchofjesuschrist.org/study/manual/revelations-in-context/a-school-and-an-endowment?lang=eng.

3. "Discourse, 7 April 1844, as Reported by Times and Seasons," p. 612, The Joseph Smith Papers, https://www.josephsmithpapers.org/paper-summary/discourse-7-april-1844-as-reported-by-times-and-seasons/1; "The Church of Jesus Christ of Latter-day Saints teaches that all human beings, male and female, are beloved spirit children of heavenly parents, a Heavenly Father and a Heavenly Mother. This understanding is rooted in scriptural and prophetic teachings about the nature of God, our relationship to Deity, and the godly potential of men and women. The doctrine of a Heavenly Mother is a cherished and distinctive belief among Latter-day Saints." "Mother in Heaven," Gospel Topics, https://www.churchofjesuschrist.org/study/manual/gospel-topics-essays/mother-in-heaven?lang=eng.

4. Abraham 3:22–4:18; Moses 7:28–33.

5. "Race and the Priesthood," Gospel Topics, https://www.churchofjesuschrist.org/study/manual/gospel-topics-essays/race-and-the-priesthood?lang=eng; Paul Reeve, *Religion of a*

Section 88 included not only a revelation on establishing a school but also a directive to build "a house of God" that, in 1836, was dedicated as the Kirtland Temple. This sacred space was more than just a shrine where God could dwell. It was also a place where the Saints could do all kinds of godly work, including prayer, fasting, and learning the alphabet.[6] After it was dedicated, both the School of the Prophets and its offshoot, the Hebrew School, held their meetings in the Kirtland Temple.[7]

In the context of these commandments to establish a school and build a temple—a joint intellectual and spiritual venture—we find the expansive scriptural injunction that gives this book its name:

> And as all have not faith, seek ye diligently and teach one another words of wisdom; yea, seek ye out of the best books words of wisdom; seek learning, even by study and also by faith.
>
> Organize yourselves; prepare *every needful thing*; and establish a house, even a house of prayer, a house of fasting, a house of faith, a house of learning, a house of glory, a house of order, a house of God. (emphasis added)[8]

This book gathers together perspectives from scholars and professionals who demonstrate a multidimensional and characteristically Latter-day Saint approach to sacred endeavor. Attending to "every needful thing" can include wrestling with longstanding questions, walking through a meadow, reading scripture, and singing with children. Instead of confining ourselves to artificial dichotomies forcing choices between faith or reason, the past or the future, work in the home or in the community, love or law, truth within the restored gospel or in the wide world of all human experience, we must unflinchingly seek

---

Different Color: Race and the Mormon Struggle for Whiteness (New York: Oxford University Press, 2015); Julie Allen, *Danish but Not Lutheran: The Impact of Mormonism on Danish Cultural Identity, 1850–1920* (Salt Lake City, UT: University of Utah Press, 2017); Quincy Newell, *Your Sister in the Gospel: The Life of Jane Manning James* (New York: Oxford University Press, 2019).

6. Doctrine and Covenants 88:119.

7. "House of the Lord, Kirtland Township, Ohio" (place entry), The Joseph Smith Papers, https://www.josephsmithpapers.org/place/house-of-the-lord-kirtland-township-ohio.

8. Doctrine and Covenants 88:118–119.

"anything virtuous, lovely, or of good report" and learn to flourish in a world of complexity and abundance.[9]

The inclusivity of gathering "every needful thing" brings challenges. How can our limited time and energy stretch to address life's many pressing needs? How do we know we've accounted for everything within our stewardship while still preserving moments of stillness? How can we fearlessly follow reason, logic, and the pursuit of evidence along a path to truth? How can we have the courage to maintain a knowledge of things not seen?

These essays narrate journeys through challenging terrain. In many cases, authors explain how their faith led them to scientific breakthroughs, professional success, and new insights into the human story. At other times, disciplinary perspectives compelled scholars to measure and test their beliefs, along the lines of the prophet Alma's "experiment" to discern what is real.[10] Their faith, along with their research and professional achievements, is hard won. But because it has been tested not only through life's hard knocks but also through the rigor of their own critical faculties, it is resilient, mature, and generous.

The polyphony of voices in this collection is a rare gift. Not only particular fields of knowledge but also distinctive ways of thinking, writing, and expressing themselves come through as these scholar-disciples from different backgrounds introduce us to how they investigate the world and cultivate faith. The writers are all accomplished academics or professionals who have made significant contributions within a single discipline (a research paper, a legal ruling, a mathematical proof, a book, etc.). While earning an advanced degree or becoming a professional scholar is not the only way to succeed in life, we suggest the members of this group have particular perspectives and sets of challenges that reward examination. This is especially true because here they speak not only with their minds but also from their hearts, drawing on their life experiences and cultural heritage. These scholars are all skilled teachers. In this role, they have worked to make their

9. Article of Faith 13.

10. Alma 32:27, 35.

insights accessible and have also challenged readers to exert the effort required to learn from their distinctive positionality, epistemology, and values.

This accomplished group claims a diversity of cultural backgrounds, citizenships, native tongues, and personal circumstances. Voices from the Philippines, Samoa, Aotearoa New Zealand, Peru, Argentina, Nigeria, the People's Republic of China, the Seneca and Navajo Nations, Hawai'i, and the continental United States speak of the Latter-day Saints as a global people. By recentering this scholarly conversation to include many experiences of those who are Black, Indigenous, people of color, or who reside outside of North America, we hope to reflect "Latter-day Saint thought" more accurately than projects with a much narrower conception of who the Latter-day Saints are.

Many will also notice that this volume's editors and authors are all women. This circumstance ought to be unremarkable, but we concede that it is not. For too long, the top tiers of professions and also nearly all the shelves of Latter-day Saint "gospel libraries" have been mostly a male-only domain. This volume shows that women's voices are as needful in faith conversations as they are in law, medicine, business, and the academy. This foray into the territory of published gospel scholarship proves the indispensability of women's voices and authority in the ongoing Restoration.

Of course, countless Latter-day Saint women, though they did not choose a professional path, have dedicated their lives to cultivating wisdom and skill and have shared their gifts with their families, communities, and the wider world. We wish to acknowledge that Latter-day Saint women in different generations and regions have experienced different opportunities and expectations with regard to life choices and that these generational and global gaps can be a source of pain. One of our aims of this book project was to establish a large net for belonging and include some of the diverse voices that haven't adequately been included in similar projects. But then to promote a sense of continuity among the essays, we established criteria for contributors that may make a new group feel that they don't belong.

We sincerely hope that readers (male, female, of varying ages, and with different education and professional backgrounds) will see the commonalties that can foster belonging in the context of this book. In our own experiences with belonging and not belonging, we've come to see belonging as being a choice both on the part of the group and the individual. There are groups that just won't let us belong, full stop. But there are also times when we can choose to belong even when all aspects of the group aren't fortuitous. Many Church members, including some contributors to this book, have set us an example of making this good and hard choice. We hope all can rejoice in our sisters, daughters, and friends whose varied circumstances and desires have moved them to achieve in the professional world and to gain increased capacity for the work of building Zion. Such work benefits us all.

These essays are held together by the wonderfully encompassing language of the revelation in Doctrine and Covenants 88:78–80. This passage of Section 88 sets out a menu of all kinds of godly knowledge that will set a person on the path toward becoming more like our Mother and Father in Heaven. We have used these categories to group contributions. First, with "my grace shall attend you, that you may be instructed more perfectly," we introduce scholars who testify how spiritual gifts have helped them make intellectual discoveries and teach with inspiration. Second, the section "in theory, in principle, in doctrine, in the law of the gospel, ... of things both in heaven and in the earth, and under the earth" gathers scholars in the sciences, including a botanist, a psychologist, a geologist, and a mathematician. A third section on "things which have been, things which are, things which must shortly come to pass; things which are at home, things which are abroad" features historians. The fourth section, "the wars and the perplexities of the nations, and the judgments which are on the land," contains insights from those who deal with trauma and conflict: an emergency room doctor whose career was inspired by Mormon, the soldier-historian; two legal scholars; and the judge of a high court. Finally, in the fifth and final section, "a knowledge also of countries and of kingdoms—that ye may be prepared in all things when I shall send you again to magnify the calling whereunto I have called you," we meet scholars who cross national and cultural boundaries as they answer the Spirit's call to serve and understand their fellow beings.

All of the contributors—while plainly acknowledging their shortcomings, the default of imperfection, and their ongoing need for grace—exemplify this passage's broad and fearless exhortation to learn, teach, and endeavor. They have served in the armed forces while in graduate school, tended small children while performing cutting-edge research, and broken new intellectual ground by drawing on knowledge and values embedded in their own cultures and family histories. They model how to think and how to be, how to analyze something up close and how to see the big picture. With this holism in mind, why should we silo ourselves into one narrow disciplinary or epistemological mindset when, as Joseph Smith taught, the diligent pursuit of intelligence of all kinds will enrich God's children eternally?[11]

Contributors recount numerous shared challenges, such as disillusionment when Church members behaved uncharitably; disorientation trying to satisfy Church, family, and professional obligations; and resilience in pursuing "every needful thing." Chieko Nishimura Okazaki—a teacher, school principal, and beloved Latter-day Saint general leader—taught, "Be spiritually independent enough that your relationship with the Savior doesn't depend on your circumstances or on what other people say and do."[12] In explaining how their faith functions in the midst of messy human relationships, the book's authors model this independence. Faith is a commitment. While a lifeline, faith also complicates life. But we as editors add our voices to those in this volume who say that of life's needful things, faith is a rewarding one.

As editors, we envisioned this book as particularly useful for Latter-day Saints navigating the vortex of young adulthood. We hope readers beginning life's educational and vocational journeys in earnest will find gems of wisdom in these compelling essays, which are not only about *what* to learn but *how*. Just as Joseph Smith organized instruction for

11. Doctrine and Covenants 130:18–19.

12. Chieko N. Okazaki, *Lighten Up* (Salt Lake City, UT: Deseret Book, 1993), 99.

the whole person in the School of the Prophets, these accounts offer guidance for navigating the challenging but rewarding terrain where all kinds of useful work takes place, including the work of faith. Here are teachers, mentors, and models. With humility and candor that belie their significant accomplishments, these authors relate the twists and turns of their intellectual and spiritual journeys, giving readers confidence to make their own ways and pursue every needful thing.

PART ONE

My grace shall attend you, that you may be instructed more perfectly

(Doctrine and Covenants 88:78)

Grace is divine love that transforms people by opening them up to God's presence and possibilities.

God's grace opens scholars up to the possibilities of new understanding—in themselves and in those they teach.

Solid and Whole in a Messy Universe

ASTRID S. TUMINEZ

Astrid S. Tuminez was born in a farming village in the Philippines and grew up in the slums of Iloilo City. She was educated by Catholic nuns and teachers as a child and later received a bachelor's degree in international relations from Brigham Young University, a master's degree in Soviet studies from Harvard, and a PhD in political science from the Massachusetts Institute of Technology. She is the author of Russian Nationalism Since 1856: Ideology and the Making of Foreign Policy *and* Rising to the Top? A Report on Women's Leadership in Asia, *as well as many other publications. She loves to travel, read, dance, run, and spend time with her family and students at Utah Valley University, where she serves as president.*

I WAS EDUCATED by Catholic nuns. When I was five years old, sisters from the Daughters of Charity found me and my family in our hut in the slums of Iloilo City, Philippines. After talking to my mother and older siblings and deciding that we had some talent, the nuns offered us places for free at their expensive convent school. We said yes. As a young girl, I linked learning, leadership, and professional work with faith. I did not separate secular pursuits from my religion. My lessons in English, math, speech, biology, physics, and earth science—taught at the Colegio del Sagrado Corazon de Jesus—all melded with early morning mass, rosaries, confession, communion, Christian living lessons, and great reverence (bordering on fear!) for God and his servants. The nuns especially loomed large in my imagination. Draped in long, white habits with their waists encircled by long rosaries that dangled down the front and heads adorned in perfectly pressed wimples, they were God's angels and authority figures—scolding me, molding me, and teaching me to read, write, and dissect frogs.

When I was ten years old, I converted to The Church of Jesus Christ of Latter-day Saints. I began to look at faith as separate from secular learning and pursuits. I had to be *in* the world but not *of* the world. However, this dichotomy was difficult to sustain. My new beliefs actually powered up my desire to excel, do well in my studies, and explore the world and all that it had to offer. In my new faith, "whatever principle of intelligence [I attained] unto in this life, it [would] rise with [me] in the resurrection" (Doctrine and Covenants 130:18). The glory of God is intelligence, and intelligence is light and truth—with eternal consequences. I believed sincerely that my mortal life was about preparing to become like God. I read more books, got better grades, and became more ambitious. I read my scriptures diligently and prayed without ceasing. I wanted, on Judgment Day, to be one of those souls commended for unceasing work and achievement and, therefore, worthy of even greater opportunities. Progression was endless. I wanted to be knowledgeable and accomplished and also kind and good.

My formal education and career have enriched my faith by helping me see that goodness and the influences of the Holy Spirit are varied, vast, and profound. My education positioned me for a global professional experience that, in turn, shaped my faith. As a sixteen-year-old college student in the Philippines, I began learning Spanish, French, and Russian, adding these languages to the Ilonggo, Tagalog, and English that I already knew. Studying languages, literature, history, and politics gave me a foundation to appreciate my encounters with people whose ethnicity, religion, political persuasion, and life experiences were vastly different from my own. I have lived and worked in five different countries, traveled to many more, and worked across a range of industries. In my last job in Singapore, I oversaw government and legal affairs in fifteen countries. My global experiences helped me develop respect and empathy for God's many children. I realized that people connected with the divine and made sense of life and the world in diverse ways.

In the former Soviet Union, for example, where I first lived as a student in 1985, religion was severely restricted. But standing in one of Moscow's infamously long lines for goods that were perennially in short supply, I met my very first friends—young Russian women from the Baptist church. Attending church meant jeopardizing their social, political, and economic prospects in a communist society where religion was denigrated and practically outlawed. They could not talk about church while we rode the bus. They had to be very circumspect about being "believers." It was difficult to follow Christ openly. And yet, they persisted. They worshipped with joy. Their courage taught me about what it means to be a true disciple—one that was willing to sacrifice worldly respect, honor, and even safety for something of eternal worth.

After the Soviet Union disintegrated and ethnic tensions worsened, my senior ethnologist friends in Moscow invited the Dalai Lama to speak at a conference on conflict prevention. The Dalai Lama seemed to walk, speak, and move in complete hope, light, and joyfulness. That encounter sparked my initial curiosity to study Buddhism. Reading books on Buddhism, practicing meditation, and visiting Buddhist sacred places in Asia led me to discover new ways to interpret my own faith. The concepts of nonself and interbeing reminded me of the injunction "If ye are not one[,] ye are not mine" (Doctrine and Covenants 38:27). As humans, we are indeed more connected than disconnected, but we tend to fail in understanding the implications of oneness and connection. Learning about the practice of mindfulness and being present in the moment reminded me of the Sermon on the Mount: "Take therefore no thought for the morrow: for the morrow shall take thought for the things of itself. Sufficient unto the day is the evil thereof" (Matthew 6:34). The practice of meditation helped me reinterpret what Christ did in the mountain for forty days and forty nights. The emphasis on suffering as the central problem of the human condition reminded me that Jesus wept in the Gospel of John, that God wept in the book of Moses, and that the Savior understood the human condition best because he suffered it most.

One of the most interesting jobs I ever had was doing Track II diplomacy, or nongovernmental, informal peacemaking, in Mindanao in the southern Philippines. After 9/11, the presidents of the US and the Philippines met, with the former expressing concern that Al-Qaeda might have infiltrated the Moro Islamic Liberation Front, a group fighting for Muslim rights and autonomy in the Philippines. The US government then commissioned the US Institute of Peace, with the guidance of a group of former senior US diplomats, to get involved in the Philippines. I was one of two principals leading the project. I had been raised Catholic but was blind to my lack of Christian kindness and empathy toward Filipino Muslims when I was growing up. Pejoratively called Moros (for "Moors") by Spanish colonists in the sixteenth to nineteenth centuries, the Muslims of the Philippines had become a minority estranged in lands they used to rule. The Christian majority had denigrated their religion for a long time and excluded their story from history books. The term *Moro*, once pejorative, has since been reclaimed by Philippine Muslims as a legitimate term to signify their unique collective identity and history.

Widespread corruption, ignorance, and rapacious leadership meant many ordinary Muslims suffered from both intra- and inter-group violence, including an intermittent conflict with the government that had killed tens of thousands of people since the 1970s. Over the four years that I worked with Moro leaders, citizens, and young professionals, I learned to be "no more strangers" with those whose religion I had been told in childhood was alien and wrong. I learned to understand more deeply what it meant to weep with those who weep, mourn with those who mourn, and bind up the brokenhearted. I spent a considerable amount of time in remote villages, sometimes shedding tears as I witnessed the brokenness of children and families displaced from their homes and farms after fleeing from battle. I learned to pray at dawn just as the Muslim prayers and chanting began in local mosques. I learned the greeting of peace and blessing (*Assalamu alaikum, warahmatullahi wabarakatuh*) that my Moro friends used, and I broke fast with them during their fasting month of Ramadan. My experiences with my Moro friends helped me understand the yearning that many people feel to connect with their own internal spiritual light, worship God, and recognize that which is holy in the universe. I came to appreciate better one of the Articles of Faith in my church, formalized in the claim that all should have the privilege of worshipping the "Almighty God according to the dictates of [their] own conscience" and should be able to worship "how, where, or what they may" (Article of Faith 11).

Besides academia and philanthropy, I also spent a decade in the corporate world, first on Wall Street doing venture capital and then in Asia as regional head of corporate, external, and legal affairs for Microsoft. These experiences influenced my faith by reminding me to be less judgmental and revealing that service to others can happen in any context. Having been trained in the humanities and social sciences, I was initially quite biased against business. I thought that corporate leaders cared only about money and had underdeveloped souls. But my stint in finance and technology introduced me to some of the most educated, innovative, and—yes—caring colleagues I have ever had. In venture capital, I met individuals whose education encompassed an MD, PhD, and MBA all at once. I met scientists whose discoveries held great promise to alleviate human illness and suffering. I was reminded that divine gifts manifest in many ways and that I had to repent of being so judgmental. Quite a few of the people I had previously judged as soulless actually had as much faith and soul as I. They were harnessing their gifts, time, and energy to build and create solutions for existing human needs. I had no need to idealize the business world, but neither did I need to judge it blindly. Christ, after all, did caution much about the perils of judging.

As a corporate leader, I wanted to care personally about my team while also expecting great accountability and results. When I conducted team retreats, I tried to balance routine business conversations with deeper explorations of common human struggles. After I left the corporate world to return to academia, I was surprised to get a note from someone who used to report to me. He had made a big life decision to quit his corporate job and move to Barcelona to be a full-time tennis coach to his daughters. He said, "I've decided that it was time to take a leap of faith.... You know the funny thing I discovered during this whole difficult process? The constant thing that always circles back to my decision was the well-being of the soul and spirit of the person and his family. I believe all of the spiritual workshops you organized for us have finally paid off in a big way." I did not realize that the corporate retreats I led were also "spiritual workshops." Then it dawned on me that my corporate work was, at the end of the day, also service. I had opportunities to directly influence the quality of life of my team and also leverage corporate resources to bring technology, education, and capital where they were needed. "Faith without works is dead" (James 2:20), and I was lucky that my work allowed me to inject life into my faith.

Finally, my education and professional pursuits have taught me to think more openly and embrace ambiguity while simultaneously grounding myself in a set of core principles that align with my conscience and life experiences. I have learned to welcome doubt without dismissing faith. I have learned that people outside of my faith live just as full, happy, and topsy-turvy a life as I do. I have learned to be solid in my own hope and faith while accepting that the world is wobbly and complex. I have learned that absolute certainty is less interesting than a humble openness to life's uncertain trials and gifts. My faith has needed to become less brittle, less prideful, less bigoted, less insecure, and *more* curious, joyful, open, and alive. My work has given me a broad exposure to ideas, people, industries, and cultures that has helped me understand the humility that Christian faith demands, as embodied in this quote from Aleksandr Solzhenitsyn (whom I read as a student of Russian literature) in *The Gulag Archipelago*: "If only there were evil people somewhere insidiously committing evil deeds, and it were necessary only to separate them from the rest of us and destroy them. But the line dividing good and evil cuts through the heart of every human being. And who is willing to destroy a piece of his own heart?"[1] I have become more sensitive to the many ways divine love and grace manifest in human life, strivings, and interactions. I have learned to embrace a life and a world whose complexities I don't fully grasp. I am more or less solid and whole in a messy and unpredictable—but ultimately also joyful and endlessly interesting—universe.

1. Aleksandr Isaevich Solzhenitsyn, *The Gulag Archipelago*, trans. Thomas P. Whitney (London: Collins & Harvill Press, 1974), 168.

The Two-Way Street of Faith and Scholarship

A Political Scientist's Experience

VALERIE M. HUDSON

Valerie M. Hudson is a University Distinguished Professor and holds the George H. W. Bush Chair in the Department of International Affairs of the Bush School of Government and Public Service at Texas A&M University, where she directs the Program on Women, Peace, and Security. Her research foci include foreign policy analysis, security studies, and gender and international relations. She is the author or editor of several books, including (with Andrea Den Boer) Bare Branches: The Security Implications of Asia's Surplus Male Population *(MIT Press 2004), which won the American Association of Publishers Award for the Best Book in Political Science. Hudson is a cofounder and principal investigator of the WomanStats Project (http://womanstats.org), which includes the largest compilation of data on the status of women in the world. Her latest book, with Donna Lee Bowen and Perpetua Lynne Nielsen, is* The First Political Order: How Sex Shapes Governance and National Security Worldwide, *which was published in 2020 with Columbia University Press. Hudson is the president of a nonprofit organization producing peer-reviewed research on cystic fibrosis and has been a La Leche League leader for over thirty-five years. She is married to David Cassler and is the mother of eight children.*

I NEVER ASPIRED to be a political scientist. As a child, I felt a great love for paleontology and pored over my books on fossils and dinosaurs until the pages were tattered all along the edges. Today, in my sixties, I still have a killer rock and mineral collection, my loupe, and my rock pick, but I never became a paleontologist. It was not for lack of trying—as a freshman at BYU, I declared geology as my major and spent that year going on field trips all across Utah to diagram rock formations and strata. Alas, it was not to be—maybe in the next life. In the meantime, I discovered you can buy some seriously exotic rocks on eBay if you know where to look.

No, I was fortunate enough to take two general education courses at BYU that altered my direction in life, one from Merlin Myers in anthropology and one from Ray Hillam in international relations. I discovered that people and the societies they build were much more interesting than rocks, which were typically only dynamic if one lived far longer than the average human being. With nations and peoples, on the other hand, a lively soap opera of change fixed my gaze. It was almost impossible to look away once I understood the players, their interests, and their histories.

From that detour as a young college student came an unexpected journey as a social science researcher. Much like Bilbo Baggins, I received an education I could never have foreseen, an education acquired through trying to answer good and important questions using social science techniques.

Foreign policy analysis

When I was studying international relations (IR) at both the undergraduate and graduate levels, most courses on the paradigms shaping the field omitted human agency as a variable of interest. Frameworks such as realism, neo-realism, liberalism, geopolitics, and so forth all took the nation-state as the fundamental unit of analysis. In doing so, explanatory variables were also of the human-less sort, such as national interest, balance of power, power capabilities distribution, and geography. Outcomes, too, tended to be defined at the most macro of levels, such as end states of war and peace. Large impersonal forces were blamed for large impersonal outcomes in the world system.

I found myself rebelling intellectually against this human-less construction of the world, and I think in large measure this rebellion stemmed from my belief in the restored gospel of Jesus Christ. This world was created by God to be a showcase for human agency. There is ample room, then, for creativity and learning, change and innovation. No soul is completely locked into its circumstances, unable to exercise any agency. Large impersonal forces actually boil down to small, very personal forces. That is why God is justified in judging every human soul according to that soul's desires, and that is why national leaders can be held accountable for the wars they cause.[1] Indeed, I was one of the cofounders of what was originally known as the LDS National Security Society, which seeks to integrate what we know of war and peace across the divide between religion and the academy.[2]

More expansively, I rebelled against the impersonality of IR theory by researching in and advocating for the IR subfield of foreign policy analysis (FPA). FPA takes as its unit of analysis not the nation-state but individuals acting singly and in groups in the realm of foreign policy. It examines the personalities and cognitions of leaders, of the small groups in which the most important decisions are made, and delves

1. Mark Henshaw, Valerie M. Hudson, Eric Jensen, Kerry M. Kartchner, and John Mark Mattox, "War and the Gospel: Perspectives from Latter-day Saint National Security Practitioners," *SquareTwo* 2, no. 2 (Summer 2009), http://squaretwo.org/Sq2ArticleHenshawNatSec.html.

2. The Society hosts a listserv and also held symposia in 1993, 2003, and 2013, and symposium proceedings of each were published; see, for example, *A Time of War, A Time of Peace: Latter-day Saint Ethics of War and Diplomacy* (Provo, UT: David M. Kennedy Center for International Studies, 2018). We hope for a symposium in 2023.

into the organizational process and bureaucratic politics of the executive branch, the domestic political contestation among the branches of government and the broader polity, the cultural background of those making decisions, and so forth. FPA is a radical vote for individual human agency in a world of structural explanations. In addition to writing many pieces in this field, I also penned a best-selling FPA textbook.[3]

The relevance of individual agency within structures is not restricted to international relations. After having spent over thirty-five years as a professor in both secular and faith-based universities, I can testify that which individual occupies which position in an institution does matter tremendously, that groupthink is real, that dysfunctional cultural norms such as passive-aggressiveness are readily observable and even predictable. Academic units jealously guard their turf, budgets, and essences.

With these understandings of human agency in place, I could better understand the Church of Jesus Christ. Many think of the Church as some monolithic structure within which all agree and all march in lockstep. That is simply not true. I came to understand that, at least below the highest levels of Church authority, there were bureaucratic politics, small group dynamics, cultures, and individual personality forces at work.

It could not be otherwise since those making decisions are fallible mortals bound by their culture's understandings. As Elder Jeffrey R. Holland has said, "Except in the case of his only perfect Begotten Son, imperfect people are all God has ever had to work with. That must be terribly frustrating to Him but He deals with it. So should we. And when you see imperfection, remember that the limitation is not in the divinity of the work."[4]

Because in my research I study these micro-levels of decision-

3. Valerie M. Hudson, *Foreign Policy Analysis: Classic and Contemporary Theory* (Lanham, MA: Rowman & Littlefield, 2007); the third edition is coauthored with Benjamin Day.

4. Elder Jeffrey R. Holland, "Lord, I Believe," *Church News*, April 7, 2013, https://www.thechurchnews.com/archives/2013-04-07/elder-jeffrey-r-holland-lord-i-believe-46398.

making, such as personality, perception, group dynamics, and culture, the fact that these forces are at work in the Church's bureaucracy has not dampened my testimony one whit. What it has done, however, is appropriately lower my expectations of Church institutional behavior. Using my FPA skills, I am able to see the fallible humans within Church institutions and the dysfunctional group decision-making that sometimes ensues. I honor the doctrine and revelations of the Church even as I recognize that many of the Church's policies and programs seeking to instantiate those doctrines and revelations have been created much like the proverbial sausage. In times of keen disappointment, I have consoled myself that the Lord does hold individuals accountable for how they carry out their work responsibilities and stewardships. However, because as a fallible mortal I am hoping for mercy from the Lord myself, I feel to forgive, for I have finally learned that this world was *meant* to be a messy, hurtful learning experience and was never meant to be a place run efficiently or justly. But my dearest hope is that there is such a Place.

Women and nations

Another focal point of intersection between the restored gospel of Jesus Christ and my work as a social scientist has been in the area of male-female relations. During my undergraduate and graduate training in international relations, there was virtually no mention of women at all, except perhaps for one or two famous women, such as Margaret Thatcher. The idea that women were literally half the world's population and had both important and unique experiences of war and peace and leadership was completely absent. There was no curiosity whatsoever; my professors painted a truly "womanless world" for their students and were content to do so. It goes without saying that all of my professors were male.

But life has a funny way of making you see what your professors do not teach you. As part of my financial strategy to get through school, I wound up in the 11th Special Forces Group as a wheeled vehicle and power generator mechanic. There, doing push-ups and running miles in combat boots alongside Vietnam vets who spent summer vacations as mercenaries in Rhodesia, I became intimately acquainted with masculinist ideologies.

These experiences opened my eyes. Though male scholars in my field of study thought of their insights as objective, I was beginning to discover they were actually infected by a deeply gendered mode of thinking. Our security doctrines were utterly male in conception and logic. I'll never forget one critical turning point in my career. I was at a political science conference in DC around the time the Cold War was ending. It was a panel on NATO strategy, and a male audience member wanted one of the (all-male) panelists to explain NATO's "follow-on-forces strategy." The young male panelist who rose answered blithely with an unintended double entendre that explicitly conflated sex and military strategy (and which, unfortunately, I cannot repeat here), whereupon I burst out laughing, could not stop, and had to leave the room.[5] The funny thing was not the double entendre itself but the young man's complete unawareness of it. That experience spurred me to realize that if we are locked into narrow masculinist thinking, we will never truly understand what is or what could be.

My first foray into researching the linkage between what was going on with women and what was going on with national and international security came in the 1990s when I was teaching a graduate methodology course as director of graduate studies at the David M. Kennedy Center for International Studies at BYU. We were reading a book that mentioned, in an offhand way, the work of historian Elizabeth Perry who had noted a relationship between female infanticide and the rise of rebel groups in historical China. That is, the worse the sex ratio within a given area of China, the more likely that area was to spawn rebel movements due to the sense of grievance experienced by the men who would never be able to form families because the girls who should have grown up to become their wives had been killed

5. Valerie M. Hudson, "But Now Can See: One Academic's Journey to Feminist Security Studies," *Politics & Gender* 7, no. 4 (December 2011): 586–90.

at birth. Knowing of the dreadfully skewed sex ratios of the People's Republic of China resulting from the one-child policy established in 1980, I began to wonder how secure even a modern nation could be if it culled 15 percent of girls from the birth population due to structural pressures such as cultural traditions, economic disincentives, and political coercion.[6] Because of my membership in the Church of Jesus Christ—which preaches that we have a Heavenly Mother as well as a Heavenly Father, that Eve did not sin but transgressed in the Garden of Eden, and that women and men stand as equals before God and before each other—I sincerely doubted whether such treatment of God's daughters could have salutary effects on a nation's security, given the wording of the Family Proclamation about "the calamities foretold by ancient and modern prophets" for, among other things, harming women.[7]

That hunch turned out to be correct. My coauthor Andrea Den Boer and I spent years investigating the effects of profoundly skewed sex ratios on national and regional security outcomes, resulting in the award-winning book, *Bare Branches: The Security Implications of Asia's Surplus Male Population*. Through this research, we demonstrated that the "womanless world" of my security studies professors was an inaccurate depiction incapable of analyzing—or even articulating—important security trends.[8]

From that initial effort came a broad research program developed under the WomanStats Project.[9] Our aim was to bring rigorous empirical evidence to bear on the proposition that when you subordinate, exploit, and harm women, you experience worse outcomes at the nation-state level. That this project originated at BYU still seems to me something very apropos, given the deep equality of women and men

6. This one-child policy was in place for decades, from 1980 to 2016.

7. "The Family: A Proclamation to the World," The Church of Jesus Christ of Latter-day Saints, 1995.

8. Valerie M. Hudson, "Why the Academy Needs Female Political Scientists: Examples from International Relations," *APSA 2011 Annual Meeting Paper* (2011); available at SSRN: https://ssrn.com/abstract=1902778.

9. WomanStats Project, http://womanstats.org.

before God as expressed in the restored gospel of Jesus Christ. In addition to creating an immense online database of information concerning women in 176 nations, we also conducted cutting-edge research on how the character of male-female relations within a society affects many different dimensions of national security, stability, and resilience. Most recently, this work was funded by the Minerva Initiative of the US Department of Defense, resulting in the tome *The First Political Order: How Sex Shapes Governance and National Security Worldwide*.[10]

Once again, this intersection had a dual directionality. As my research began showing beyond a doubt that nations where women are treated badly struggle to achieve stability and prosperity, I became convinced that my own faith community still labored somewhat under the shadow of that same struggle. There were continuing misconceptions and false traditions concerning women in the Church despite the revolutionary doctrine of the restored gospel of Jesus Christ. However, any church asserting that it is the true church of Christ has the absolute obligation to restore women to their rightful place as the full, equal partners of men in the plan of happiness, to restore Mother Eve to a position of respect and admiration, and to restore the principle of companionate marriage as the celestial ideal in emulation of our Heavenly Mother and Heavenly Father. I can only conclude, then, that the restored Church of Jesus Christ must undertake this work as an integral part of the Restoration, and I believe that work has begun in earnest.

As a result of these conclusions, I began to translate my research into the context of the Church, for example through the book *Women in Eternity, Women of Zion*, coauthored with the political philosopher and Church member Alma Don Sorensen.[11] I have been delighted to see this line of argument take root among orthodox members of the

10. Valerie M. Hudson, Donna Lee Bowen, and Perpetua Lynne Nielsen, *The First Political Order: How Sex Shapes Governance and National Security Worldwide* (New York: Columbia University Press, 2020).

11. Valerie Hudson Cassler and Alma Don Sorenson, *Women in Eternity, Women of Zion* (Springville, UT: Cedar Fort, 2004).

Church,[12] as well as to see forward movement in Church policies and programs so that Church doctrine more fully matches Church practice. I remain an active commentator on these matters in our faith community's public square.[13]

Conclusion

There are many other things in and of this world that also fascinate me, such as the radical discretization of matter. But I understand that some work may have to take place after this life: mortality focuses the mind wonderfully, and I am now in my sixties. When I was an undergraduate at BYU, I taped on my wall a Latin invocation from Danish astronomer Tycho Brahe, who uttered these words in his dying breath in 1601: "*Ne frustra vixisse videar.*" Translated, it means, "Let me not seem to have lived in vain." I suppose I was drawn to that saying in my youth as a measure I could one day use at the end of my life to gauge my feelings about my time here on earth. Though the most important part of my life's work revolves around my family and children, I am deeply grateful to God for granting me professional work that satisfies both my intellectual and my spiritual curiosity. I feel happy that political science has strengthened and informed my testimony. At the same time, my understanding of the restored gospel of Jesus Christ has prompted meaningful questions in my field of study, and my relationship with God has provided the grace, the strength, and the means necessary to pursue answers. It's been a wonderful life as a female Latter-day Saint political scientist—I could not have asked for a better "unexpected journey."

12. See, for example, Joseph M. Spencer, *First Nephi: a brief theological introduction* (Provo, UT: Neal A. Maxwell Institute, 2020), 100–15; and Melinda Wheelwright Brown, *Eve and Adam: Discovering the Beautiful Balance* (Salt Lake City, UT: Deseret Book, 2020).

13. Valerie M. Hudson, "Updating My Old Lists! The Status of Diarchy in the Church of Jesus Christ, 2019," *SquareTwo* 12, no. 3 (Fall 2019), http://squaretwo.org/Sq2ArticleCasslerUpdateList.html.

Faith as a Scientist

EMILY BATES

Emily Bates earned her bachelor of science degree in biology from the University of Utah. After serving a mission in Geneva, Switzerland, for The Church of Jesus Christ of Latter-day Saints, she earned her PhD in genetics from Harvard Medical School. Dr. Bates completed a postdoctoral fellowship at the University of California, San Francisco School of Medicine. She taught biochemistry at Brigham Young University in Provo, Utah, for four years before joining the faculty at the University of Colorado School of Medicine. She has authored several research articles that are published in scientific journals. She enjoys running, hiking, and skiing and considers her two children and her husband a great blessing.

I TEACH AND CONDUCT research to understand the laws of biology. My profession has shaped the way that I see God and what I expect from my Heavenly Father and Heavenly Mother.[1] From my own education and my experience teaching, I have come to understand that learning is most exciting and enduring when students are led to their own discoveries. A good teacher facilitates discovery by providing students

1. "Heavenly Mother," Gospel Topics, https://www.churchofjesuschrist.org/study/manual/gospel-topics-essays/mother-in-heaven?lang=eng.

with opportunities to learn concepts for themselves. When they are empowered to solve problems, students feel ownership of concepts and are motivated to delve further into the subject. When I was an undergraduate student in Dr. Anthea Letsou's laboratory at the University of Utah, I used genetics to try to figure out when and how a signal is received for limbs to develop correctly. I was so excited by the process of discovery that I would come to the lab late at night and on weekends. The techniques I used in the lab I could remember fifteen years later when I needed them as a professor starting my own lab. In contrast, I do not remember much from my cell biology class where I listened to lectures, frantically taking down notes that I reread and studied so that I could ace my exams. The classes that provided opportunities for me to discover something new had the greatest impact on my education.

When I was an assistant professor at Brigham Young University, I was assigned to teach a lab class that focused on certain lab techniques, like making lots of copies of DNA and measuring whether a gene is turned on in cells. A few students complained to me that the class was boring because they felt that they were being evaluated on whether they could follow directions in a cookbook. In response to their complaints, I redesigned the experiments so that students used the same techniques, but this time, they used them to discover something new. We copied DNA and looked at how much a cancer-related gene turned on to test the idea that blocking one protein in a cell could affect a cancer-related pathway. Some students from the newly designed class told me that they had changed their career plans because they enjoyed the class so much.

I believe our Father and Mother in Heaven are master teachers. They want us to learn through our own experience because the lessons we learn in this way will help us remember what we have learned and know how to use it.

I grew up believing in a loving God who could do all things. "Ask and ye shall receive" was a concept I was taught in Sunday School but also that the receiving part was dependent upon my faith and obedience. My faith meant that I would not only believe but would act accordingly. I heard promises of health that hinged on obedience to the Word of Wisdom, a religious law of health: no smoking, no drinking alcohol, and no recreational drugs. To keep the spirit of the law, I also ate healthy foods and ran daily, except for Sundays. To me, the Word of Wisdom sounded like a recipe for a life without health problems. As a teenage girl surrounded by other Church members, I kept my side of the bargain as best as I could, maybe even a little too zealously.

Migraine headaches challenged my childhood view of God. I kept all of the rules of health according to the Word of Wisdom. I used my migraine-free time engaged in good causes. Because I also struggled with dyslexia, I had to work extra hard in school to earn good grades. It took longer for me to read required material and to complete homework assignments. I did not feel I had time to waste suffering through migraines that came as often as once a week. I prayed fervently to be cured. But I could not rely on being healthy when it came time to take an exam at school, run in a track meet, or play my violin at a recital. During times that I considered critical to my life and schooling, I would lose my sight, the contents of my stomach, and my ability to speak clearly or stand upright. The pain in my head was intense. If God loved me and could intervene, I could not understand why my prayers to have my migraines taken away were not granted. Now, with the perspective of knowing the greater suffering of others who do not find relief despite their faith and goodness, my challenge seems small, but at the time, my pain and the disruption to my life seemed insurmountable. It challenged my belief in God. I prayed to ask if God was real and if God loved me. That is when I felt the love of my heavenly parents. Feeling that love taught me that God is real. Knowing that God loved me gave me comfort. Feeling God's love is a miracle. The miracle of feeling God's love gave me strength and motivation to use my own experience to help others. Our Father and Mother in Heaven intervened by inspiring me with their love.

My migraines motivated me to study genetics and to devote my professional life to understanding the reasons that biological processes go wrong. Working hard throughout my education to overcome my dyslexia gave me good study habits that have served me well throughout my career. As I have studied the principles that underlie how bodies grow and develop, I have seen that sickness and health are consequences that follow laws of biology, chemistry, and physics. Those laws are constant. Whether God makes the laws of nature or is bound by these laws, I think they are rarely, if ever, broken to shield us from difficult experiences. Mistakes (mutations) in our genetic material, our DNA, are not avoidable. Those mutations can happen just from living. For example, errors in the chemistry of replicating the DNA can cause mutations. Once a mutation is replicated in new cells, the chances of repairing the mutation in multiple cells is close to zero. Mutations can be responsible for devastating health struggles, such as birth defects or cancer. A baby who has a mutation in a gene that is important for face development has done nothing to deserve a cleft lip and palate. Similarly, in most cases, a person who suffers from cancer did nothing to deserve cancer. Cancer occurs because of mistakes that crop up in DNA. If the genetic change occurs in a gene that is important for fixing mutations before they are passed on, more mistakes go unchecked, and they accumulate in cells until the cells grow out of control and take over organ systems. God did not make cancer happen. The God that I worship only does that which is good. No one deserves either of these afflictions or one of the many other diseases.

One of my favorite scriptures tells us that God invites all of us to goodness. I read this to mean that we can all take inspiration from our heavenly parents to do good: to love, to learn, to create, to nurture, to contribute and participate in God's work, bringing to pass good for humanity.

> For he doeth that which is good among the children of men [and women]; and he doeth nothing save it be plain unto the children of men; and he inviteth them all to come unto him and partake of his goodness; and he denieth none that come unto him, black and white, bond and free, male and female; and he remembereth the heathen; and all are alike unto God, both Jew and Gentile. (2 Nephi 26:33)

This scripture tells us that God does only "that which is good," and that includes inviting us, no matter who we are, to come and receive goodness. This tells us that the goodness that God provides is ours to receive if we choose. We can decide to turn to God for comfort when we are troubled by sickness or sorrow. We can look to God to learn how to succor those who stand in need of succor. We are all invited to partake of God's goodness. The goodness that God provides is not something that passively comes to us. We are all invited to receive the love of our heavenly parents and then give that love to others.

Whether God creates the laws or abides by them, the idea that God would physically intervene to keep people from suffering began to seem less likely as I studied genetics and molecular biology. Of course, I cannot know for sure that physical divine intervention does not happen, but as my view of God shifted to that of master teachers, I began to believe that our heavenly parents expect us to learn from our own earthly struggles and to learn to care for our sisters and brothers during theirs. I think our heavenly parents expect us to do our best to make life better for each other. In my view, disease is not a punishment. In my view, a cure from disease is not a reward for the faithful. Disease and healing follow the laws of nature. The belief that God physically intervenes is common, and I respect that viewpoint. I still pray daily for loved ones who suffer, but my faith is no longer challenged by the lack of a magical cure for a good, faithful person.[2] My perspective on how God helps us during challenges changed as I realized we all grow while we participate in miracles by following inspiration.

I believe that our heavenly parents have invited us to physically, emotionally, and spiritually help each other so that we can learn to become like them. We discover compassion by experiencing suffering. We discover love by serving others. We discover generosity when we practice giving to someone who is in need. I believe God inspires us to give the right words of encouragement, money, meals, hugs, and other signs of

2. See, for example, Elder Anthony D. Perkins, "Remember Thy Suffering Saints, O Our God," October 2021 General Conference, https://www.churchofjesuschrist.org/study/general-conference/2021/10/53perkins?lang=eng.

love to those who need comfort. When my migraines were not miraculously or medically healed, I searched and discovered gaps in medical knowledge that motivated my studies, my career, and my progress as a scientist. I believe that God has inspired me with ideas. I work to test the ideas, which teaches me a method of learning and increases my ability to understand. I believe that God inspires scientists to find new remedies for sickness. I believe that God inspires and guides doctors to find the best available treatment. As we are inspired to help each other, both the person inspired to give and the person on the receiving end can learn and grow.

The COVID-19 pandemic has been devastating to many of us. Millions of people lost their lives or lost loved ones, health, income, or financial security. My family was spared the most severe losses. But nevertheless, the pandemic has been difficult for me as well. I gave birth to my son on the day our city and my university shut down in response to COVID-19. In the hours before I was admitted to the hospital, the rules changed to restrict visitors, excluding my husband from joining me and not allowing my daughter to meet her new brother until I came home. Nurses and doctors seemed scared to come close to check on me. In my postpartum vulnerability, we were isolated. I did not have my church community, my friends and colleagues, or my neighbors. We lost the majority of our incomes for 2020. I felt I was failing my students because we did not have reliable childcare due to COVID-19 closures and exclusion for any potential symptom while the youngest kids had no access to vaccines. Even though my losses were not as great as many in the world, I struggled. I do not believe the devastation of the pandemic came from God. But I believe that God inspired people to work together to reduce the negative effects of the disease.

As we experienced the early stages of the COVID-19 pandemic, people from all over the world worked together to stop the spread of a devastating and often fatal disease. People who belong to many different religions united in prayer for a common cause. People sewed masks to donate. Scientists devoted their individual expertise to search for helpful information about COVID-19 and to develop vaccines and treatments. Artists created beauty for us to watch or listen to from home so that we could be inspired and comforted while isolated from one another.

Is this collaboration a miracle? It feels like a miracle to me. Our heavenly parents invite us to be part of a miracle by inspiring us to do good and unite in love for all humanity, who are created in their image. We all grow through participating in their divine cause.

In my belief system, God gives guidance that helps us to have the healthiest and happiest life that we can with our individual constraints (our biological and economic situations). For example, following the Word of Wisdom protects us from some difficult mental and physical challenges, but it does not give a charmed life, free from all mental and physical health struggles. God inspires goodness, progress, kindness, learning, understanding, and wisdom. Moroni 7 reads,

> But behold, that which is of God inviteth and enticeth to do good continually; wherefore, every thing which inviteth and enticeth to do good, and to love God, and to serve him, is inspired of God.... For behold, the Spirit of Christ is given to every man, that he may know good from evil; wherefore, I show unto you the way to judge; for every thing which inviteth to do good, and to persuade to believe in Christ, is sent forth by the power and gift of Christ; wherefore ye may know with a perfect knowledge it is of God. (Moroni 7:13, 16)

God helps us to see our greater potential and motivates us to reach that potential. As a young girl who struggled with dyslexia, I never would have had the confidence to see my own potential to be a scientist, but I felt called to this career by the direction in my patriarchal blessing. I have worked really hard to fulfill what I saw as a calling. As I have worked toward my career goals, I have seen that I could do much more than I would have imagined. Perhaps something that I discover will be part of someone's healing. For each of us, God inspires us with ideas of how to help each other and care for one another. We learn by ministering to others in their suffering.

Our Heavenly Father and Heavenly Mother love us through our challenges and give us strength and comfort. I have felt that love in some of the times I have needed to feel it most. For me, that was a miracle.

Faith and My Life as a Medical Scientist

ELIZABETH HAMMOND

Mary Elizabeth Hale Hammond completed her medical education at the University of Utah, followed by post-graduate research and residency training at the Karolinska Institutet in Stockholm, Sweden, Massachusetts General Hospital, and Harvard Medical School in Boston, Massachusetts. After serving briefly on the faculty of Harvard Medical School, she and her family moved to Utah. She established an electron microscopy laboratory at LDS Hospital and provided specialty services to laboratories throughout Utah. She served as medical staff president at LDS Hospital, chair of Pathology at Intermountain Healthcare (Urban Central Region), and professor of pathology and internal medicine (cardiology) at the University of Utah. She is the author of 250 original publications. She has received numerous honors, including distinguished alumna from the University of Utah and University of Utah School of Medicine, Legacy of Life Award from Intermountain Healthcare, and the Pioneer Award from the International Society for Heart and Lung Transplantation. She enjoys grandmothering, walking, cooking, and reading. She and her architect husband share a passion for urban neighborhoods and pacific beaches.

❖

WHEN I WAS IN COLLEGE, my sister and best friend suffered a potentially fatal head injury in an auto-pedestrian accident. I was in the room when the eminent surgeon told my parents that she was likely to die despite his efforts to save her. Elder Harold B. Lee, an apostle at the time, was also in the room with his arm around my father, his friend. He listened quietly to the surgeon, went to my sister's bedside, and pronounced a simple, direct blessing upon her, promising her healing and a long life. As he spoke, my parents and I received the calm assurance that he spoke the truth. Although she was comatose for a week, she ultimately recovered completely. This experience taught me that there was a marked difference between scientific knowledge and God's knowledge. Fine physicians could do their best with their knowledge, skills, and experience, but only God knew complete truth. Furthermore, that complete truth was available only by prayer and faith. Faith in God's truth drove the fear from the room that day.

I have always had a firm knowledge that my Father in Heaven was a trusted advisor and friend, just like my own parents did. They knew that God was their father, and their heartfelt, frequent prayers to that familiar, loving father helped to cement my own faith in him. God was their partner in making all-important decisions, so he also became mine. My path as a woman of faith and science is a response to my knowledge that God has "not given us the spirit of fear; but of power, and of love, and of a sound mind" (2 Timothy 1:7).

I have always loved to learn almost anything and have spent large amounts of time doing just that. When I studied biology in junior high school, I knew that I had found an intellectual home. I was thrilled and amazed by the harmony and symmetry of natural things, and I began to think about careers in science. At the time, I had a female pediatrician. She was an excellent physician who found great joy in her service to patients. I also found satisfaction in serving my family. I loved to help my siblings with their homework, cook with my mother, and work with my father in the garden. Medicine seemed a natural career to combine service and science.

My parents were very supportive of my decision and helped me prepare myself by guiding me to appropriate course work in high school in the late 1950s. There were others in my extended family and neighborhood who were critical of my goal to become a physician. "Would you be able to get married and have a family if you were a physician?" they asked. A demanding career like that seemed to be in conflict with my Latter-day Saint upbringing. When faced with this negative advice, I turned to my usual source of support: my parents, my sister, and Heavenly Father. All were supportive, so I stayed the course.

As I studied more about medicine and science, I marveled at the infinite knowledge of God. Biologic processes are preserved across all species of animals and are designed to have almost infinite flexibility that allows variation in character and function. They are clearly the work of God rather than random chance happenings. Our earthly knowledge of these processes is limited. In my studies, I learned that there were still many unanswered questions about human physiology and disease. Our understanding was constantly changing as new methods and ideas emerged. I loved thinking about these unanswered questions, so I engaged in research, both as an undergraduate and as a medical student. Being part of that process of discovery and refinement was an exciting prospect.

After medical school, I was granted the opportunity to spend a year in Sweden doing a postdoctoral fellowship in cancer biology with an amazing scientist, Georg Klein. Although he professed no belief in God, he possessed a deep respect for truth and the process of finding it. He opened new scientific vistas to me that informed my future research efforts. He was humble, honest, open, and collaborative. I resolved to follow his example in my research efforts.

As I sought to become both a scientist and a physician, I encountered numerous influential mentors along my path who, like Georg Klein, refined my thinking and my approach to scientific questions. I have often asked myself why these individuals appeared in my life. In retrospect, I believe that God had a role in their appearance. I believe that my openness to being taught made it possible for me to learn from them effectively and use those lessons to grow and develop as a scientist. I continued to apply the lessons I learned in Sweden to my research endeavors in Boston and then in Salt Lake City, guided and taught by other pivotal individuals.

God gave me a wonderful intellect that I could use to find answers in my pathology and research endeavors. Refusing to succumb to fear of failure was an important aspect of my faith. I was willing to seek new answers and new directions without fear. I believed that God would direct my path if I tried honestly and diligently. When I became confused while seeking answers, I often felt either confirmation or confusion that helped to define the next steps. When I became convinced that antibodies (protein molecules of defense in our blood and tissues) were causing a more damaging form of heart transplant rejection, I conducted research and published my findings. At the time, most transplant experts believed that only immune cells influenced transplant outcomes. My results were disparaged and rejected when they were published. I was publicly shamed and derided for my work, but I continued to publish and refine my ideas because I knew that they were correct. The experimental evidence of the role of antibodies in this process had been highlighted since the 1970s but had been overlooked by cardiac transplant experts. Despite the international opposition, my colleagues in Utah strongly supported and encouraged me because my findings were important to their care of patients. I found that when antibodies were present in the heart, the patient had an increased risk of death despite the absence of immune cells. This form of rejection led to a nine-fold increase in risk of death compared to patients who had more typical transplant rejection caused by immune cells. Ultimately, other groups recognized and published similar findings, and my recommendations were accepted by the international cardiology community twenty-two years after my original publication. My faith in the process of discovery drove out my fear of failure.

I used the same scientific principles and diligence in my service to patients when solving difficult diagnostic dilemmas. Often, I would receive a strong confirmation or denial that my diagnoses were correct, and that guidance would lead me to answers. My compassion for the patients whose problems I was addressing drove me to keep seeking even when it was inconvenient or when I was pressured to give up. Finding these answers for patients has brought me great personal satisfaction and occasionally changed a patient's disease trajectory.

When I became the leader of my department, I experienced significant rejection and aggravation as a woman in a position of leadership in a male-dominated profession. At times, I became angry and depressed by this adversity rather than focusing on the lessons it was teaching me. Although my anger was justified, I let it consume me, and I put distance between me and God. I chose to nourish my grievances instead of my faith. I stopped regularly seeking God's help, choosing to rely only on my own thinking as a guide. My family noticed the change in my behavior and emotions. I eventually acknowledged to them that I felt unworthy of God's help because I had ignored his guidance. Lovingly and patiently, they helped me return to God through daily prayer and scripture study. I am so grateful for their guidance that allowed me to return to the blessings of having the Spirit as a guide in my life and in my profession.

Staff leaders in my department regularly tried to make decisions without my input. My return to prayer led me to ask God for his help, and he guided me to change my behavior so that I could more effectively relate to these staff members. The Spirit helped me identify my weaknesses and modify them. It was a painful and slow process, but the change in my approach made it possible for me to become their trusted leader. The Spirit taught me to look first at my own weaknesses to find solutions rather than focus on blaming others, however justified.

On another occasion, fear stalked the hospital corridors when we had a serious laboratory computer failure. We were reduced to manually recording important laboratory results twenty-four hours a day. Laboratory results are critical to define disease and predict responses to treatment. Physicians and nurses were clamoring for a quick resolution. I had no idea how to solve the issues that we faced, but I knew how to avoid fear and find answers. I went frequently into my office, locked the door, and prayed for inspiration. After one long day, the beginning of solutions emerged as individuals with various crucial expertise came to me with powerful, specific suggestions that averted a total crisis. Although I had experience, scientific knowledge, and the will to solve the lab problem, it was only through prayer and the guidance of others that the answers came. My understanding that only God had complete access to all knowledge and truth led me again to turn to him when confounded.

Finally, faith in God has guided my life as a wife and mother. I married my architect sweetheart while I was in medical school. When faced with challenges of managing life as a dual-career couple, he prayed with me and gave me a priesthood blessing, helping to relieve my fears and give me courage to continue my studies and my work. When we had three children as busy young professionals, our faith and reliance on the Spirit helped us find answers to our challenges to get appropriate childcare, solve trials faced by our children, and decide what was the best career path for each of us. It was often a difficult process. Competing priorities raged for attention, leading to stress and frustration. Early in our marriage, we committed to maintaining our activity in The Church of Jesus Christ of Latter-day Saints regardless of convenience. Each week in church meetings or in attending to our callings, we were reminded of God's love and the power of prayer to heal wounds and calm roiling emotions. We were strengthened by the examples we saw. That commitment helped us weather many of life's storms.

Now as I look back on fifty-plus years in science and medicine, I am filled with gratitude for the blessings bestowed upon me by a loving Father in Heaven. He knows me. He helped me find my way so that I could help others and develop answers to scientific challenges. I can easily see his hand in my life. Through the influence of his other children on earth, he helped me find my way to science and medicine, guided me to mentors who could influence my thinking, and led me to those who needed my help and scientific expertise. Reliance on inspiration allowed me to avoid fear of failure, as well as danger in relationships and obligations, and gave me courage to face my mistakes and weaknesses. Through the grace of the Savior's influence, I was gently prodded to acknowledge my mistakes and errors and was guided to better ways of living when I stumbled along the way.

Faith in God was given to me as a gift. I recognized the power of that gift and the obligation it represented to use it wisely. As President Nelson reminded us in April 2020, we can know God's priorities for us individually if we strive to be righteous and listen to his personal messages for us. In that way, we can have his power to guide our own lives and provide blessings to those around us, free from the paralysis of fear.

Singing as a Teacher

LANEY McCLAIN ARMSTRONG

Laney McClain Armstrong is a singer and conductor who has made choral music and education her life's work. Dr. Armstrong has worked with singers of many ages, teaching middle school and high school students, serving as the associate artistic director and director of Musicianship at the Cantabile Youth Singers of Silicon Valley, and working in many capacities at the San Francisco Girls Chorus. She currently works as a music teacher at the Renaissance International School in Oakland, is the artistic director of the San Francisco-based women's ensemble Musae, and is the director of choral studies at the San Francisco Girls Chorus. Dr. Armstrong holds a bachelor of arts from Harvard University in Afro-American studies and a master of music in choral conducting from the University of Oregon under the direction of Dr. Sharon Paul. In 2013, she received a doctorate in musical arts in choral conducting from the University of Washington, where she studied with Dr. Geoffrey Boers. Dr. Armstrong, her spouse, and their four young daughters live in Oakland, California.

IMAGINE A GROUP of children on a playground. You might observe some of them using the steady beat of a jump rope to keep time to a chant. At the same time, there might be another group taunting each other in melodic tones. And yet another pair might be singing a song while keeping time with a hand game. All around you, rhythms and melodies would be bouncing off the blacktop and ringing around the play structures as children played in their natural way.

This was what the musicologist, composer, and music educator Zoltán Kodály observed when he watched children play in early twentieth-century Hungary. He realized that children learned music by and through play and that those songs could be used to teach them musical concepts. His philosophy of music education grew into a method of teaching music theory and literacy that is now used worldwide: the Kodály method. Based on rhythm and solfège syllables,[1] his eponymous method can begin with the smallest of children starting with the simplest and most basic of concepts: a steady beat and the minor third between *so* and *mi*.[2] Building on this foundation, students add concept by concept, one note or new rhythm at a time, until they are reading, writing, and dictating music fluently.

What makes the Kodály method revolutionary is that each new concept is introduced with a folk song from the children's culture. First, they learn the song by rote, then they repeat it with a dance or game before any written version of the song is introduced. Once the children are able to sing the song without assistance, it is used to teach a new musical concept. At that point, the song is in them so thoroughly that making the leap to the new concept is natural and simple.

Primary songs, written for children to learn and sing at church and at home, ingrain in us concepts in the same way as Kodály observed in Hungarian children. But while Kodály used folk songs to teach music theory concepts, Primary songs teach children gospel truths. The songs are taught usually by rote, using play, visual aids, and a lot of repetition. As children repeat and learn the songs and their concepts, they become a part of them, music and lyrics inextricably linked. A repertoire of Primary songs, carefully chosen, can teach a child the foundations of

1. Solfège is a method of naming notes using the syllables *do*, *re*, *mi*, *fa*, *so*, *la*, and *ti*.

2. To hear that minor third between *so* and *mi*, think of the sound of a doorbell "ding-dong" or a child's teasing chant.

the gospel of Jesus Christ in a way that reaches the core of their being. I know this because I was one of these children.

I started attending a ward in Oakland, California, with my parents and infant sister when I had just reached Primary age. My mother grew up in a household with parents who were members of the Church, but though she was baptized at age eight, her family did not attend church regularly. My father, a Black man raised in segregated Kansas City, Kansas, was wary of the racial history of the Church, all while being drawn to its messages of following Christ and focusing on family. After a few years of meeting with missionaries, my father was baptized, and I attended church each week throughout my childhood.

As a child who loved to sing from a very young age, Primary was great fun to me. I loved learning the songs and being able to engage in one of my favorite activities in a new place.

One of my favorite Primary songs was "I'm Trying to Be Like Jesus." I loved its soaring melody and its simple message. I loved the simple illustration of one child comforting another that appeared below the title in the *Children's Songbook*, a constant fixture on the piano in our home. Singing "I'm Trying to Be Like Jesus" transports me back to the hours I spent at that piano in our living room teaching myself to play and sing simultaneously. I thought I was honing my musical abilities; it wasn't until much later that I realized I was building a core part of my testimony of the gospel of Jesus Christ.

"I'm Trying to Be Like Jesus" teaches in simple and compelling ways. Singing in the first-person point of view, the singer states that "I'm trying to be like Jesus; I'm following in his ways" and "trying to love as he did." It is after those opening phrases that the song, both lyrically and musically, reminds me that—despite how hard I may try to follow the Savior—things do not always go my way. I will be "tempted," get lost, or have the path obscured. I will have to work hard to "remember the lessons he taught." With this reminder that things will be hard, the song shifts to uncertain, minor harmonies in contrast to the sunnier, major harmonies of the opening phrases. Yet, it does not stay there long. As the text reminds me to "listen as the still, small voice whispers," the melody climbs and harmonies surge back toward the home key, leading to the apex of the line: "Love one another as Jesus loves you." This is not just the apex of the melodic line; it is the thematic heart of the song. The melodies and harmonies lead us right to the message at the core of the gospel of Jesus Christ, shining a light on the second great commandment to "love thy neighbor as thyself" (Matthew 22:39).

As I moved through childhood, adolescence, and into adulthood, the truths at the heart of "I'm Trying to Be Like Jesus" and other simple Primary songs continue to speak to my soul. They are a part of me and continue to teach me simply by being a part of my consciousness and being. They remind me, comfort me, and help me to identify and live the core parts of the gospel of Jesus Christ. And as I teach familiar Primary songs to my children, I rely on them to teach truths that will reach them in ways that my words cannot. I know the songs they learn will continue to teach them in their minds and hearts, especially in difficult and solitary moments when I cannot be there to buoy them.

According to my parents, I have been singing constantly since I was tiny. My mother remembers my knowing every word to a Culture Club album as a two-year-old and, not much later, pointing out that a certain Sesame Street song playing in the car was, in fact, a combination of two different songs. I would perform standing on the hearth of my grandparents' home and make up my own songs to narrate my toddler life. Seizing on my love of singing, my mother enrolled me in the San Francisco Girls Chorus just after my seventh birthday, and it was there I found my true love: choral singing. Now, choral music is my profession and vocation.

Vocal music is a unique form of music. Only with the voice are you able to combine music with words to express meaning and emotion. With only one singer, that additional avenue for expression is powerful. With choral music, there is another level of connection: the singers connect not only to the words and the music but to each other. The voices join together to express the same sentiment, amplifying the messages of the text and the music.

I have always found this amplification to be powerful as a choral singer, and it is even more potent in a religious context. When I am singing in a choir or a congregation, the songs and hymns allow me to raise my voice in a coordinated way with those around me. When we sing the same words at the same time, with the added benefit of beautiful music amplifying our words, we are able to express the sentiments of our hearts simultaneously. It is this combination of music, text, voices, and belief that provides a direct conduit to my heart and mind for the Spirit.

As the Savior commands Emma Smith to gather hymns for the new church, he tells her in Doctrine and Covenants 25:12, "The song of the righteous is a prayer unto me." I often feel more able to express the sentiments of my heart when singing than when praying, writing, or speaking. Singing "Nearer, My God, to Thee" at the funeral of my young nephew helped me to find a way to plead for peace for our family in a way I felt inadequate to do with mere words. Joining others in singing "Christ the Lord Is Risen Today" at a glorious Easter service lifts my heart with the hope of the Resurrection more than any scripture or thought has been able to do. And joining with a room full of Primary children singing "I'm Trying to Be Like Jesus" reminds me that the gospel of Jesus Christ may not be easy, but it is simple.

In a choir, it is essential that all members work together, pulling in the same direction and with the same intent. If not all the singers are following the conductor, working toward the same goal, the music cannot be performed as intended. Notes and tempos may clash, entrances and cutoffs will be uncoordinated, and singers and audience alike will be left unsatisfied without the fulfillment of the promise of the music. As congregations and classes sing hymns together, with our minds turned toward the same ideas, our hearts speaking the truths of the gospel together, we create a unity that may not be available to us in other ways. Our songs rise to heaven together, focused on our testimonies of gospel truths that rise above our differences and disagreements. When the hymn is over, we are just a bit more unified, knowing that our pew partner, our Relief Society sister, our bishop, all were joined in the same song. It allows us to be unified together under the direction of our Heavenly Father, working together to follow the gospel of Jesus Christ laid out in the lyrics of the songs we have sung.

In my life, there have been many times when I did not care to sing along or join in with those beside me. There have been times when my faith flagged and joining in with others seemed disingenuous, when I was in a place where I felt I could not honestly sing the words of the hymn with my heart and soul. As a choral conductor, I can look back on those moments with a tiny iota of the perspective of our Heavenly Father. When I prepare a choir, I set out a plan. I help the singers to learn the music, and we practice thoroughly so that it is in our bodies and souls. But when the performance is upon us, as the conductor, all I can do is hope that the singers remember all our work and follow the plan. If they choose to do something different, there is nothing I can do to stop them. So it is with our Heavenly Father. He gives us a path to follow and countless opportunities to rehearse the principles we are taught, but ultimately, we have our agency and can choose to follow or not. He must stand by, observing, watching, and hoping we return to the plan he has given us.

While our agency is ours, music is one of the tools God uses to remind us of the plan he has for us. To regain our footing on his path, sometimes just hearing the music is enough to stir a remembrance in our souls of the love of our Heavenly Father. When I was in my early twenties, I was struggling with the direction my life would take, feeling like my God was far from me, and wondering if he heard me and understood what I needed. I was going through the motions of church attendance, but I did not feel the connection I once had. One Sunday, when attending Sunday School, the teacher played the Tabernacle Choir recording of "It Is Well with My Soul." That music, those words, those hundreds of voices joined together tapped straight into my heart:

> When peace like a river attendeth my way
> When sorrows like sea billows roll
> Whatever my lot, Thou hast taught me to say
> It is well, it is well with my soul.

As tears streamed down my face, I felt the reassurance that my Savior loved me, my God knew me, and I was seen and heard. I knew that things could be well with my soul even as life felt dark. I knew that it was the music that was able to penetrate my uncertainty more than any other method I had tried. To this day, when I hear that song, I sing along and am reminded of that moment when I knew things could be well with my soul.

The hymns and songs of The Church of Jesus Christ of Latter-day Saints, especially those I learned as a child, are etched into my soul in both word and melody. Their tunes come to my mind in difficult times and bring with them the comfort and reminders of the important teachings of their texts. I can remember that "I am a child of God" and that he is there to "strengthen me, help me, and cause me to stand." I can constantly be reminded, through lilting melodies, that "I know Heavenly Father loves me." Most of all, my soul is lifted along with the melody to remind me that, while I may not always be perfect, I can listen to the whisperings of the Holy Ghost to remember all of the "things Jesus taught."

Desde el Perú

Mi desarrollo académico de la mano con la fe

ANA MARÍA GUTIÉRREZ VALDIVIA

Ana María Gutiérrez Valdivia nació en Arequipa y creció a tres horas de la capital de la región, en el valle de Majes. Recibió sus títulos de MD, MS y doctorado de la Universidad Nacional de San Agustín donde se desempeñó como vicerrectora académica del 2015 al 2021. Durante su tiempo como vicerrectora se enfocó en el desarrollo y transformación curricular. También realiza investigaciones en salud sexual y reproductiva, así como en educación médica. Ana considera su bautismo en la Iglesia de Jesucristo de los Santos de los Últimos Días como un evento trascendente que la ayudó en su camino de discipulado. Ella ha servido como presidenta de la Sociedad de Socorro de su estaca y barrio y ayuda a los futuros misioneros a completar sus solicitudes médicas. Durante su tiempo libre, le gusta leer, servir y visitar el campo donde creció. El crecimiento académico de Ana no hubiera sido posible sin la ayuda de su esposo Luigi y sus cuatro hijos Diego, Luis, Coco, y Ximena y espera compartir la eternidad con ellos.

Ana María Gutiérrez Valdivia was born in Arequipa, Peru, and grew up three hours away from the main city in the valley of

Majes. She received her MD, MS, and doctorate degrees from the Universidad Nacional de San Agustín, where she worked as the academic vice chancellor from 2015 to 2021. During her time as the vice chancellor, she focused on curricular development. She also does research in sexual health, reproduction, and medical education. Ana considers her baptism into The Church of Jesus Christ of Latter-day Saints a transcendent event that helped her start her path of discipleship. She has served as the Relief Society president of her stake and ward and helps future missionaries fill out their medical applications. During her free time, she enjoys reading and visiting the green farms where she grew up. Ana's academic growth would not have been possible without the help of her husband, Luigi, and four children, Diego, Luis, Coco, and Ximena. She looks forward to eternities close to them.

Ana María wrote her essay in Spanish. An English translation follows the original essay.

En medio de las difíciles circunstancias que me han rodeado, el éxito profesional en mi vida está basado en el apoyo de mi familia, mi fe, y esfuerzo. En todo el camino recorrido, tuve la mano de Dios ayudándome en las decisiones más importantes. He confiado en él con humildad y esto me ha traído paz.

Nací en 1961 en un hospital de Arequipa lejos de la zona rural donde vivían mis padres, porque necesitaron atencion medica para una cesarea. Debido a que ellos eran personas de fe, me nombraron Ana María. Ana por la abuela de Jesús (y patrona de la zona), y María por mi abuela materna. Mis padres fueron industriosos, honestos, sencillos y caritativos. Ellos tuvieron escasa instrucción académica; en la provincia de Aplao, donde se criaron, sólo había educación primaria. Mi abuelo paterno y mi abuela materna fallecieron prematuramente, lo que formó el carácter y fe de mis padres. Los dos muy devotos católicos me enseñaron a servir a otros a través del ejemplo.

Crecer con poco pero suficiente me ayudaría por el resto de mi vida a vivir enfocada en lo más importante. Me crie en el hermoso valle de Majes, una provincia de la región de Arequipa, área agrícola con aire puro y cielo estrellado. Vivíamos de lo que producía la tierra y de la crianza de ganado. Cultivar el campo es un acto de fe porque dependíamos de la naturaleza y de un mercado inestable. Compartí mi niñez y experiencias con mis queridos hermanos Nery, Tulita y Niltón.

Mi interés en los estudios comenzó desde pequeña. Yo asistía como alumna libre a la escuela antes de cumplir seis años. Por la falta de luz eléctrica, tenía que estudiar con lámparas de kerosene y velas por la noche o cuando podía aprovechar la luz del día. Fue difícil, porque debía ayudar en las tareas domésticas de la casa y con el cuidado de los animales (gallinas, pavos, patos, gansos, cerdos, ovejas, y cabras). Sin importar las limitaciones, recibí muchos reconocimientos académicos en la escuela y comúnmente me asignaban enseñar a mis compañeros. Mis padres rezaban diariamente, y me enseñaron a encomendarme a Dios. Aprendí a confiar en él. Me sentí acompañada toda mi vida y especialmente cuando mi padre fue injustamente encarcelado temporalmente por reclamar con otros padres de familia el maltrato físico que una maestra infringió a un niño en la escuela.

Estudiar nunca fue fácil y siempre requirió sacrificio. A los diez años migré a la ciudad de Arequipa, a casi cuatro horas de distancia de mi familia, para continuar mi educación. Viví por un año con unos compadres de mis padres. Esto fue difícil para mí porque tuve que enfrentar barreras sociales y culturales al estudiar en la escuela de una zona urbana y de clase económica media alta. Después de un año, mi madre vino a vivir conmigo y me cambié a un colegio parroquial. Lamentablemente vivimos muy incómodos por más de dos años en una vivienda tugurizada con baño compartido y nunca pude invitar a mis amigas a visitarme porque me incomodaba la situación en la que vivíamos. Al cumplir mis 15 años, como un regalo por este acontecimiento, nos mudamos a una casa que mis padres con mucho esfuerzo edificaron en una urbanización. A pesar de las dificultades, logré el primer puesto al terminar la escuela secundaria, di el discurso de graduación y obtuve ingreso directo a la universidad.

Mi tiempo en la universidad trajo la bendición del evangelio. Ingresé a la Universidad Nacional de San Agustín (UNSA) a la carrera de Medicina. Mi hermana Tulita vivía conmigo y estudiaba Economía en una universidad privada. Las dos compartimos las responsabilidades del hogar. En esta época conocí la iglesia por medio de Ricardo Gonzales, un amigo de la universidad. Recibí las charlas misionales, leí el Libro de Mormón y oré. Recibí mucha paz y calor en mi ser, confirmando la veracidad de lo que había aprendido. Al bautizarme sentí como nunca antes el amor de Dios y de Jesucristo y nací literalmente de nuevo.

La iglesia trajo mucha alegría, cambios y responsabilidades a mi vida. Ahora tenía nuevas reuniones y costumbres. Aprendí a guardar la palabra de sabiduría a pesar de que el café y el vino eran parte de mis costumbres familiares. El vivir con mi hermana, quien también se bautizó, nos ayudó a apoyarnos mutuamente, y podíamos ser nuestros propios agentes. Con el tiempo, mis parientes y compañeros respetaron mis creencias. También aprendí a interesarme y amar a las hermanas asignadas como maestra visitante, y a ser fiel en ese servicio, por amor al Salvador. Además, experimenté compartir el evangelio y ayudé en la conversión de una amiga.

Mi tiempo universitario fue incesante y ocupado. Solía vender tarjetas en navidad, libros, material quirúrgico e instrumental médico para enseñar con el ejemplo a los jóvenes, que era posible estudiar, trabajar y servir en la iglesia. Guardar el día de reposo era difícil. A veces no podía terminar de estudiar para algún examen, pero esto edificó mi fe en el día de reposo. Este mandamiento fortaleció mi matrimonio y es una tradición familiar que nuestros hijos también comparten en sus nuevos hogares.

El servicio en la iglesia me llevó al matrimonio. Serví de representante de jóvenes adultos solteros (JAS) de Estaca y visitaba a los líderes y jóvenes de los barrios. Durante ese tiempo conocí a mi esposo, Luigi

Morales Velásquez. Los dos compartimos el mismo llamamiento. Nos casamos en el templo de Lima Perú en 1987 sin nuestras familias porque mis padres no eran miembros y la familia de mi esposo, miembros de la iglesia, no contaban con recursos para el viaje. La madre de mi esposo quedó viuda mientras él servía una misión, y él decidió continuar hasta concluirla. Sabíamos que el Señor no nos dejaría de lado al ver nuestro sacrificio.

Es posible ser fiel y salir adelante con nuestro desarrollo académico. Los frutos de mi esfuerzo en mis estudios por fin llegaron. Al terminar mi pregrado, antes del internado, conseguí el tercer lugar de 125 alumnos. Mi sacrificio dado al servicio del Señor no afectó mi rendimiento académico. Sin embargo, el inicio de la vida matrimonial coincidió con un exigente internado con guardias nocturnas y diurnas, y se volvió aún más difícil porque quedé embarazada. Fue un gran sacrificio para toda la familia. Cada paso que di en esta etapa fue con la ayuda de mi Padre celestial. No hubiera podido cuidar de mi primer hijo sin la ayuda de mi esposo y su familia. En esa época el interés en geriatría había comenzado en el Perú, y mi tesis de graduación, "Función renal en el anciano," recibió reconocimiento nacional. Me gradué en enero de 1989 después de un internado dificultoso.

Con la ayuda de Dios y gracias a las enseñanzas de la iglesia logramos superar tiempos muy difíciles en el Perú. Después de titularme, me dediqué a cuidar de mis hijos, pues tuve al segundo bebe en marzo de 1989. Enfrentamos grandes desafíos económicos durante una gran depresión nacional. Afortunadamente, teníamos un huerto y un pequeño almacenamiento. Pasamos esta época gris consumiendo vegetales de nuestro jardín y de las cosechas de mis padres. Económicamente fueron los años más oscuros, pero gracias a esta experiencia ahora puedo comprender y ayudar a otros en circunstancias similares.

Mi carrera como docente universitaria comenzó en 1991 como asistente ad honorem de Salud Pública en la UNSA. Luego de un riguroso proceso, me seleccionaron para una plaza en 1992. No hice especialidad clínica por priorizar el tiempo con mi familia. La docencia me permitía tener un horario flexible para dedicarlo a mis hijos que ya eran tres durante esa época. En 1996 decidí continuar mis estudios con una maestría en Salud Pública. Lamentablemente, esto recortó mi dedicación a mi niña, nacida en 1996. Siento que debí haber postergado el inicio de la maestría para pasar más tiempo con mi bebe. Sin embargo, opté por pasar tiempo de calidad con ella y lo hemos compensado con experiencias compartidas.

Sé que el amor de Dios no hace acepción de género. En medio de estos desafíos, envié mi proyecto titulado "Factores asociados a la invisibilidad de la violencia contra la mujer en establecimientos del MINSA" a un concurso de tesis de maestría en Salud Pública a nivel de Latinoamérica y el Caribe. La Organización Panamericana de la Salud la seleccionó, financió y publicó. La posición y el valor de la mujer en el plan de Nuestro Padre celestial me inspiraron a enfocarme en este tema, especialmente al ver las desigualdades en mi país. Este proyecto abrió una línea de investigación en la que trabajé con estudiantes de pregrado. Fortalecimos y enseñamos a grupos afectados por violencia doméstica. Después hice una consultoría en políticas de equidad de género para una ONG apoyada por la Cooperación Canadiense propiciando una participación más activa del varón en el proceso de paternidad.

Después de mi maestría aprendí más, de maneras inesperadas. Mi madre falleció en el 2005 después de luchar por tres años contra un cáncer pulmonar. Mi padre también partió con ella después de sufrir un accidente cerebrovascular. Ellos me inspiraron a escribir poemas, que es uno de mis talentos, y leí en ambos entierros unos dedicados a ellos. Muchos asistieron a sus velorios y sepulturas porque admiraban su servicio y devoción a la comunidad y a Dios. Mi padre recibió la medalla de la ciudad de Castilla por su contribución al desarrollo local y ser un ciudadano dedicado.

Decidí desarrollarme en el área de Salud Pública pues me interesaban los problemas poblacionales y su prevención. Por ello, inicié un doctorado en Salud Pública en el 2006. Fue arduo y largo terminar la tesis debido a las responsabilidades y las labores de un hogar de seis personas y el trabajo en la universidad. Orienté mi tesis a la educación médica con mi proyecto sobre "El ejercicio de la docencia en medicina según la percepción de los estudiantes." Incursioné en la investigación cualitativa aprendiendo a profundizar y explicar el comportamiento de individuos y grupos.

Poco a poco oportunidades políticas/administrativas comenzaron a surgir. Integré una lista como tesorera del Consejo Directivo del Colegio Médico Regional. Yo no tenía experiencia en este tipo de roles ni en elecciones, pero tenía fama de persona íntegra y confiable, y eso era lo que muchos buscaban al votar por nosotros. Salimos elegidos y trabajamos por dos años (2009–2010) ejerciendo con justicia y equidad, siempre procurando brindar lo mejor a los médicos de nuestra región. Esta posición me hizo una persona pública y mucho más ocupada con grandes retos frente a diversas instituciones y personas, pero lo que más atesoro son las lecciones aprendidas sobre el servicio.

Tomé un periodo de fortalecimiento espiritual y familiar después de terminar mi gestión en el Colegio Médico. Trabajé como Directora de la Unidad de Investigación de la UNSA con el objetivo de promoverla, y continúe enseñando Salud Pública. Por algunos años rechacé muchas oportunidades porque quería más tiempo para mí, mi familia y Dios. Serví por cuatro años como presidenta de la Sociedad de Socorro de estaca, así como otros llamamientos en la Sociedad de Socorro, Mujeres jóvenes y Escuela Dominical de barrio. Para el 2014 ya todos mis hijos varones habían regresado de sus misiones, fortaleciendo mí testimonio fuertemente. Su fidelidad y progreso trajeron gran gozo y paz a mi alma. Ha sido un gozo acompañarlos a ser sellados en el templo, y a algunos verlos perseguir sus sueños en el extranjero con la única compañía de nuestro Señor. Todas estas experiencias me ayudaron a considerar que la felicidad se encuentra en el hogar.

La Universidad donde laboraba requería una transformación y quería ayudar. La UNSA por muchos años estuvo estancada; necesitábamos hacerla resurgir. En diciembre del 2015, la lista de la que fui parte ganó las elecciones. Yo asumí el cargo de Vicerrectora Académica. Me invitaron por causa de mi carácter, convicciones, ideales de justicia y solidaridad y no por alguna influencia externa o interna. Agradezco lo que soy en la vida, a mis padres y la iglesia que me ayudaron a forjar metas y valores. Deseaba usar toda mi experiencia para devolver algo a la universidad que me brindó tantas oportunidades de desarrollo, y así ayudar a estudiantes, profesores, y administrativos.

Un gran problema requiere un gran cambio, y un gran cambio requiere mucho trabajo. El cargo de vicerrectora académica fue abrumador. Este periodo fue de transición debido a los cambios normativos, modificación de reglamentos, actualización de 59 programas académicos, licenciamiento institucional y acreditación, capacitación docente, cambios a los paradigmas de enseñanza, incorporar las Tecnologías de Información (TIC) y educación virtual. El primer año, dormía muy pocas horas, pero fui adaptándome a las largas jornadas diarias. La más grande bendición y decisión fue rodearme de personas buenas, capaces, motivadas y comprometidas que me ayudaron en momentos difíciles. Cada mañana y noche me arrodillaba en oración solicitando guía divina. Me sentí pequeña e inepta ante las grandes tareas que surgieron por casi 6 años en ese oficio, pero con la ayuda de Dios salí adelante. Ame sentarme a escuchar a todas las personas que conforman la universidad e intentar encontrar soluciones a sus necesidades.

Como Vicerrectora Académica pude ayudar en el desarrollo de docentes y estudiantes, lo que me alegra, porque al servir a mis semejantes siento que estoy al servicio de Dios. La posición de liderar académicamente una universidad de más 27000 estudiantes y 1700 docentes fue grandemente desafiante. Ahora después de casi seis años puedo mirar atrás y decir que luchamos la buena batalla e hicimos un gran trabajo para mejorar la calidad universitaria. La UNSA es ahora una de las cinco mejores universidades públicas del país. Durante nuestra gestión capacitamos a la mayoría de los docentes, y nuestros esfuerzos en generar competencias en Tecnologías de Información nos permitió ser la primera universidad pública en el Perú en iniciar el año académico 2020, durante la pandemia del COVID-19.

Sin embargo, el gozo más profundo proviene de mi familia porque implica ser parte de la vida de cada uno de ellos, al acompañarlos e influir en su formación y desarrollo espiritual y académico. Estoy satisfecha de tener una familia con cuatro hijos fuertes en el evangelio, quienes sirven fielmente en sus barrios y estacas. La familia ha crecido con nueras y nietos, así como logros académicos y profesionales. Pero la tranquilidad de vivir con esperanza en Cristo y la eternidad lo hace todo aún más grandioso. Tenemos la confianza de saber que tenemos lazos imperecederos, y que estamos construyendo una relación que va más allá de la muerte.

Mis experiencias profesionales me permiten ahora tener más definido lo que deseo hacer en el futuro. Yo quiero ayudar a otros a crecer, sobre todo en localidades rurales donde no hay muchas oportunidades para romper el círculo de la pobreza y la falta de capacitación. Me siento tranquila y agradecida por todo lo que me ha llevado a este punto. Quién hubiera pensado que la niña de campo lograría esta posición y viajaría a través del mundo aprendiendo de educación superior en Europa, Latinoamérica, Estados Unidos y mi propio país. Durante las decisiones más importantes, las variadas experiencias y acontecimientos, he sentido la influencia del Santo Espíritu, quien me sigue inspirando. El conocimiento en verdad es la gloria de Dios y él lo comparte libremente con nosotros si estamos dispuestos a dar y recibir.

From Peru, My Academic Development Hand in Hand with Faith

ANA MARÍA GUTIÉRREZ VALDIVIA

translated by D. Morgan Davis, Lori Forsyth, and Jorge Morales

THE PROFESSIONAL success I have achieved is based on the support of my family, faith, and effort in the midst of the difficult circumstances that surrounded me. All along the path I have traveled, I have had the hand of God to guide me in my most important decisions. I have humbly trusted in him, and this has brought me peace.

I was born in 1961 in an Arequipa hospital far from the countryside where my parents lived because they needed special medical attention for a C-section. As they were people of faith, they named me Ana María. Ana for the grandmother of Jesus (and patron of the region) and María after my maternal grandmother. My parents were industrious, honest, simple, and loving. They had scant education because in the province of Aplao, where they were raised, only elementary education was offered. My paternal grandfather and my maternal grandmother both passed away early, which was formative for the character and faith of my parents. Both devout Catholics, they taught me by their example to serve others.

Growing up with little, though enough, would help me throughout my life to be focused on what is most important. I was raised in the beautiful valley of Majes, a province of the Arequipa region, an agricultural area with pure air and a sky full of stars. We lived off what the land would produce and the animals we raised. Cultivating a field is an act of faith that depends on nature and on an unstable market. I shared my childhood and experiences with my beloved siblings, Nery, Tulita, and Niltón.

My interest in studying began when I was a very young girl. I was already attending school as a free student before I turned six. Due to a lack of electric lighting, I had to study by kerosene lamp and candles at night or when I could take advantage of the daylight. It was difficult because my help was also needed around the house with the domestic animals (chickens, turkeys, ducks, geese, pigs, sheep, and goats). Despite many disadvantages, I received several academic awards in school, and I was regularly assigned to teach my classmates. My parents prayed daily and taught me to commend myself to God, and I learned to trust in him. I have felt his company all my life, including when my father was unjustly jailed for several months for speaking out, along with other parents, against the physical abuse that a teacher inflicted on a child at the school.

Studying was never easy and always required sacrifice. At ten years of age, I moved to the city of Arequipa, nearly four hours away from my family, in order to continue my education. I lived for a year with some friends of my parents. It was hard for a girl facing social and cultural barriers as I was, studying in an urban school in an upper-class neighborhood. After a year, my mother came to live with me, and I transferred to a parochial school. Unfortunately, we lived very uncomfortably for a little more than two years in impoverished housing with a communal bathroom, and I could never invite my friends to visit me because I felt uncomfortable about our living situation. When I turned fifteen years old, we moved to the house that my parents had built, through much effort. Despite all the difficulties, I was awarded first place at the end of secondary school. I gave the valedictory address and received direct admission to college.

My time at college brought the blessing of the gospel. I enrolled at the National University of San Agustín (UNSA), majoring in medicine.

My sister Tulita lived with me while studying economics at a private university, and we shared household responsibilities. It was during this time that I came to know of the Church through Ricardo Gonzales, a friend at the university. I took the missionary discussions, read the Book of Mormon, and prayed. I received so much peace and warmth within my being, confirming the truth of what I had learned. When I was baptized, I felt the love of God and of Jesus Christ as never before, and I was literally born again.

The Church brought much happiness, many changes, and new responsibilities to my life. Now I had new meetings and customs. I learned to keep the Word of Wisdom despite the fact that for my family, coffee and wine were a part of their customs. Living with my sister, who also was baptized, helped us to support one another in being agents unto ourselves. With time, my extended family and friends came to respect my beliefs. I learned to take an interest in and love the sisters I was assigned to as a visiting teacher and to be faithful in that service out of love for the Savior. I also experienced sharing the gospel and helping in the conversion of a friend.

My time at college was busy and nonstop. I used to sell Christmas cards, textbooks, surgical supplies, and medical instruments to friends and acquaintances in order to teach young people by example that it was possible to study and work while also serving in the Church. Keeping the Sabbath day was difficult. At times, I could not finish studying for a Monday exam, but this built my faith in the Sabbath, which strengthened my marriage and is a family tradition that our children also share in their new homes.

Service in the Church brought me to marriage. I served as a stake young single adult (YSA) representative, and I would visit leaders and young people in the wards. It was during this time that I met my spouse, Luigi Morales Velásquez. The two of us held the same calling. We were married in the Lima Peru Temple on February 20, 1987, without our families. My parents were not members, and though my husband's family were members of the Church, they did not have the financial resources for the trip. My husband's mother had been widowed while Luigi was serving a mission, and he decided to stay and finish his service. We knew the Lord would not let us down, having seen our sacrifices.

It is possible to be faithful and move ahead in our academic development. The fruits of my academic efforts came at last. Upon completing my undergraduate degree, before my medical residency, I was third in my class of 125 graduating students. I felt that effort made in the service of the Lord had not hindered my academic preparation. Nevertheless, starting married life at the same time as a demanding residency with night and day shifts was even more difficult because I became pregnant. It was a great sacrifice for the whole family. Every step that I took during that time was with the help of my Heavenly Father. I would not have been able to care for my oldest child without the help of my husband and his family. At that time, in 1988, interest in the field of geriatrics had increased in Peru, and my senior thesis, "Renal Function in the Elderly," received national recognition. I graduated in January 1989 after completing this residency.

With the help of God and thanks to the teachings of the Church, we were able to overcome very difficult times in Peru. After finishing my residency, I focused on caring for my children, as I had had a second infant in March of 1989. It was a time of huge financial challenges—the country was suffering from an economic depression. Fortunately, we had the garden and some food storage, and so we weathered that gray time eating vegetables from our garden and also from the harvest of my parents. Economically, they were very dark years, but thanks to those experiences, we can now understand and help others in similar circumstances.

My career as a university lecturer began in 1991 as assistant *ad honorem* in public health at UNSA. Following a rigorous vetting process, they chose me to fill a slot that was created the next year, in 1992. I did not have a clinical specialty because I wanted more time with my family, and the lectureship allowed me to have a more flexible schedule. This helped me to spend a little more time with my three children during this period. In 1996, I decided to continue my studies with a master's in public health. Unfortunately, this would not allow me to spend much time with my fourth child, my only daughter, born in 1996. I have felt that I should have postponed the beginning of the master's program; nevertheless, I chose to spend quality time with her rather than increasing the quantity of time. We compensated for this later with shared experiences.

I know that the love of God does not discriminate based on gender. In the midst of these challenges, I sent my project, entitled "Factors Associated with the Invisibility of Violence Against Women in MINSA Establishments," to a master's thesis seminar on public health for Latin America and the Caribbean. The Pan American Health Organization selected it, financed it, and published it. The position and value of women in the plan of our Heavenly Father inspired me to focus on this theme, especially seeing the inequalities in my country. This experience opened up a line of research that I worked on with undergraduates. We strengthened and taught groups affected by domestic violence. Afterward, I consulted on gender equality policies for an NGO with support from a Canadian organization working toward gender equality through promoting more active participation by men in their role as fathers.

After my master's degree, I learned even more about life in unexpected ways. My mother passed away in 2005 after a three-year battle with lung cancer. Soon my father joined her in death after suffering a cerebral-vascular accident. They inspired me to write poems (one of my talents), and I read a poem dedicated to each of them at their funerals. Many helped at their wakes and burials because they admired their service and devotion to the community and to God. My father received a medal from the city of Castilla for his contribution to local development and for being a committed citizen.

I decided to pursue further study in the field of public health as I was interested in population problems and their prevention. Accordingly, in 2006, I began a doctorate in public health. I focused my dissertation on medical pedagogy: "The Employment of Medical Residency According to Student Perceptions." I got involved in qualitative study, which allowed me to deepen concepts and explain behaviors of individuals and groups.

Little by little, political and administrative opportunities began to arise. I was added to a roster as treasurer of the board of directors of the regional chapter of medical professionals. I had no experience with this kind of role nor with elections, but I was known as a trustworthy person of integrity, and I believe that this is what many were looking for in supporting the candidacy. We won and worked for two years (2009–2010) on several committees, always seeking to provide the best to the healthcare workers of our region with fairness and opportunity. This position made me a public person and much busier, which in turn brought great challenges with various institutions and people, but I treasure the lessons learned, especially of service.

I spent some time in spiritual and family strengthening after the end of my term in administration in the medical chapter. I worked as director of the research unit of UNSA with the objective of promoting it, and I continued teaching public health. For some years, I turned down many opportunities because I wanted more time for me, my family, and God. I served for four years as the president of the Relief Society in my stake, in other Relief Society callings, in Young Women, and in Sunday School in the ward. By 2014, all of my sons had returned from their missions, greatly strengthening my testimony. Their faithfulness and growth brought great joy and peace to my soul. It has been a joy to accompany them to be sealed in the temple and to see them pursuing their dreams abroad with only the company of our Lord. All of these experiences helped me to remember that happiness is found in the home.

The university where I worked required a transformation, and I wanted to help. UNSA had been stagnant for many years; we needed to facilitate a resurgence. In December of 2015, I was part of a roster of professors who won the university elections. I was to be part of this group as academic vice chancellor. They invited me not because of some external or internal influence but because of my character, convictions, and ideals of justice and solidarity. I am grateful for my life, my parents, and the Church, which have helped me to forge my goals and values. I desired to use all of my experience to give back to the university that had given me so many opportunities for development and thus to help students, professors, and administrators.

Great problems require great change, and great change requires great effort. The burden of being academic vice chancellor was overwhelming. This period was one of transition due to regulatory changes, modification of regulations, updating of fifty-nine academic programs, institutional licensing and accreditation, teacher training, changes to teaching paradigms, incorporating information technology (ICT), and virtual education. The first year, I slept very little but gradually adapted to the long working hours. The greatest blessing and decision was to surround myself with good, capable, motivated, and committed people who helped me through difficult times. Every morning and night, I knelt in prayer requesting divine guidance. I felt small and inept in the face of the great tasks that arose for almost six years, but with God's help, I have succeeded. I loved sitting down to listen to all the people that make up this university and to take time to find solutions to their needs.

As academic vice chancellor, I helped in the development of teachers and students, which brought me happiness because in serving my fellow beings, I feel that I am in the service of God. The position of academically leading a university of over 27,000 students and 1,700 faculty was challenging. Now, after six years, I can look back and say that we fought the good fight and did great work in improving the university's quality. UNSA is now one of the five best public universities in the country. During our presidency, we trained the majority of teachers, and our efforts to develop competencies in information technologies allowed us to be the first public university in Peru to open the 2020 academic year virtually during the COVID-19 pandemic.

However, my deepest joy comes from my family by being part of each one of their lives, accompanying them, and influencing their spiritual and academic formation and development. I am pleased to have a family with four children strong in the gospel who serve faithfully in their wards and stakes. The family has grown, adding daughters-in-law and grandchildren, as well as academic and professional accomplishments. But the tranquility of living with hope in Christ and in eternity makes everything even greater. We have trust in the knowledge that our ties are everlasting and that we are building a relationship that goes beyond death.

My professional experiences now allow me to better define what I want to do in the future. I want to help others grow, especially in rural areas where there are not many opportunities to break the cycle of poverty and where there is a lack of training. I feel at peace with and grateful for everything that has brought me to this point. Who would have thought that a little girl from the countryside would achieve this position and travel the world learning about higher education, coming to know Europe, Latin America, the United States, and my own country? During my most important decisions, through a variety of experiences and events, I have felt the influence of the Holy Spirit, who continues to inspire me. Knowledge indeed is the glory of God, and he freely shares it with us if we are willing to give and receive.

PART TWO

In theory, in principle, in doctrine, in the law of the gospel ... of things both in heaven and in the earth, and under the earth

(Doctrine and Covenants 88:78–79)

God placed us into a world governed by natural and moral laws.

The truth of the Creators' laws harmonizes beautifully with the truth of our divine nature.

Faith as a Complex Ecosystem

KYRA N. KRAKOS

Kyra N. Krakos is a professor of biology and director of the sustainability program at Maryville University and a research associate at the Missouri Botanical Garden. She earned her BS and MS at Brigham Young University and her PhD at Washington University in St. Louis. She was named Science Educator of the Year by the Academy of Science of St. Louis in 2016. Her lab focuses on the need to understand the dynamics of the natural world in a changing environment. You can find her TEDx talk from 2015 under "Plants, Pollinators and People: A Love Story." Originally from California, Kyra is a happy St. Louis, Missouri, native-by-choice, where she lives with her husband and three children in a home that is "very, very nerdy."

IT IS EARLY MORNING, and I am petting bees.

During the growing season, my job shifts from professor to field pollination biologist, and the balance of indoors and outdoors suits me. There is a faint steamy morning fog still hovering over the prairie, lending an air of magic to my morning. The bees are sluggish before the full sun hits them, so I can reach out and stroke their fuzzy bellies. I whisper to them that I can relate—I too am not a morning person.

My student team will arrive soon to join me at our research site, and we will have several hours to collect data before the heat of a summer prairie sun convinces most living things of the wisdom of a siesta. Until then, I am Eve, walking in my Garden, enjoying the peace of anticipated discovery.

I have been studying pollination systems for over fifteen years. Understanding pollination is important to human survival: over 85 percent of wild flowering plants depend to some extent on pollination. Honeybees alone pollinate about 66 percent of the world's 1,500 crop species, accounting for 15–30 percent of food production.[1] Economically, up to $577 billion worth of annual global food production relies on direct contributions by pollinators.[2] Pollination is also important to human happiness since chocolate requires a pollinator!

Some people would look out over a prairie field like this and drive on. Others would appreciate the seasonal explosion of wildflowers. Hikers might look at the tall grasses and shiver at the lurking ticks and chiggers. That is not what I see. I see a competitive battlefield of seduction and promiscuous rivalry, the field teeming with sexual tension and diversity. Here, the shape of the flowers, the nectar, the scent, and a hundred other different flower characters have raced down evolutionary paths of every direction to entice and lure in a pollinator. The plants face an old problem for their biological kingdom—they cannot move, but they must mate. The competition for pollinators is fierce, and all is fair in this war. There is no weird tactic for survival or reproduction that is not worth an evolutionary attempt by a plant species. The story of a plant and its pollinator is rarely the simple one-to-one interaction taught in grade school, like the sweet story of a red, dangling, long-tubed flower that is visited only by a hummingbird that has just the right tongue length to access its nectar. "Look how lovely and orderly the natural world is as it works together!" The reality is that a member of the pollination web is more likely to have multiple shifting partners, and many plants, as a last resort, can self-pollinate. I regularly run experiments to test who is dallying with that risky inbreeding option.

For me, pollination is a fascinating complex system to be discovered and understood. Like many complex systems, it can lose many of

1. J. Ollerton, R. Winfree, and S. Tarrant, "How many flowering plants are pollinated by animals?," *Oikos* 120 (2011): 321–26.

2. "Summary for policymakers of the assessment report of the intergovernmental science-policy platform on biodiversity and ecosystem services on pollinators, pollination and food production," in *Secretariat of the intergovernmental science-policy platform on biodiversity and ecosystem services*, ed. S. G. Potts et al. (Bonn, Germany: IPBES, 2016).

the interacting flowers and pollinators of the network to extinction or climate change but hold together because of the redundancies built into the system. However, shake the network too long and hard, and it will collapse. The pollination web is intricate, in peril, and in need of our care, understanding, and active preservation.

My faith is a complex system. The fragile web of answers from parents, teachers, and Church leaders that sustained my childhood faith could not withstand the shaking of my questions as I grew. As I learned to think critically, I had to build a new system with redundant mechanisms for nurturing faith and spiritual growth in the face of new information and more complex questions. My spiritual identity was ground down and rebuilt again and again. My understanding comes in agonizing incremental steps.

My whole life, I have been intent on gaining new information—it is a defining characteristic. I was the one looking for the secret garden, the wardrobe that led to another world, the key to a mysterious book; my hunger to open a forbidden box rivaled Pandora's. I was certain that the magic, the answers, the *more information* was going to be revealed soon. Growing up as a Latter-day Saint in the 1980s and 1990s, the promise of that bigger reveal was a key part of the narrative. We were the generation that would usher in the Second Coming of Christ. There was a promise of secret and sacred knowledge, of more to be had, if we hit all the proper milestones. I grew up dissatisfied.

My dissatisfaction at the lack of big new knowledge showed up early in Primary and Sunday School, where, in retrospect, I'm sure my endless questions were exhausting to my poor teachers. When I was in my tweens, my father was called as bishop. The day my father brought home his newly minted bishopric material, I quietly slipped the for-authorized-priesthood-holders-only *Handbook 1* out of the stack and squirreled away to read it cover to cover. Hoping for revelation, I found only bureaucracy. I was too young then to see some of the problematic assumptions underlying teachings on topics such as birth control or how to counsel a rape victim in those dry words. I went away still unsatisfied, still wondering where I would find the key to the secret garden.

> The sweetest thing in all my life has been the longing—
> to reach the Mountain, to find the place
> where all the beauty came from—[3]

Prior to my mission, these lines hung on my wall, centering all my hopes on the promised knowledge of the temple. Coupled with my dissatisfied hunger was also the perpetual anticipation of new information. I had spent years preparing for the temple rituals, as earnest Latter-day Saint kids do, by participating in early-morning seminary, earning the Young Women medallion, and attending temple preparation classes. Here at last, I thought, I would find the knowledge I had been seeking for so long. The day finally came, and I went to the temple with my parents and other family members. Afterward, I smiled and nodded as my excited family asked what I thought of the experience and kept silent about my deep disappointment at the lack of new information about our theology that I had expected from the temple experience.

That hunger for a place in this world that had new information inevitably drove me to science. But science did not suddenly reveal a new world to me—it taught me new, laborious ways of seeing and knowing. My faith and hope are rooted in the Church, and this background ran into a tension with scientific thinking. At church, I had been raised to not question the authority of leaders and taught that obedience to the established rules was a high ideal. In the world of science, I was taught that authority and status quo are to be challenged, aggressively, with constantly renewed and reexamined data. Something had to give.

Despite all the lessons of a girl raised in the Church in the 1980s, I ended up a scientist instead of a stay-at-home mother. It took me a decade to shed guilt and a sense of failure and just embrace that I was more authentic and a better mother as a working-mom botanist. The natural world of plants was the secret world that I craved as a child. Botany is not reverent, so it was a good fit. I am one for loud laughter and natural rowdiness. I wove the parts of my life together, tracking plant-pollinator networks all over the world with my babies in tow. There are pictures of my ten-week-old daughter at a research

3. C. S. Lewis, *Till We Have Faces: A Myth Retold* (London: G. Bles, 1956), 75.

site in my smiling mother's arms while I hover nearby tagging a plant.

Science transformed me in bone-crushing ways. I suspect if there is an eternal day of judgment, it is something akin to the experience of the agony and indifference of a qualifying exam or dissertation defense when getting a PhD. You stand with nothing but what you carry inside you. The committee of established scientists is the unmerciful bar of judgment, and for as long as they see fit, they can ask you anything. They drill down on your abilities, find the edges of your knowledge, and peel it back. The committee sniffs out your fear and trills for the blood in the water. (Or so it felt; in reality, they were doing their job, and they were very supportive during my schooling.) It leaves you raw, exhausted, and transformed. The scabs form, you heal, and the scars are yours. You are reborn, a peer, a newly minted PhD. Congratulations, you now know a lot about one small thing.

> Lord of dimensions and the dimensionless,
> Wave and particle, all and none,
>
> Who lets us measure the wounded atom,
> Who lets us doubt all measurement,
>
> When in this world we betray you
> Let us be faithful in another.[4]

While these changes in the way I interacted with the world and ideas impacted my faith, they also gave me new pathways of understanding faith. The different ways of knowing in science and in my spiritual life became redundancies, strengthening me, making my wisdom durable. The complex pollination networks I was studying became my new personal analogy for caring for my spiritual well-being. I focused on how small things can be very important, on the ways that both the emergent properties of a system as well as the grubby details require attention. Natural systems are both fragile and capable of resiliency, and it is vital to identify the crucial parts of a network if you want to keep it intact. I explored what parts of my faith were key in

4. Mark Jarman, "Five Psalms," in *To the Green Man* (Louisville, KY: Sarabande Books, 2004), 47.

the health and strength of my personal spiritual network. I once sat in a meeting listening to a colleague talk about how the years of careful detailed data collection were finally going to pay off in testing a new mathematical model, and I gravely said, "This is excellent, and it really illustrates how we learn the bigger concepts line upon line, precept upon precept." I loved my own private joke, but it was also true. Whether in a Sunday School class or a lab, we learn step by step.

When I teach evolution every spring semester in the Midwest, there is always more than one student who comes haltingly to my office only to melt down over their own struggle between faith and science. In these cases, the education I received as a young person in the Church surfaces to help me out in unanticipated ways. A student in my office recently was weeping, saying that perhaps her desire to go to medical school is impossible to reconcile with her faith tradition. I may not have wisdom to share, but I can be in the place of tension with my students. I can empathize with their pain and share the ways that I have learned to live joyfully with unresolved questions. I draw on older lessons in my life in these instances, such as the New Testament and Old Testament classes I had at BYU that academically opened the nuance of scriptural language and helped me forge new paths of understanding.

Often, the lessons I teach fall under the heading "science is a how; faith is a why." For example, photosynthesis is the mechanism for how a tree is made, but it isn't mentioned in the creation story in Genesis. Genesis will tell you why there was a creation and that it was good. Science lets us understand the hows. Being a disciple means being a better scholar of both the hows and the whys. You might need to study different translations of the scriptures. You will need to read primary scientific literature, dig deep on understanding genetics and what Darwin really taught to see that the mechanism of evolution leads to a world of wondrous biodiversity but does not challenge your identity as a child of God. Remember not all parts of your humanity can be measured as quantifiable data.

I tell my students that are struggling what I tell myself: be patient. Understanding in any area comes in small steps, and I have to be content with that. Revelation rarely comes all at once. Science is the most satisfying for me because data is, or can be, "real"—it isn't dependent on what I think. The math of gravity exists outside of human paradigms or constructs, and learning to understand it is a way of touching realities larger than myself. A universe of order and consistency speaks to me of a Creator who is not arbitrary or careless.

In the front of every field journal I have had since the age of eighteen, I have written the last few lines of a poem I discovered my freshman year at BYU. I read them to the student in my office and hope they are enough. Perhaps they will hold her together while she grows, as they do for me.

> I have not found the Islands
> of the blest, Islands of peace;
> but would believe in them,
> would search for them, would
> keep them floating
> with my breath.[5]

Those islands, those secret worlds of more knowledge, elude me still, but there are moments I glimpse a balance that makes me feel whole. I was only twenty-four years old when I held my firstborn. In awe, I watched him snuffling hungry mammal sounds as he lay in my arms, and in that moment, I felt the first understanding of what the love of God might be. I was also a female mammal holding her young, overwhelmed with the flood of biochemicals that would ensure my care for the next generation of my genetic line. I love my new little son. I am biologically programmed to care for him. One is the how; the other is the why. Which is true? I take joy and solace that both are true.

The sun is climbing higher, and the bees are moving faster. They are no longer patient with me—it is time to get to the business of bee work. I inhale the dark earth smell of the prairie and feel the humidity burrow down in my lungs. I love it tangibly. Here is the secret world unfurling its answers one data point at a time. Here is the garden where I walk with God. Here is where I find that my humanity is part of my divinity.

5. Leslie Norris, "Islands of Peace," in *The Complete Poems* (Brigend, Wales: Poetry Wales Press, 1985), 248–51.

In Search of the Wise

KIMBERLY APPLEWHITE TEITTER

Kimberly Applewhite Teitter, PsyD, is a licensed clinical psychologist, a published author, an adjunct professor, and an entrepreneur in the Salt Lake City area. She received a BA in psychology from New York University (New York, NY) and an MS in school psychology and a doctorate in psychology in school-clinical child psychology from the Ferkauf Graduate School of Psychology of Yeshiva University (Bronx, NY). Kimberly received the Leadership Education in Adolescent Health psychology postdoctoral fellowship at Boston Children's Hospital Division of Adolescent/Young Adult Medicine (Boston, MA) and was a fellow at Harvard Medical School before moving to Utah. Kimberly is a bishop's wife and mother of two daughters, as well as the assistant director of the Debra Bonner Unity Gospel Choir.

❖

As a child, I was always attracted to wisdom. My family lore goes that I taught myself how to read when I was three years old and was often found with a book in hand. Fortunately for my parents' peace of mind, we did not have much in the way of salacious media; there were mainly the encyclopedia sets that door-to-door salesmen used to peddle, whatever pamphlets were brought home from the hospital or the pharmacy where my mother and father worked, and the scriptures.

As I learned the simple gospel messages of God's love and mercy, I also read about the side effects of emerging medications and the developing technology of holograms. I drank everything in and wanted to know more. When I read, I felt a fullness and an increase of light; it would have been intoxicating if it hadn't felt so holy to me. I figured as long as I was continuously seeking for that light, that wisdom, I would be on a fulfilling path that God wanted for me.

I grew up on the outskirts of a small North Carolinian town. Most African American families like ours lived inside the city limits, but my family lived in the country. Being a Black child, especially one that was so precocious about learning, was, shall we say, complicated. I can vaguely remember being trotted out to read for people when I was a young child or being put in the center of my local Church leaders' visions of diversity and unity, enough that I understood that there was a suspicion around people who looked like me being able to do what I could do. I heard rumors about the kids who went to city schools (most of whom looked like me)—that their schools were dirty, their behavior was poor, and they weren't the type of people I would want to be around. I also was aware that there weren't many other Black families at church either, and though I didn't know the history of why this was the case, I certainly found the lack to be conspicuous.

Being a member of The Church of Jesus Christ of Latter-day Saints, which was the only religious tradition I personally had known, meant that in many ways, we were cut off from Black cultural practices, which often centered around their home churches. I can remember being so shocked to see my mom swaying back and forth to the beat of gospel music when we'd ride in the car to church on Sundays or when we'd visit my grandmother at her Baptist church. *This isn't in the hymnal!* I would think. *Should we really be clapping in church?*

I could not make sense of how to reconcile my own ethnic identity with what everyone else seemed to expect of me. My heart often filled with fear as I tried to make sense of these things, but the feeling felt almost like a fear without grounding, a fear I couldn't really commit to because it didn't make sense. Part of me was afraid that people would see me like they saw those city kids, part of me worried about how those city kids would see me, and part of me felt like I wanted to hide from the whole endeavor and not be paraded around. The rest of me was frustrated at myself for not wanting to let my light shine like the scriptures said. I often felt like I was trying to hold to what made sense to me in the way that Nephi envisioned people moving toward the tree of life in his dream, but mists of darkness and confusion threatened to cover my way.

To figure out how to make meaning of my life, I started to orient myself to whatever feeling of light I could find; when I sought after that light, I often felt that feeling of centeredness and fullness that I felt as a child in the midst of all my books. It would be years before Elder David A. Bednar would give his address on revelation being like the growing light of a sunrise rather than a bulb on a switch, but that was akin to how I learned to experience the influence of the Lord in my life.[1]

There were two major sunrise periods in my life as a teenager that influenced my spiritual journey as well as my career path and kept them growing side by side. The first, guided by my parents, was my journey to understand the intersection of my identity as a child of God and a Black woman through various cultural immersion experiences. I felt my eyes open to the inherent divine connections that were found in the elements of worship from my parents' previous traditions and in our family sense of spirituality. When I came to understand myself in context, I saw how the Lord's love could extend past the worldly conceptualizations of marginalization, prejudice, and hatred. I began to find value in the strengths of my heritage and how those strengths had led me to increased light in my life. And as my heart grew to love myself, my heart could "[swell] wide as eternity" (Moses 7:41) for my

1. David A. Bednar, "The Spirit of Revelation," April 2011 General Conference, https://www.churchofjesuschrist.org/study/general-conference/2011/04/the-spirit-of-revelation?lang=eng.

fellow heavenly siblings—first for the kids who looked like me across town in the city and then for the Lord's sheep in different lands and circumstances. When I read in a magazine about safe spaces for queer youth, I felt that increase of wisdom and light witness to me that the Lord wanted that for them too. I developed a firm testimony that the Lord loves all his children and that the gospel has a place for everyone in it.

I decided that I wanted to find a way in my life to help foster that development of divine potential in other people, and this came to be through my second "sunrise" moment of revelation. I initially planned to go into teaching, until I felt the darkening of the path when I couldn't ascertain how to have the most influence. In high school, I felt an urge to follow my love of learning to a residential magnet school for science and mathematics, even though I had never felt that those were my strongest academic areas. I lived across the hall from a girl who mentioned that she planned to take a psychology class from a teacher with a reputation for leniency, hoping to get an easy grade in between her more rigorous coursework. I had never had an interest in psychology before, but I felt a sense of fullness and clarity when I decided to join her. And through taking that class, I came to believe that much of the world's systemic disparities are perpetuated by unresolved mental health issues that become misinterpreted, just like with the rumors I had heard about the kids across town. Without a fair amount of research, only seeking after the light I had always striven to follow, I pursued the path of becoming a clinical psychologist.

When I work with patients today, I often tell them that if I had known that being a psychologist would require going through the psychology major, I wouldn't have made it. I was in for a rude awakening when I entered my first psychology classes as an undergraduate at New York University. I had gone down this road thinking that I would be working with people, but instead, I was learning about the *brain*—neurons, impulses, synapses, lobes, and pathways. I struggled to move past my expectations and engage in the work before me. It was easy to get distracted by other things that felt more fulfilling. To top it off, getting a psychology degree in the late 2000s was a unique kind of gamble. I can remember classmates walking out to join the protestors at Occupy Wall Street. I recall a prominent donation to my college being compromised when a donor was arrested in a financial scheme related to the subprime lending crisis. My loving but worried father sent me an article talking about how psychology was one of the least lucrative fields due to needing a doctorate degree in a lengthy program to have optimal flexibility in your career path. I tried to disregard what he said, but then our department hosted a meeting that said even a terminal degree in psychology wasn't very fruitful in the economy of the day. I didn't know what to do—I was trying to follow the ways I had felt light and wisdom guide me in my life, but this didn't seem like the path I needed or wanted to be on.

Years after I graduated from college, I listened to a prominent gospel musician speak on how he turned his life from what could have been a successful touring career in popular music to the gospel music path he chose. At the time that he was at his fork in the road, he told us, he felt it would have been crazy to give up the financial freedom that pursuing the more glamorous option would afford him. But he quoted the Lord speaking in Isaiah, saying, "For my thoughts are not your thoughts, neither are your ways my ways, saith the Lord" (55:8). The musician said that often we are quick to acknowledge the words of that scripture and understand the divine wisdom of the Lord, but when we feel directed in our lives to pursue a surprising or unexpected path, we are quick to say that that path must *not* be of God.

I wish I had that wisdom back as a confused undergrad, but my willingness to follow the light, even as dim as it was, helped me navigate a school experience that stoked a passion for psychology again. In my last years of school, NYU opened their state-of-the-art Child Study Center for evidence-based therapy treatments and developed a child and adolescent mental health studies minor. I was able to align with the values of shaping the minds of youth that had given me the initial interest in psychology and developed a love for the growing youth brain in context of the holistic self, including youth behavior and lived experiences.

After finishing my undergraduate work and while moving through my doctoral program in psychology, I was tasked with finding what my primary orientation would be. In therapy work, an orientation comes across as the language you speak but has as much connection to identity as language does to its home culture. Orienting yourself gives you a primary way to conceptualize the problems or concerns of a patient when they enter the room, determine the best course of action for intervention, and assess and predict behavior in the future. My program was psychodynamically oriented, which meant that it borrowed from the intellectual descendants of Freud to look at inner drives and early relational patterns. I could speak that language, but it often came out with an accent. When it came time to choose a supervisor for my research project, I had no idea whom to choose until I felt inner clarity about going with one of the prickliest professors in our program. At that point, my fatigued and frantic grad school brain didn't feel remotely capable of wisdom, but I figured that following that sense of light had not failed me up to this point. It turned out that this professor was the strongest ally to all kinds of diverse humans who have come through my program and was especially cognizant of mentorship of BIPOC (Black, Indigenous, People of Color) students. She navigated complex client situations with a skill that I grew to admire. She worked through a multicultural family systems lens and was quickly being wooed over to a dialectical behavioral approach. These models ended up being the defining hallmarks of my own clinical conceptualization and have helped me align my spiritual life with the professional even more clearly as I work to bring the ethics of mercy and compassion into balance with the need for change.

In a family systems perspective, behavior is examined relative to its function in the context around it; in other words, rather than look at a behavior and judge it as good or bad, right or wrong, we ask questions of a tone familiar to those immersed in the gospel: *What is this behavior? What is its purpose here? Where is it going?* In facilitating change, it is recognized that a behavior exists because it has served a purpose and filled a need. Family systems theory emphasizes the interconnectedness of people within families and through the generations in an eternal ebb and flow of seeking for balance in relationships. In this view, so many behaviors that seem unforgivable are understood in context which helps provide insight that leads to movement and growth. It is akin to how the Savior ministered to the woman caught in adultery, first condemning her accusers, recognizing the prevalence of sin and interconnectedness of behavior between the woman and her accusers, and then encouraging the woman to "go, and sin no more" (John 8:11).

From my perspective as a clinical psychologist, Latter-day Saints believe in an interconnected eternal family system in which we inherit traits both human and divine. It is a comfort to me to think of my own progress and that of those around me as part of a continuous ebb and flow in the quest for eternal growth and balance. I can have behavior that helps my progress just as easily as I can have behavior that is *less* helpful, but all behavior is held in context and understandable in the system as a whole. It allows me to be more forgiving of myself and others as it deemphasizes finding the fault in our actions in favor of seeking to understand their purpose or function.

One of the first jobs I had when I moved to Utah was in a setting with many White members of the Church. I had seen many people I grew up with back East who moved to Utah for this very reason, to finally get a sense of relief to be "amongst the Saints." However, I struggled to find a place of belonging, particularly when my identity as a Black woman or my desire to advocate for marginalized groups felt conspicuous. The first person I called was my grad school supervisor, who listened patiently through my tears. She then reminded me, "These are human primates, mainly White men, maintaining the system of power they know. This place is working just as you would expect." As I internalized those words, I held compassion for the persecution narratives that have been transmitted generationally from Latter-day Saint pioneers and onward and understood why some today might still feel the need to be hypervigilant of anyone who might be different enough from the group to be a threat. I placed this in context with the national strife that has used racial phenotype as a signal for insider and outsider status. As I looked at the whole system, it gave me the wisdom I needed to let go and move on. This is one of many ways that a family systems perspective has helped me to make sense of the systemic issues of the world that affect my life and those I love—racism, classism, homonegativity and homophobia, power and privilege; these forces, while causing pain, are products of a system where behavior has function.

My primary mode of working with clients today is in the dialectical behavior therapy model, which was developed to intervene with chronically suicidal individuals or people whose experience of emotion leads to difficulty in their lives. Some of these people experience negative emotion more strongly than other people; others find it hard to keep their emotions from fluctuating too quickly in crisis situations; still others find it hard to return to a place of calm after their emotions have been provoked. The people I see have often experienced traumatic events (a singular instance or chronically over time) or don't have the experience of having a safe and validating space. Many of them come to me when they've tried every other medication, been to multiple therapists, and have been in and out of hospitals for most of their lives. These clients come with a profound level of hopelessness that often feels like a mist of darkness. Together, we go through the process of seeking for glimpses of light, those sunrise moments of insight.

In a way that I feel can only be explained by the synchronicity of the universe and the divine truth inherent in all things, the place where insight is held and peace is found is in the synthesis of reason and emotion, the middle path between being and doing—just as I have experienced in the truths of my own life. There are many ways that I guide clients to finding this place for themselves: imagining that they are a light flake of a stone, drifting slowly down to the bottom of a lake, feeling full and satisfied; picturing themselves descending down a spiral staircase, growing more and more centered; or, most simply and most truly, asking the question—*is this wise?*

Faith in Science

JULIE BARROTT WILLIS

Julie Barrott Willis was raised in Idaho as the third oldest of ten children. She earned BS and MS degrees in geology from Brigham Young University and a PhD from the University of Utah; she did her doctoral field research in Alaska toting a shotgun given to her for Mother's Day. She is a professor and associate dean at BYU–Idaho, where she has mentored several undergraduates in active tectonics research. Her 2012 BYU–Idaho devotional address, "Gaining Light through Questioning," is published in the online version of At the Pulpit: 185 Years of Discourses by Latter-day Saint Women. *Her life was strongly influenced by parents who encouraged her to explore and question and by her Grandmother Barrott who, despite educational disadvantages, stepped out of traditional 1940s norms to be a business leader. Julie and her husband have three children and two grandchildren. She likes to hike, ski, bike, and camp with her family, play the piano, and read in front of a fire.*

"IT'S TRUE!" As a newly declared geology major, I set down my textbook with a deep sense of awe and reverence. My intellect working in tandem with the Holy Ghost, a verifier of *truth*, confirmed plate tectonics as a unifying concept in geology.[1] The implications were equally

1. John 14:26; Moroni 10:5.

clear: earth's tectonic and hydrologic processes have shaped the earth for a very long time.

My study of geology was fueled by curiosity about the diverse features I observed in the physical world. I was raised on the flat Snake River Plain yet could see the rugged Teton Mountains rising abruptly to the east; I played on black basalt that looked vastly different in color and texture from pebbles I picked up in creek beds; I swam in the Snake River, which ranged from calm river bends to waterfalls within sight of my home; and yearly, we drove the short distance to explore Yellowstone National Park with its otherworldly landscape.

How did this geologic variety happen? Were the Teton Mountains built and the Grand Canyon carved in one day? Was the ocean created salty, while rivers were not? Was the earth's diversity created in seven days? Logic and reason suggested not. Could my faith support reason? Could faith and reason work together?

Gaining knowledge is a principle doctrine of The Church of Jesus Christ of Latter-day Saints. Scriptures state that the "glory of God is intelligence" (Doctrine and Covenants 93:36) and that "if a person gains more knowledge and intelligence in this life ... [they] will have so much the advantage in the world to come" (Doctrine and Covenants 130:19). Scriptures and prophets encourage pursuing all sources of knowledge, including science. As select examples, we are to teach each other "of things both in heaven and in the earth, and under the earth" (Doctrine and Covenants 88:79). Brigham Young, referring to the youth of the Church, stated, "When they are old enough, place within their reach the advantages and benefits of a scientific education. Let them study the formation of the earth, the organization of the human system, and other sciences."[2]

My purpose in sharing this essay is to help non-scientists and scientists see faith in science and faith in God not as adversarial but as inclusive sources of truth. Viewing them in tandem can help scientists preserve faith in God and non-scientists cultivate faith in science.

2. Brigham Young, "Cease to Bring in and Build up Babylon ...," in *Journal of Discourses* (Liverpool: F. D. and S. W. Richards, 1875), 17:45.

Revelatory and scientific methods are valid truth-seeking tools

Revelatory methods and scientific methods are both valid tools, useful within their own spheres for seeking knowledge. They both follow a pattern of asking questions, seeking answers, interpreting information, and sharing newfound knowledge.[3]

The key to gaining any new knowledge is to actively ask questions and seek answers.[4] Scientists ask questions based on empirical observations, then collect empirical data to answer them. An example from my own research is asking questions about the relationship between earthquake faults observed at earth's surface and the subducting tectonic plates underneath them. Empirical observations include the types and magnitudes of earthquakes and how they change from one end of a fault to another.[5] As explained by Moore and others, "Empirical observations [and data] are factual descriptions of the physical world.... Their validity does not depend on an observer's philosophical perspective, personal opinion, or mood."[6] After making sufficient observations, scientists use logic and an understanding of fundamental scientific principles to make an interpretation. They then submit their work for review by peers who evaluate the observations, methods, and interpretations to ensure the work is unbiased and accurate. Studies that are not peer reviewed are not accepted as science.

Not all questions can be answered by empirical methods. Those of a religious nature require subjective approaches such as prayer,

3. Dan Moore, Brian Tonks, and Alan Holyoak, "Seeking Truth through Science and Religion: Being Disciple Scholars," *Perspective: Understand Great Teaching* 12, no. 2 (2012): 16–22.

4. Julie B. Willis, "Gaining Light through Questioning," BYU–Idaho devotional, 2014, and in online version of *At the Pulpit: 185 Years of Discourses by Latter-day Saint Women*, ed. Jennifer Reeder and Kate Holbrook, https://www.churchhistorianspress.org/at-the-pulpit/bonus-chapters/bonus-7?lang=eng.

5. J. B. Willis, P. J. Haeussler, R. L. Bruhn, and G. C. Willis, "New Holocene Slip Rate and Revised Characteristic Earthquake Parameters, Castle Mountain Fault, Alaska," *Bulletin of the Seismological Society of America* 97, no. 3 (2007): 1019–24, doi: 10.17850120060109.

6. Moore et al., "Seeking Truth through Science and Religion," 17.

discussion, and studying and seeking insights from both religious and non-religious sources.[7] Subjective methods enable revelation of new knowledge, but unlike empirical observations, they cannot be replicated by a peer and thus are more open to varied interpretations. This does not invalidate them, but it does highlight a key difference between revealed and scientific knowledge: peer review can neither confirm nor disprove a subjective experience, its interpretation, or the truth it revealed.

As a science professor, I encounter students who do not trust science because some of its interpretations or recommendations differ from their personal worldview. I strive to help them increase their faith in science by separating empirical-based evidence from opinion. I often share this advice from my husband and fellow geologist: "No one person or scientist is an expert in all areas. So, on any topic, find the experts, and determine what the majority of experts conclude." A clear expert majority lends credence to scientific conclusions and should be weighed against personal, religious, or political bias.

Finding truth is an evolving pursuit of knowledge

Science is an iterative process of continued discovery and adaptation. Interpretations of empirical data and recommended procedures based on them change as new data are collected and interpreted. As an example, most Western doctors in the 1700s believed that bloodletting cured disease. But new observations proved them wrong—in the case of a patient with a high fever and abdominal pain (empirical observation), their appendix might be infected (new data gained through medical dissections), and surgical removal, which had proven more effective than bloodletting, would be indicated (procedural change).

As a more modern example, little was known about earthquake hazards when unreinforced stone and brick buildings were constructed

7. Alma 5:45–46.

during the nineteenth century in the flat valley of the Great Salt Lake. However, mounting empirical evidence, gathered in the twentieth and twenty-first centuries, indicates that the seemingly innocuous Salt Lake Valley is subject to large periodic earthquakes that will intensely shake unconsolidated sediments and collapse the nineteenth- and early twentieth-century masonry buildings, killing or injuring the occupants.[8] In response to published and peer-reviewed articles about the pending earthquake, community and Church leaders joined efforts to seismically retrofit several historic, unreinforced stone and brick public buildings, including the historic Salt Lake Temple and the Utah State Capitol; their leadership to mitigate death hopefully will be joined by others who own unreinforced masonry homes, apartments, and schools.[9] Other life-saving measures that resulted from earthquake research include implementing building codes that no longer allow construction of unreinforced brick and stone buildings in earthquake country and developing scientifically tested ways to inexpensively mitigate seismic-induced collapse of adobe homes—a global problem impacting millions of people in South and Central America, Africa, and India.[10]

Modern societies owe much to the continual discovery and adaptation of scientific knowledge. Science provides the foundation for humans to solve problems and progress toward a more equitable global society including many issues that tend to unfairly impact the economically challenged of all races and in all countries. As a few limited examples, scientists help engineers identify areas of the world that are most

8. M. N. Machette, S. F. Personius, A. R. Nelson, D. P. Schwartz, and W. R. Lund, "The Wasatch Fault Zone, Utah—Segmentation and History of Holocene Earthquakes," *Journal of Structural Geology* 13, no. 2 (1991): 137–49.

9. S. J. Weaver, "President Nelson Outlines Plans for Salt Lake Temple during Its Four-Year Closure for Renovation," *Church News*, April 19, 2019, https://www.churchofjesuschrist.org/church/news/president-nelson-outlines-plans-for-salt-lake-temple-during-its-four-year-closure-for-renovation?lang=eng.

10. See, for example, D. M. Dowling, "Adobe Housing in El Salvador: Earthquake Performance and Seismic Improvements," in W. I. Rose, J. J. Bommer, D. L. López, M. J. Carr, and J. J. Major, eds., *Natural Hazards in El Salvador* (Boulder, CO: Geological Society of America, 2004): 281–300.

vulnerable to sea level rise and will most benefit from innovative flood mitigation; they have helped medical professionals globally eradicate diseases such as smallpox and polio and find solutions for malaria; and they help develop and determine how to responsibly use fertilizers, irrigation, and modern seeds so farmers at all levels can grow more crops on limited arable land to feed the world's nearly 8 billion people.

Just as ongoing scientific discovery leads to progress in society, the evolving pursuit of knowledge known as continuing revelation—a core tenet of The Church of Jesus Christ of Latter-day Saints—helps humanity progress toward a more Christlike society. Examples of this progress include building small, local temples or issuing a proclamation on the living Christ, as well as individual efforts to develop a personal relationship with knowledge and truth. I have learned that continued discovery of revealed knowledge is the privilege of any who invest in asking questions and seeking answers.

Studying science has enabled my personal pursuit of knowledge. It has given me the tools to ask questions, look for both empirical and subjective evidence, and understand the iterative nature of unwrapping truth. That said, I must acknowledge that faith-based questions are not always answered satisfactorily. Studying science has taught me that the more difficult the question, the longer and harder the process of finding an answer. Persistence is required to find subjective evidence that may enlighten the darkness of unanswered questions.

Science and revelation answer different questions

In studying geology, I sometimes encounter questions whose answers seem to contradict some interpretations of scriptural passages. I have learned to defer to scientific experts questions regarding the physical earth and to religious experts questions regarding salvation. I find insight from this statement by James E. Talmage, a geologist, theologian, and former member of the Quorum of the Twelve Apostles:

> Let us not try to wrest the scriptures in an attempt to explain away what we cannot explain. The opening chapters of Genesis and scriptures related thereto were never intended as a textbook of geology, archaeology, earth-science, or man-science.... We do not show reverence for the scriptures when we misapply them through faulty interpretation.[11]

This statement, written by the same man who authored the book *Jesus the Christ*, suggests that my knowledge of a 4.6-billion-year-old earth, based on empirical observations and rigorous scientific interpretation, does not contradict Church doctrine whose rightful focus is personal salvation and spiritual growth. My geologic studies help me gain knowledge about *how* the earth operates, *how* it was created, and *how* it became geologically varied; my religious studies help me know *why* it was created. I tell my students, "If I didn't read the scriptures, I would never know the why; if I didn't study science, I would never know the how."

Science illuminates the nature of God

Studying science has taught me the accuracy of Alma's declaration: "All things denote there is a God; yea, even the earth and all things that are upon the face of it, yea, and its motion, yea, and also all the planets which move in their regular form do witness that there is a Supreme Creator" (Alma 30:44).

Our heavenly parents and their son Jesus Christ, as master scientists, positioned the earth at a distance from the sun where the tilt of its axis ensures that the hydrologic system effectively distributes life-sustaining water in its liquid, gaseous, and solid forms. They similarly ensured earth's diameter is sufficient to maintain the internal energy needed to drive plate tectonics. Over billions of years, this tectonic system formed ocean basins and continents with diverse geographic

11. James E. Talmage, *The Earth and Man: Address Delivered in the Tabernacle, Salt Lake City, Utah. Sunday, August 9, 1931* (Salt Lake City, UT: The Church of Jesus Christ of Latter-day Saints, 1931).

niches where plants and animals in all their variety would have reason to evolve.

As scientists, they recognized that the natural operation of earth's hydrologic and tectonic systems would provide the ideal setting for their children both to develop and be tested. The natural processes that bring the blessings of continents on which to plant crops and rainstorms to water fields also bring the curse of disasters. We cannot have mountains without earthquakes, rivers without floods, or oceans without hurricanes.

Latter-day Saint doctrine teaches that I am on earth to learn to use my agency to choose joy despite the hazards of life.[12] Logic, honed by my scientific training, implies this task is so vital that my heavenly parents limit protecting me from the perils of the natural world. They allow both human and physical laws to operate, seldom stepping in to prevent tsunamis, divert hurricanes, or stop wars. They let us experience life as it happens and celebrate our stumbling first steps toward godhood. As examples of parenting perfection, they provide comfort and support when life goes awry. They may not remove a trial, but if asked, they will support us through it. As the Savior states, "In me ye might have peace. In the world ye shall have tribulation: but be of good cheer; I have overcome the world" (John 16:33). Faith in science has helped me understand my heavenly parents and their abilities as master scientists to create the world in such a way that it perfectly meets their goal to bring to pass the immortality of their children.[13]

Science generates awe and faith

Studying science increases the sense of awe and wonder in my life. The Jewish philosopher Heschel wrote that "[awe] is at the root of faith. We must grow in awe in order to reach faith."[14] My faith is rooted in awe,

12. 2 Nephi 2:25.

13. Moses 1:39.

14. Abraham Joshua Heschel, *Who Is Man* (Stanford, CA: Stanford University Press, 1965), 89.

and my awe is rooted in science. I cannot look at a mountain, a glacier, or even a pebble without thinking about its origin and the processes that shaped it. These thoughts lead to awe—for the natural processes at work, for our Creator, and for the scientists who came before me. That awe is generated equally by science and faith. The renowned scientist Carl Sagan wrote,

> How is it that hardly any major religion has looked at science and concluded, "This is better than we thought! The Universe is much bigger than our prophets said, grander, more subtle, more elegant. God must be even greater than we dreamed"? Instead they say, "No, no, no! My god is a little god, and I want him to stay that way." A religion, old or new, that stressed the magnificence of the Universe as revealed by modern science might be able to draw forth reserves of reverence and awe hardly tapped by the conventional faiths.[15]

I believe my heavenly parents are the god Sagan describes. They have mastered science, understand the power of natural laws, and rejoice in their application. And I believe they stand in awe themselves as they look at stars sweeping across the universe or hold in their hands a tiny, flawless garnet created by the perfect combination of heat and pressure applied to aluminous shale along converging tectonic plates.

The reverence and awe I feel from studying science began with a geology textbook, and it continues today. For me, science inspires awe, and awe inspires faith. So when someone asks if science can support faith and if faith can support science, my answer is a resounding yes.

15. Carl Sagan, *Pale Blue Dot: A Vision of the Human Future in Space* (New York: Ballantine Books, 1994), 50.

Eternal Principles of Reasoning

NOEMÍ LUBOMIRSKY

Noemí Lubomirsky was born and raised in La Plata, Argentina, and earned bachelor and doctoral degrees in mathematics from the National University of La Plata, where she currently is an adjunct professor. She also takes part in different projects that promote the articulation of mathematics between the high school and university levels. She has authored several research articles that have been published in scientific journals. In addition to math, she is passionate about family history, which led her to learn some of her ancestors' languages and travel to their countries to look for documents to complete her family tree. She has served in the Primary, Young Women, and Relief Society organizations both in her ward and stake. During her free time, she enjoys knitting, reading, and hiking.

MOST PEOPLE think that mathematics is the study of numbers. However, nowadays, the most accepted definition of mathematics is that it is the science of patterns. Mathematicians work with abstract patterns, using logic rules to find new relationships between them and to see whether those relationships say something useful about the original things.

That definition probably fits me. Since my early childhood, I have loved patterns. My mother told me that before I turned one year old, I could spend many hours building towers of cubes by size or by color. The idea of numbers and operations between them came some years later, and even though I liked it, I think I have never been really good at mathematical calculations. However, that interest grew through the years, and soon the math hour was my favorite one at school; studying math was a natural decision when the time to choose a career came. During college, I found that algebraic logic was the area I loved the most, so I decided to study for a doctorate to further learn about that topic. Algebraic logic is part of the foundation of mathematics. We try to find connections between logic statements and their algebraic interpretations.

Let me give you an example. Consider classical propositional logic. In that logic, we work with propositions—statements which are, by themselves, either true or false—such as follows:

p = *It is May*
q = *General Conference was held last month*

Both p and q are propositions because it is possible to determine their truth or falsity. p is true during May and false in other months, while q is only true in May and November (there have been exceptions, but it is always possible to decide whether this sentence is true or false depending on the date of the last General Conference). In logical systems, the propositions can relate through connectives like negation ($\sim$), implication ($\rightarrow$), or disjunction ($\vee$), resulting in propositional formulas like the following:

$\sim p$ = *It is not May* (the negation of p)
$p \rightarrow q$ = *If it is May, then General Conference was held last month* (p implies q)
$p \vee q$ = *It is May, or General Conference was held last month* (p or q)

Finally, we work with a set of inference rules, such as modus ponens, which says that if p implies q and p happens, then q should happen. For example, using the previous propositions, if we have $p \rightarrow q$ and p, by modus ponens, we can conclude q:

If it is May, then General Conference was held last month ($p \rightarrow q$)
It is May (p)

General Conference was held last month (q)

If I see the sun shining, then it is daytime ($p \rightarrow q$)
I see the sun shining (p)

It is daytime (q)

There are interesting examples of modus ponens. Doctrine and Covenants 130:20–21 and 132:5 can be symbolized with the following scheme:

If we obey, then we will be blessed ($p \rightarrow q$)
We obey (p)

We will be blessed (q)

This being the case, we might be tempted to ask why righteous people have problems if blessings follow obedience. It is important to note here that the logic scheme of our lives has many propositions interacting at the same time. Another proposition which is true for every human being can be found in Alma 42:4: "There was a ... probationary time." So in our life's scheme, we also have the proposition r = *this life is a probationary time*. The scheme can be something like this:

If we obey, then we will be blessed ($p \rightarrow q$)
We obey (p)
This life is a probationary time (r)

We will be blessed (q)
This life is a probationary time (r)

Even though the promised blessings were there, the proposition regarding trials during this mortal time stood there because you cannot eliminate any true proposition from the scheme.

Something that we do with propositional formulas is find their assignments of truth, which we call valuations. For the case of classical propositional logic, valuations are given by truth tables in which we consider all the possible truth values for the propositions. For example, for the proposition $p \vee \sim p$ (p or not p), we consider the two possible truth values for proposition p: true (T) or false (F). If p is T, then $\sim p$ (not p) should be F, and if p is F, then $\sim p$ should be T. In this logic, if we consider the disjunction of one true statement r and one false statement s, the resulting proposition is always true, so we have the following valuation:

p	$\sim p$	$p \vee \sim p$
T	F	T
F	T	T

In the previous example, we can see that no matter which truth value we assign to the proposition p, the proposition $p \vee \sim p$ is always true. Then we say that $p \vee \sim p$ is a tautology. For example, if we consider the proposition p = *today is Monday*, then the negation is $\sim p$ = *today is not Monday*, and the proposition $p \vee \sim p$ would essentially say *today is Monday or is not Monday*, which is always true, no matter which day we are on. By using tautologies and propositions, we can also give logical arguments to reach conclusions, which we call theorems.

Logic is part of the foundation of mathematics because it is the way in which mathematicians reason and prove that new results are true. It has been said that logic is the study of reasoning not only in mathematics but for every aspect of life. While that characterization has limitations, it works well enough for our purpose, which is to consider logic and reasoning as a tool to find and recognize truth.

For example, tautologies are very useful in mathematical reasoning but difficult in real life. In math, when you have a tautology, you know that two statements are equivalent. For example, in classical logic, the proposition *p implies q, and q didn't happen* is equivalent (there is a tautology) with the proposition *then p didn't happen*, which, in mathematical terms, can be written as such:

$$(p \rightarrow q) \wedge {\sim}q \text{ is equivalent to } {\sim}p$$

That is very useful to reason and prove results in math (and many other contexts). However, we also tend to reason this way in everyday life, which is less reliable because there are so many independent variables governing human behavior. Here is an example of a tautology that is common but dangerous because the first statement is not incontrovertibly true, and therefore, it is an unstable basis for further reasoning:

If he likes me, he would write to me.
He didn't write to me.

Therefore, he doesn't like me.

If something is true in an absolutely incontrovertible way, then the contrapositive (${\sim}q \rightarrow {\sim}p$) is also true. If something is true in a mathematical proof, it's true, end of story. But non-mathematical language is imprecise, and it's hard to find a statement that's absolutely incontrovertibly true in messy, complicated human life.

For these and other reasons, in this mortal state, we cannot completely comprehend the heavenly reasoning. In Isaiah 55:8–9, the Lord said, "For my thoughts are not your thoughts, neither are your ways my ways, saith the Lord. For as the heavens are higher than the earth, so are my ways higher than your ways, and my thoughts than your thoughts." In my view, we cannot think in the same way that he does because we are so limited in this state. For example, we cannot deeply understand eternity because all that we know here seems to have a beginning and an end, or at least that's what we can perceive with our limited senses.

Nevertheless, just like a small child can perfectly understand the concept of numbers, count from one to one hundred and perfectly do some sums with those numbers without knowing that there are infinite numbers and infinite operations between them, I hope I can understand in this mortal state at least some of the principles from all the eternal truths that the Lord knows and maybe reason between them in a way that is correct and compatible with his perfect reason.

A perfect reasoning

If a person were able to be perfectly objective and would only accept true propositions as axioms (basic statements that we assume to be true) and theorems, then logic could be a perfect model of reasoning. In fact, there is someone whose reasoning is perfect. Recently, I found in the scriptures an interesting invitation from the Lord: "And now come, saith the Lord, ... let us reason together, that ye may understand; let us reason even as a man reasoneth one with another face to face.... I, the Lord, reason with you that you may understand" (Doctrine and Covenants 50:10–12). Another example is "I will show unto you my strong reasoning" (Doctrine and Covenants 45:10).

Surely, I would speak to the Almighty, and I desire to reason with God (Job 13:3). There are other scriptures where this invitation can also be found, including Isaiah 1:18, Job 13:6, and Doctrine and Covenants 61:13. Those scriptures give me the idea that there is, in fact, a correct and perfect way of reasoning, a supreme logic where every theorem is an eternal truth.

On the other hand, there are incorrect ways of reasoning. An important property in logic is the property of consistency. We say that a set of statements is logically inconsistent if they cannot all be true at the same time. For example, suppose that we consider that the statement p is true and that the statement $\sim p$ is true as well. Isn't that inconsistent? We cannot believe p and $\sim p$ at the same time because they have opposite truth values. Moreover, if there are circumstances where we believe both p and $\sim p$, then our logical system is inconsistent, in which case, in that flawed system, any statement q would appear to be true. For example, I believe that the Word of Wisdom is a law of health revealed by the Lord. Then, for me, the proposition p = *I should not drink alcohol* is an axiom. If, in some situation, I consider it okay to have a drink, then I am adding to my logic system the axiom $\sim p$ = *I may drink alcohol*. At that point, we have a problem with our logic system. The presence of such a problem might lead me to mistrust what I thought I knew to be true. It may reject other true statements I had previously believed related to the Word of Wisdom: for example, if it is okay to drink alcohol, then why not coffee?

In other words, if we add to our system something false but we consider it true, it can make us believe that something else is true when maybe it is not because we have a "failure" in our system of beliefs. I think sometimes that happens when Satan confuses us, and we decide to categorize as true something that is false. The confusion it provokes can lead us to other mistakes. The text of Doctrine and Covenants 78:10 describes Satan's desire to turn our hearts away from the truth so that we become blinded and then don't understand things. That is why we need to be careful about the things we believe. Moreover, when we turn our hearts to the truths that we know, our minds are enlightened, and it is easier to understand new truths.

I deeply understood that principle a few years ago as I was struggling with a complicated math problem. One afternoon, after serving many hours in the Buenos Aires Argentina Temple, I was enjoying the view of the beautiful gardens and the warmth of the sun. I felt a deep peace as I pondered on the things that I had learned that day. Since I had to wait for my parents, I decided to return to a very difficult problem related to my thesis. I took a sheet of paper, and once more, as I had done many times in the previous months, I wrote out my problem. As I worked, I began to see relations between many principles I had studied before, and I was finally able to prove one of the main theorems of my thesis. It was not that I found the proof in any principle that I learned in the temple, but I think it was not a coincidence. I needed a clear mind, full of light and truth, to find more truth.

Having that idea in mind, it is interesting to read the scripture in John 8:32: "And ye shall know the truth, and the truth shall make you free." It is important to reason on the basis of true principles. In logic, we use the term *axioms* for such principles, and the term *theorems* for statements which can be deduced from axioms by reasoning. The main problem here is how to know if our axioms are true.

Valuations to recognize the truth

In mathematics, the axioms are very few and seem obvious. For example, one axiom is that if a is a natural number and $b = a$, then b is a natural number. Every theorem in math can be demonstrated through reasoning (giving a proof) based on those axioms. But in our minds and lives, our axioms might be of a different character since they are not only about math but also about human relationships, nature, emotions, faith. We all have different views of the world, and they are strongly based on our system of beliefs, our axioms. How can we know if our axioms and theorems are true? Are there ways to reason about these things that we assume to be true?

If we want to know if something is true, then it would be useful to first understand what truth is. In Doctrine and Covenants 84:45–46, we read, "For the word of the Lord is truth, and whatsoever is truth is light, and whatsoever is light is Spirit, even the Spirit of Jesus Christ. And the Spirit giveth light to every man that cometh into the world; and the Spirit enlighteneth every man through the world, that hearkeneth to the voice of the Spirit." There, we learn that truth is light which comes through the Spirit. The Holy Ghost is a revelator; that is one of his main purposes. The Holy Spirit can act as a truth table for us—we look to him to know what is true. He is the logical guide for our lives.

How can we access that guidance or valuation from the Spirit? In the same way that, in classical logic, there are some rules for making truth tables, there are also some rules to allow the Spirit to tell us whether something is true or false. In Moroni 10:4, we learn that to know the truth, we should study it out in our minds (identify and study the statement) and "ask with a sincere heart, with real intent, having faith in Christ, [and] he will manifest the truth of it unto you, by the power of the Holy Ghost." Moreover, in verse 5, we learn that "by the power of the Holy Ghost ye may know the truth of all things." The Holy Ghost can give us the proofs for our theorems and axioms in life. Those theorems include not only our beliefs and other things connected with our faith but also any principle of truth, comprising "things both in heaven and in the earth, and under the earth; things which have been, things which are, things which must shortly come to pass" (Doctrine and Covenants 88:79). Through the Spirit, we can find the proof of any truth. We are not expected to just believe; the Lord wants us to know. He is the one who invites us in those verses in Moroni to find out our own proof of the truth of the statement "the Book of Mormon contains the word of the Lord, and the principles we find there are true."

There are other scriptures where the Lord teaches us this model. For example, in Alma 32:26, someone identifies an axiom and wonders about the truth of it: "Now, as I said concerning faith—that it was not a perfect knowledge—even so it is with my words. Ye cannot know of their surety at first, unto perfection, any more than faith is a perfect knowledge." In the next verse, we are taught to study it with a sincere desire to know the truth of it: "But behold, if ye will awake and arouse your faculties, . . . and exercise a particle of faith, yea, even if ye can no more than desire to believe, let this desire work in you." Then, in verse 33, the proof from the Spirit comes: "Because ye have tried the experiment, and planted the seed, and it swelleth and sprouteth, and beginneth to grow, ye must needs know that the seed is good." And lastly, in verse 34, the person has a perfect knowledge of the truth of it, and it becomes a theorem: "And now, behold, is your knowledge perfect? Yea, your knowledge is perfect in that thing, . . . and your mind doth begin to expand."

Interestingly, logic allows a valuation to show us the truth of any theorem independently of other ones. It is easy to understand that principle as we read Doctrine and Covenants 93:30: "All truth is independent in that sphere in which God has placed it, to act for itself." Moreover, understanding that the Spirit is our guide, which can give us the proof of any truth, helps us to understand that "the righteous ... love the truth" (2 Nephi 9:40) because the righteous have the Holy Ghost with them. For me, gaining my own testimony was like a math equation, following these principles:

1. I try to identify the truth I want to know (find the proposition).
2. I develop a sincere desire to know it (prayer helps me for that).
3. The Spirit comes and testifies.
4. Then I know.

No matter what we study or which area of knowledge we are interested in, there is a way to know the truth. Our Heavenly Father, the one whose "glory ... is intelligence, or, in other words, light and truth" (Doctrine and Covenants 93:36), provided a way. As we read in Doctrine and Covenants 93:26, "The Spirit of truth is of God," and through that Spirit, we can learn eternal principles of truth. I hope we can all continue our journeys on earth learning more eternal principles of truth because "whatever principle of intelligence we attain unto in this life, it will rise with us in the resurrection" (Doctrine and Covenants 130:18).

PART THREE

Things which have been, things which are, things which must shortly come to pass; things which are at home, things which are abroad

(Doctrine and Covenants 88:79)

The past is a foreign country.

Historians labor to discover and empathize
as well as to interpret and account.

Walk in Beauty Every Step

FARINA KING

Farina King, a citizen of the Navajo Nation, is the Horizon Chair in Native American Ecology and Culture and associate professor of Native American Studies at the University of Oklahoma. She earned her PhD at Arizona State University in US history. King specializes in twentieth-century Native American studies. She is the author of The Earth Memory Compass: Diné Landscapes and Education in the Twentieth Century. *She earned her MA in African history from the University of Wisconsin and a BA from Brigham Young University with a double major in history and French studies. She has studied several languages, including French, Portuguese, Yoruba, Wolof, and Navajo, and she plans to learn more languages in the future. Other than learning different languages and having fun with her family, Farina loves to sing, dance, and travel. Learn more about her at farinaking.com.*

❖

SHÍ ÉÍ Bilagáanaa nishłį́ dóó Kinyaa'áanii báshishchíín. Bilagáanaa dashicheii dóó Tsinaajinii dashinálí. Tónaneesdizídi shi'dizhchį́. My elders taught me that we introduce ourselves by our clans in *Diné Bizaad*, the Navajo language. We call ourselves *Diné*, "the People," but Europeans and European-Americans refer to us as Navajos. I am *Bilagáanaa* of White settler English-American maternal descent, and

I am born for the Towering House clan of Diné. My maternal grandfather was *Bilagáanaa*, and my paternal grandfather was of the Black-streaked Woods People clan of Diné.

Since *shízhé'é*, my father, is enrolled as "full-blood" Navajo, he and his children, including me, are citizens of the Navajo Nation. I have a Navajo blood certificate with a census number, which marks me as legally "half degree Navajo Indian blood." Native Americans are among some of the only people in the United States who are required to prove their identity through constructs of "blood quantum" and pedigrees, like dogs. People have asked me: "How much Indian are you?" I am a Diné woman who constantly seeks to educate all people about what that really means to me.

I am also a baptized and endowed member of The Church of Jesus Christ of Latter-day Saints. I am the Horizon Chair in Native American Ecology and Culture and associate professor of Native American Studies at the University of Oklahoma. These introductions provide context of my positionality—or social position based on identity and lived experiences—and connect me with my relations and *shik'é*, my kin.

A friend, who is also Native American and baptized in the Church, once asked me how I reconcile my faith with all I know about the past. In many ways, my answer to this question is evolving, but my perspective as a Diné Latter-day Saint scholar stems from various facets of my identity and background. I reconcile my identities because my ultimate faith lies in Jesus Christ and not in mortal beings of the past or present. Many of the teachings that I learn in the Church correlate with the faith of my Diné ancestors, and these teachings have inspired my research as a historian of Native American and Indigenous studies.

My focus on studies of culture and history began and continue with *shizhé'é*. He is an example of one who seeks knowledge and truth. My father was raised in *Diné Bikéyah*, Navajo lands, in a family that lived according to Diné ceremonial and ancestral ways. As a young adult, he converted and joined The Church of Jesus Christ of Latter-day Saints while attending Brigham Young University (BYU) between 1968 and

1969, where he also met my mother. My parents taught me that we are all born from a Creator and that we are connected as five-fingered beings.

My father once told me what the Diné concept *hózhǫ́* means to him: "being in the right place at the right time, doing the right things." In Diné teachings, we learn prayers of *Hózhǫ́ǫ́jí*, the Blessingway, that emanates beauty in front of us, behind us, below us, above us, all around us, and within us. This beauty, *hózhǫ́*, evokes meanings of harmony and balance, a guiding principle and ideal of our life journey. *Si'ąh Naagháí Bik'eh Hózhǫ́*—live a long life in beauty. "Walk in beauty," as many translations of this Diné teaching emphasize, embodies cycles of restoring harmony through recurring struggles with disorder and imbalance.[1] Clara W. McMaster's lyrics from "Teach Me to Walk in the Light," a Latter-day Saint Primary song and hymn, resonate with me because of Diné conceptualizations of *hózhǫ́*: "Teach me to walk in the light of his love; / Teach me to pray to my Father above; / Teach me to know of the things that are right; / Teach me, teach me to walk in the light."[2] Life is a learning journey to restore *hózhǫ́* and, one day, to reunite with our heavenly family by walking in the light, which prayer and proper guidance enable. Prayer brings discernment of "things that are right." Prayer is also essential for *T'aa Sha Bik'ehgo Na'nitin*, which represents a Diné sense of direction on the "Road of Beauty."[3] As a Diné Latter-day Saint, these corresponding teachings guide me on my

1. For more about these Diné teachings, see Farina King, *The Earth Memory Compass: Diné Landscapes and Education in the Twentieth Century* (Lawrence: University Press of Kansas, 2018), 20–21.

2. Clara W. McMaster, "Teach Me to Walk in the Light," in *Hymns* (Salt Lake City, UT: The Church of Jesus Christ of Latter-day Saints, 2002), 304, https://www.churchofjesus christ.org/music/library/hymns/teach-me-to-walk-in-the-light?lang=eng&__r=1. The song was originally published in 1958. Clara McMaster wrote the song for children to sing at the 1958 General Conference of The Church of Jesus Christ of Latter-day Saints. The scriptures inspired her, as she noticed that "the scriptures are filled with this great, important message—'walk in the light.'" See "'Teach Me to Walk in the Light' Was Written by a Member of the Choir," *The Tabernacle Choir Blog*, February 26, 2014, https://bit.ly/McMasterSong.

3. King, *The Earth Memory Compass*, 21–23.

learning journey. Church teachings inform us that Christ can heal us. Through his atonement, he not only paid a debt for sin but he took upon himself our hardships and pain. I see Christ as a road to restoring beauty by making us "at one," in balance, or walking in *hózhǫ́* because he paid the ultimate price of sin.

As a scholar, I have hesitated to discuss my religious background in the workplace because many in Native American and Indigenous circles hold negative perceptions of the Church. I am working on a manuscript about Navajo Latter-day Saints, *Diné dóó Gáamalii*, which will inevitably open a discussion about my positionality and subjectivity to a wider audience. In my research, I navigate various communities that sometimes intersect and even collide; they present their own layers and meanings including but not limited to family, profession, ethnicity, gender, and religion.

As a person of mixed cultural background and ancestry, I have struggled to understand the complex intersections of my identity throughout my life. I have also been pressured to not identify as both Native American and Latter-day Saint. However, I have found that my faith has drawn me closer to my Diné identity. My personal background and layers of identity have prompted me to explore diverse histories of Native Americans, including the stories and experiences of my father and family. I have pursued understandings of what it means to be Latter-day Saint and Native American, specifically Latter-day Saint and Diné. Diverse perspectives and histories, including oral histories and stories, of Latter-day Saint Native Americans have shaped this effort. As a BYU undergraduate student, working with Jessie Embry, the past associate director of the Charles Redd Center for Western Studies, I launched these studies by interviewing about one hundred different Native American Latter-day Saints who all affiliated strongly with the Church.

Their stories have intertwined with my own in many ways. Based on my own experiences and insights from the interviews, Native Americans, in general, do not just walk between "two worlds" as many people might portray their experiences in recent literature and popular media.[4] Diverse Native Americans walk through many worlds, which overlap, correlate, and conflict. Maurice Crandall, a Yavapai-Apache scholar I interviewed, articulated this idea of navigating multiple worlds, which I have since pondered. Gina Colvin, a Māori lecturer at the University of Canterbury, stresses understanding "compound worldviews" when examining historical Indigenous Mormon experiences. She spoke at the 2017 Mormon Studies Conference, "Multicultural Mormonism: Religious Cohesion in a New Era of Diversity,"[5] and titled her keynote presentation "There's No Such Thing as 'A' Gospel Culture." Various scholars and public intellectuals have contributed such tremendous groundbreaking work that I respect. Historians Robert S. McPherson and Sarah E. Burak worked with Diné Latter-day Saint Jim Dandy to share his life journey of balancing his Diné teachings and faith in The Church of Jesus Christ of Latter-day Saints.[6] These messages impress me because they recognize that people and cultures are complicated, and that it is possible to value multiple worldviews.

Native Americans have identified plenty of reasons to distrust Latter-day Saints because of their histories and past experiences with White settlers and Church leaders who conflated religion and colonialism.[7] In my profession, I trace historical relations and dynamics of Indigenous peoples and the Church, and I study conflicts that have occurred and continued between Mormons and Native Americans in the nineteenth and twentieth centuries. (I use *Mormons* in a specific

4. For more critique of the binaries of "two worlds," see James Joseph Buss and C. Joseph Genetin-Pilawa, eds., *Beyond Two Worlds: Critical Conversations on Language and Power in Native North America* (Albany: State University of New York Press, 2014).

5. The conference took place on March 30, 2017, at Utah Valley University in Orem, Utah.

6. See Robert S. McPherson, Jim Dandy, and Sarah E. Burak, *Navajo Tradition, Mormon Life: The Autobiography and Teachings of Jim Dandy* (Salt Lake City: University of Utah Press, 2012).

7. See Gina Colvin and Joanna Brooks, eds., *Decolonizing Mormonism: Approaching a Postcolonial Zion* (Salt Lake City: University of Utah Press, 2018).

historical context, when White settler members of the Church were commonly called and identified as Mormons in the nineteenth and early twentieth centuries for example. These conflicts between the two groups bore these specific names at that time.) During this time, Mormon settlers made various efforts to remove and displace Indigenous peoples such as Utes, Shoshones, Goshutes, and Paiutes from their homelands in what became Utah. For instance, in the winter of 1850, Isaac Higbee, stake president in the region, petitioned Brigham Young to exterminate Indigenous peoples in areas that became known as Utah Valley.[8] Darren Parry, a leader of the Northwestern Band of the Shoshone Nation, recently wrote *Bear River Massacre: A Shoshone History*, which tells the history of how early Mormon settlers benefited from the attacks of the US military on Shoshone peoples in their ancestral lands of southeast Idaho along Boa Ogoi, Bear River. In 1863, the US military massacred four hundred Shoshone people in one of the largest mass killings in American history—at least half of them were unarmed elders, women, and children. Parry quotes a Latter-day Saint bishop, Henry Ballard, who said at the time of the Bear River Massacre, "The Lord raised up his foe [referring to Colonel Patrick Connor, leader of the army] to punish [the Shoshone] without us having to do it."[9] Mormons also instigated the Circleville Massacre in 1866, in which they killed no fewer than sixteen Paiutes.[10] They also captured Indigenous women and children during these violent clashes, who were often "small children too young to talk."[11] Whether scholars frame the practice of Mormons buying Indigenous children as "removing" them from their Native families or as "saving" them from cycles of

8. Thomas Alexander, *Brigham Young and the Expansion of the Mormon Faith* (Norman: University of Oklahoma Press, 2019), location 1819 [Kindle version]. For more examples, see Will Bagley, ed., *The White Want Every Thing: Indian-Mormon Relations, 1847–1877* (Norman: The Arthur H. Clark Company, University of Oklahoma Press, 2019).

9. Henry Ballard, "Journal," January 29, 1863, cited in Darren Parry, *The Bear River Massacre: A Shoshone History* (Salt Lake City, UT: By Common Consent Press, 2019), 31.

10. W. Paul Reeve, "Circleville Massacre, A Tragic Incident in the Black Hawk War," *History Blazer*, September 1995, accessible online, *History To Go*, https://historytogo.utah.gov/circleville-massacre/.

11. Ibid.

captivity and violence, many Mormon settlers did not "adopt" Indigenous children as equals in their families but used them for indentured servitude.[12]

Many in Indigenous communities also condemn how Latter-day Saints considered Native Americans to be Lamanites and appropriated Indigenous symbols and identity in Lamanite imagery that appears in pageants, art, literature, and film. They decry the Indian Student Placement Program that the Church initiated and facilitated between 1947 and 2000 in which Native American children lived away from their homes with Latter-day Saint families during the school year.[13]

To this day, Navajos still experience tremendous racism from Latter-day Saints in border towns near the Navajo reservation, such as Blanding, Utah; Flagstaff, Arizona; and Gallup, New Mexico. Recently, the child of a Navajo friend of mine from a border town came home from Primary and told her that another child in their ward said, "You're brown because you're cursed." Similarly, a Navajo convert and relative of mine once whispered to me, referring to White members of their stake in a border town region, "They love the Lamanites, but they hate the Indians."[14] Some individuals associated with the Church endorse policies and plans that desecrate and deplete sacred Diné lands,

12. See Taylor Tree, "Mary Mountain and Adoptions of Native Children in Utah Territory," *Intermountain Histories*, https://www.intermountainhistories.org/items/show/407. Mormon settlers referred to these exchanges of purchasing Indigenous slaves for indentured servitude as "adoptions." See also Brian Q. Cannon, "'To Buy Up the Lamanite Children as Fast as They Could': Indentured Servitude and Its Legacy in Mormon Society," *Journal of Mormon History* 44, no. 2 (April 2018): 1–35; and Margaret D. Jacobs, "Entangled Histories: The Mormon Church and Indigenous Child Removal from 1850 to 2000," *Journal of Mormon History* 42, no. 2 (April 2016): 27–60.

13. For more about the Indian Student Placement Program, see Matthew Garrett, *Making Lamanites: Mormons, Native Americans, and the Indian Student Placement Program, 1947–2000* (Salt Lake City: University of Utah Press, 2016); and Elise Boxer, "'The Lamanites Shall Blossom as the Rose': The Indian Student Placement Program, Mormon Whiteness and Indigenous Identity," *Journal of Mormon History* 41, no. 4 (2015): 132–76.

14. See Farina King, "Indigenizing Mormonisms," *Mormon Studies Review* 6 (2019): 3. In this sentence, I am referring to the descendants of White or European-American Latter-day Saint settlers.

such as Bears Ears, through resource development and extraction.[15] Others run businesses that prey on Navajos and Native Americans. In one memorable case, a doctor, former stake mission leader, and respected member of the Latter-day Saint community in Blanding, Utah, was found guilty of running a business where he dug graves, pillaged Indigenous artifacts, and sold them off, defying federal laws that prohibited it.[16] Amid a probe by the Bureau of Land Management (BLM), this doctor took his life.[17] Two Latter-day Saint US senators have seemingly undermined efforts to protect Indigenous land and possessions by challenging the federal government's authority to do so.[18] In 2018, a Latter-day Saint Utah House representative called the BLM's

15. A timeline tracks the movement to reduce the size of Bears Ears National Monument, created to protect sacred Indigenous sites. This movement to reduce the size of Bears Ears was supported by Latter-day Saint senator Orrin Hatch. https://www.deseret.com/2017/12/2/20634385/timeline-the-battle-over-two-of-utah-s-national-monuments. A recent example of the continuing alignment of Latter-day Saint lawmakers on the opposite side of Indigenous tribes is this op-ed by Latter-day Saint lawmakers Mitt Romney, Mike Lee, Chris Stewart, John Curtis, Burgess Owens, and Blake Moore. Published in the *Deseret News*, the op-ed opposes the expansion of protected Indigenous land. https://www.deseret.com/opinion/2021/10/8/22716955/bidens-expansion-monuments-an-insult-sens-lee-romney-curtis-moore-utah-stewart-owens-bears-ears. This puts them in direct opposition with the wishes of the Indigenous nations represented in the Bears Ears Inter-Tribal Coalition—which includes the Zuni, Hopi, Ute, Ute Mountain Ute, and Navajo Tribes—but on the same side as energy and mining interests. https://www.kuer.org/health-science-environment/2021-06-01/energy-developers-and-uranium-miners-eye-land-near-bears-ears-national-monument.

16. In 1996, this doctor and his wife were found digging at a site with human bones. A judge whose son the doctor had delivered dismissed the felony charges against him, and his wife pleaded no contest to a misdemeanor charge. In 2003, the family agreed to pay the state $10,000 for raiding a grave. https://archive.sltrib.com/story.php?ref=/news/ci__12572033. In 2009, the couple was charged again. A summary of the incident can be seen in the news report from KSL on June 10, 2009: "The defendants are accused of being part of a network that was not selling, but stealing artifacts. The artifacts came from the Four Corners region. The area is a treasure trove of significant Native American archeology dating back many centuries. Over the years, scientists estimate the majority of artifacts from the region have been looted, pillaged and sold for profit." "Dozens arrested in archaeological artifacts bust," *KSL*, June 10, 2009, https://www.ksl.com/article/6771105.

17. "A sting in the desert," *Los Angeles Times*, September 21, 2014, https://graphics.latimes.com/utah-sting/.

18. "Senators look at policing practices by federal land agencies," *Route Fifty*, May 8, 2018, https://www.route-fifty.com/management/2018/05/senate-federal-land-policing/148083/.

enforcement of laws against stealing artifacts "overkill."[19] Two Latter-day Saint senators agreed, believing that the BLM should not have protected Native American land so vigorously.[20]

A Native American scholar who has lived in Blanding once asked me how I could participate in the Church given its fraught past and recent struggles with various leaders and lay members. I pointed out that diverse peoples believe in stories and oral traditions of imperfect people that are instruments for a greater cause. In the Book of Mormon, Alma 17:11, the sons of Mosiah received this message from the Lord: "Go forth among the Lamanites, thy brethren, establish my word; yet ye shall be patient in long-suffering and afflictions, that ye may show forth good examples unto them in me, and I will make an instrument of thee in my hands unto the salvation of many souls." Humans are imperfect and make mistakes, but we are often set on paths to do marvelous works for a greater purpose.

The oral tradition of the Diné Hero Twins tells a story, similar to Pandora's Box, wherein two sons of the sun fight off different kinds of monsters but choose to leave several monsters on earth, including poverty, cold, lice, and old age. However, the twins could not defeat the monsters without help. They were not perfect beings and could only assume their important task with the assistance of Spider Woman; their mother, Changing Woman; and the sun.[21]

When I learn of prophets and listen to debates such as the recent outcries about Brigham Young's racism, I know that my faith does not reside in just a person.[22] Yet I consider the prophet to be an

19. "Blanding artifacts raid raises questions, criticism years later," *KSL*, May 10, 2018, https://www.ksl.com/article/46317366/blanding-artifacts-raid-raises-questions-criticism-years-later.

20. "Hatch and Bennett call artifacts raid overkill," *Salt Lake Tribune*, June 14, 2009, https://archive.sltrib.com/story.php?ref=/ci_12589567.

21. Jim Kristofic, *The Hero Twins: A Navajo-English Story of the Monster Slayers* (Albuquerque: University of New Mexico Press, 2015).

22. Courtney Tanner, "Statue of Brigham Young covered in paint at BYU with the word 'racist' sprayed at the base," *Salt Lake Tribune*, June 19, 2020, https://www.sltrib.com/news/education/2020/06/19/statue-brigham-young/; Joanna Brooks, *Mormonism and White Supremacy: American Religion and the Problem of Racial Innocence* (New York: Oxford University

important instrument for the Lord. I do not know all the answers; thus, I continue on the path of the learning journey with "hope for things which are not seen, which are true" (Alma 32:21). My faith is in the Lord above all else, which guides me in discerning what comes from the mortal being and what comes from the Lord's purposes and causes. I read another scripture almost every day from the Book of Mormon, 2 Nephi 4:34, that reads as follows: "O Lord, I have trusted in thee, and I will trust in thee forever. I will not put my trust in the arm of flesh; for I know that cursed is he that putteth his trust in the arm of flesh. Yea, cursed is he that putteth his trust in man or maketh flesh his arm." These verses encourage me to ask the Lord for guidance and personal revelation to know the best direction for me. This principle gives me strength through my mistakes and helps me to understand the mistakes of others to grow and continue learning like the Hero Twins and my ancestors did before me. The Book of Mormon has sustained my faith throughout my life, and it provides a map that I have used in my own spiritual healing. It has reminded me that we are all on our own personal healing journeys, and that in our unique challenges, God loves each of his children equally.

My faith has sustained me in my scholarship and learning. I pursue studies of history because I want to elevate the silenced and forgotten voices that I have come to know and love. Historical studies serve as platforms to share these voices. Faith in the great Creator and Lord has sustained me and my family. Acknowledging and respecting the protocols of Diné and Indigenous peoples, communities, and tribal nations are crucial parts of my education and development as a scholar and Diné citizen. Most importantly, my elders and relatives have given me knowledge through oral tradition by sharing their memories with me and by teaching me about kinship. I try to use whatever affiliations I have with higher education, organizations, and communities to encourage and support healing and equality wherever I find myself. I am

---

Press, 2020); and Jana Riess, "Renaming BYU buildings after nonracists, and other ways to dismantle white supremacy in Mormonism," June 19, 2020, https://www.sltrib.com/religion/2020/06/19/jana-riess-renaming-byu/.

trying to seek *hózhǫ́*, restoring balance and harmony, with all my relations. It is a long road and journey, but every step matters. The Lord shows us our blemishes along the way to heal and restore our beauty, as he teaches us in Ether 12:27: "If they humble themselves before me, and have faith in me, then will I make weak things become strong unto them." *Hózhǫ́ó naasháa doo*. Walk in beauty every step.

History Calling

Acts of Creation, Memory, and Redemption

TONA HANGEN

Tona Hangen is a history professor at Worcester State University whose research and teaching interests include modern US history, religion and media, medical history, digital humanities, and the pedagogy of history. She holds a BS from MIT and a PhD from Brandeis University and is the author of Redeeming the Dial: Radio, Religion, and Popular Culture in America *(University of North Carolina 2002), among other works. She has received her university's Excellence in Teaching Award and coordinates the master's program in history. She serves as executive secretary for the New England Historical Association. She and her husband, Don Hangen, adore time with their four grown children, two daughters-in-law, and two grandchildren. She was recently called as the stake Relief Society president of the newly formed Worcester Massachusetts Stake.*

I FEEL DEEPLY called to the work of teaching both motivated and unmotivated learners; making my university, and academia in general, a more welcoming and diverse place; and pulling ordinary people's stories out of the archives and fragmentary sources of the past. All of these, in their own way, are sacred acts. Here is one such story, surprisingly intertwined with my own life. In 2015, while on sabbatical from my university, I took a research trip to my home state of Virginia to look at archival materials related to public schools in the late 1950s after the *Brown v. Board of Education* decision had declared racial segregation unconstitutional. I vaguely knew that my mother had been a seventh grader at the first school in Virginia desegregated by court order in 1959, Stratford Junior High in Arlington. Her childhood had been divided between Pasadena, California, where she remembered meeting kids with many different racial heritages in her elementary school, and northern Virginia, which at the time had legally segregated schools.

During the fight over desegregation, a racist group called the Defenders of State Sovereignty and Individual Liberties (Virginia's version of Southern White Citizens' Councils) sent letters to all the White students encouraging them to exercise their "right" to stay out of school if they were made to attend with Black children. My grandmother, an intuitive amateur archivist, tucked the vile letter into her scrapbook from that year, preserving it for history.

During my sabbatical, I traveled to consult some records in the Special Collections Library at the University of Virginia. I happened to request the files of one William Lightsey, who, from 1959 to 1960, headed the Virginia Committee for Public Schools. In his files, I found a student pro-integration petition from Arlington Public School students, dated September 1958. It read: "We, the undersigned students of the Arlington Public Schools, believe that our schools should be preserved as public schools. We think it unfair to us that schools should be closed or turned over to private management in order to prevent a few children of a different race from attending our schools." Huh, I thought. I wonder... Several pages in—sure enough, there was my mother's neat, looping, teenage, cursive signature. Maybe I was "meant" to find it. Maybe not. But it felt like a little flashlight illuminating my research path and encouraging me to keep going. Through this small and simple act of signing a petition, my mother wrote herself into the archives—on the right side of history.

Not all people, especially not all women, are so plainly present in archival sources. Walter Benjamin wrote of the backwards-facing "angel of history" who sees that the past is a giant pile of debris but who is unable to go back and fix things because she is being pushed inexorably forward by time.[1] Out of the pile of debris that is the available past, historians do redemptive work by our meticulous reconstruction of simply what happened. Yet sometimes the work of discovering historical peoples' lives is less like recognizing the handwriting of a family member and more like reassembling something that has been through an efficient shredder. For example, sometimes women are most present in the silences of the archives, just as they are sometimes only evident in scripture passages (and many historical documents) that are carefully worded to omit them entirely. Historians like myself stitch together clues that suggest the shape and quality of their lives, like reconstructing a crime scene from the forensic evidence alone.

Developing that historian's mindset has honed my awareness of the documents and small details that might be lost in conventional recordkeeping, helping me be more fully present in my own life and more cognizant of what—and how—to remember. The scriptures are suffused with the exhortation to "remember." It is one of the most frequent things Christ said to his followers, and it's the purpose behind the weekly sacrament and so much else of what Latter-day Saints do. We are a people with habits of meticulous recordkeeping, and we tell and recount and testify about true stories that tether us to God and anchor us to each other. There is deep power in the narratives that evoke memory: power to create identity, power to cleanse and sanctify, power to create meaning and locate ourselves in the maelstrom of human history. No one is too inconsequential not to be "found" in the archives. The same theology that renders every soul worthy of salvation animates me as a historian. It turns and returns my heart to the task at hand: document humanity's presence and influence, especially those whose lives may seem insignificant or overlooked by traditional historical methods.

If I'm being honest, however, I find my time for contemplative research all too scarce in the day-to-day reality of professorial life. The movie of my life could be called *The Accidental Professor*: a series of chance encounters, lucky strikes, and choices made in the fog of intellectual war, leading from graduate studies to eventually land me

1. Walter Benjamin, "On the Concept of History," in *Illuminations*, ed. Hannah Arendt (London: Fontana/Collins, 1973), 255–66.

in the history and political science department at a public university with a high teaching load. There, I quickly learned that an acquired Latter-day Saint skill set is a tremendous asset in academia. I found that many of the talents developed in a lifetime of Church membership seamlessly transferred into my work as a college professor. Some of those were generic effectiveness skills, such as goal setting (thanks, Personal Progress!), running a meeting, being part of a small team or committee, event planning, recruiting and welcoming new members of the community, and having accountability within a vertically organized reporting hierarchy. Others have been forged in the interpersonal aspects of Church life, like being responsible and genial, getting along even when you disagree, sublimating one's ego to a common goal, returning and reporting, and giving others the benefit of the doubt.

Much of my day-to-day work life is spent in creating and teaching new classes, tweaking the ones I teach regularly, meeting with advisees, mentoring thesis writing, and endless assessing of student learning outcomes. I go round and round with the big questions, semester after semester. What are my students supposed to know or do at the end of my class? How can I measure their learning? If I want them to adopt historical thinking skills instead of just regurgitating historical facts, what kind of useful evidence of their newfound skills can I gather? Is my teaching really resulting in their learning? In the strange pandemic semesters, there were added stresses of managing campus interactions safely, tracking down students absent from Zoom meetings, and recalibrating work-life balance when working almost entirely from home. I wonder if my students have any idea how much I celebrate their small victories: when they turn things around and pass a class when failure seemed imminent, or grasp a new concept with a visible "aha" expression, or make truly original connections in discussions and in their writing.

Actually, in my mind, teaching is a holy drama of creation in three acts: from the moment a teacher decides on outcomes and topics ("let there be learning") to the messy reality (birthed in blood) to the final reckoning when the day closes ("it was good"). It's also an act of profound hope for the future. In *History: A Very Short Introduction*, John Arnold proposes three reasons for doing history: for simple enjoyment, as a tool ("something with which to think about ourselves"), and to be made aware of the possibility of doing things differently.[2]

The common cliché is that we learn history in order for it not to repeat itself, and I suppose learning cautionary lessons from the past is wise. However, we also learn history to remind ourselves that the past *could* have gone many other ways, and therefore, the future (both near and far) is not inevitable either. We who live in the present get to birth that new life into being with our gifts of agency, imagination, and diligence. We decide how good, how fair, how inclusive, and how full of joy and beauty that future might be. As historians, we are aware that agency is constrained in myriad ways, to be sure, by forces such as sexism, inertia, structural racism, and ignorance. Yet, always there is a tiny candle against the raging darkness, the spark of divinity in each of us. I love the commandment given to Eve and Adam (and therefore to all of us) to "multiply, and replenish the earth" (Genesis 1:28) because I believe it has meaning far beyond human reproduction and child-bearing. A book, an article, an essay, a lecture, a syllabus, even the arc of an entire academic life—these are things that multiply the earth and replenish its goodness and abundance.

In the celebration of the ordinary, the left behind, and the fragmentary, I find a deep religious connection which hallows even my secular work as a professional historian. Every child of God is significant; in Peter's curious phrasing in Acts 10:34, God is "no respecter of persons." Everyone deserves to have her or his story told; no one is beneath a careful historian's interest. Likewise, among my current students, everyone should be heard and everyone's human dignity acknowledged.

Some historians look for epic patterns or the hand of Providence in the unfolding of a grand design in the course of human history. The small scale interests me more; I see God's love enfolding human history on the lowest and most mundane levels. After all, I found my own mother in the archives. I find my true self when I get lost in the service of others, which is the heart of being an educator. And I hear divine love thrumming behind the tapestry of history even as we weave it—if we choose to listen.

2. John H. Arnold, *History: A Very Short Introduction* (Oxford: Oxford University Press, 2000).

A Discomforted Disciple, But Disciple Nevertheless

CARRIEANNE SIMONINI DELOACH

CarrieAnne Simonini DeLoach is a descendant of a Portuguese-Italian Catholic family and is intensely proud of their culture and appreciative of the sacrifices made by those who immigrated to America. She hopscotched through the United States and Europe during her youth as an army brat. Not having experienced quite enough camouflage, she was commissioned a Medical Service Corps officer and served with the 101st Airborne (AIR ASSAULT) Division. She earned a BA from the University of Dayton, an MA from the University of Central Florida, and a PhD from Rice University. The title of her doctoral dissertation is "Armies of Women: Gender, Religion, and Nationalism in Utah during the Spanish-American War." She loves vintage clothing, cross-stitching, her Yorkie Betty Friedan, and playing strategy games with her husband and four children.

As an angsty Catholic teenager, I read the seemingly endless genealogies in the Old and New Testaments with frustration. The women were few and, at times, depicted only by their associations with men. Even the rooftop-bathing, dynasty-building, war-fueling Bathsheba was on occasion described as "her that had been the wife of

Urias" (Matthew 1:6). As an undergraduate seeking to find a religion more generous to women, I was fortunate to fall in love with one of the only, if not the only, Latter-day Saint men at a Marianist Catholic university. Meeting him exposed me to strong Latter-day Saint women. I chose to attend Relief Society meetings to learn more about his faith. In these gatherings, I absorbed doctrinal tenets that appealed to my feminist sensibilities: the lack of original sin, the recasting of Eve as a necessary heroine, and gender equity in the plan of salvation. When the missionaries came knocking on my door, I welcomed them, and I read the Book of Mormon eagerly, hoping for a cast of plentiful and essential female actors. Yet the elders, for whom I will always feel inestimable gratitude, taught lessons with stacked paper cups about authority and restoration that featured only male faces. If dissatisfaction with one all-male priesthood had prompted my search for a new faith, how would exchanging it for another male hierarchy be a better choice?

Even with these concerns, diligent prayer resulted in personal revelation and a nascent testimony of the truthfulness of the gospel, so I chose to be baptized. A part of me hoped that entering the waters of baptism would magically wash away my deep longing to find parity between the representation of men and women in Heavenly Father's restored gospel. If I just prayed hard enough, stayed under the cleansing water long enough, I could emerge content with the status quo. My baptism and confirmation were intensely spiritual experiences. I knew entering into these covenants was the right choice. However, I had not metamorphosed from a distressed caterpillar into a mollified butterfly. I was still me, the spiritually hungry, seeking feminist.

As I served in the army immediately after 9/11, I attended church in two different worlds. The first was that of an average ward composed of a mixture of civilian and military members. The second consisted of services held during war games or "in the field." In the former, I was surrounded by women. In the latter, I was almost always the only attendee without the priesthood. In neither, I discovered, were probing questions on gender inequality welcome. My intentions in pursuing such inquiries were not to be provocative or to draw undue attention to my ignorance. I wanted access to the strength and connectivity patriarchal histories and priesthood pedigrees provided as the sinew between living men and male generations in the priesthood body of faith. I, too, wanted a theology as specific as my role and as expansive as the generations of women linking me to my Heavenly Mother.

As I earned my first master's degree focusing on Middle Eastern women's history, it occurred to me that I need not limit my pursuit of historical information on women's roles in the Church to Sundays. However, I was frequently accused within academic circles of being too religious to be a feminist, and within religious gatherings, I was too clinical to be a true believer. I was simultaneously too conservative and too liberal, too academic and too spiritual, too quiet and too vocal, too angry and too complacent. As a result, I dug a moat between my professional and private lives, placed crocodiles in its bottomless waters, and built a wall around it. I staffed the wall with mental sentries that attempted to prevent crossovers between my bifurcated realities.

Anyone familiar with Middle Eastern women's history knows this was, in large part, an exercise in futility. As I addressed the role polygamy, nationalism, and feminism played in the nineteenth-century women's and independence movements of Palestine, my mental sentries scurried from one research question to another, attempting to block the connections between my scholarly investigations and my suspicions that these same issues were crucial to early Latter-day Saint history. In texts addressing the supposedly debasing nature of Islamic polygamy on the "development" of Middle Eastern women, I found references to Joan Smyth Iversen's *The Antipolygamy Controversy in U.S. Women's Movements* and Sarah Barringer Gordon's *The Mormon Question: Polygamy and Constitutional Conflict in Nineteenth-Century America*.[1] Even in books almost devoid of women, there was evidence of the global impact of the Mormon polygamous past. As my professional and private lives collided, ideas seeped through the unattended holes.

1. Joan Smyth Iversen, *The Antipolygamy Controversy in U.S. Women's Movements, 1880–1925: A Debate on the American Home* (New York: Routledge, 1997); and Sarah Barringer Gordon, *The Mormon Question: Polygamy and Constitutional Conflict in Nineteenth-Century America* (Chapel Hill and London: University of North Carolina Press, 2002).

Therefore, when upheaval in my doctoral program made the pursuit of a PhD in Middle Eastern women's history no longer feasible, I chose to cave in the moat and knock down the wall. Changing fields offered me the opportunity to write a dissertation on the history of Latter-day Saint women, but where to start posed a problem. My university's library boasted only one shelf of "Mormon history." It included eight identical copies of the Book of Mormon, two texts on Brigham Young, several salacious novels authored by anti-polygamists, and *Mormon Enigma: Emma Hale Smith*. Staring down at the portrait of the first Relief Society president on the cover of a scholarly book was transformative. On the first page, I read, "Emma Smith was far more than an appendage and helpmeet to prominent men. She was also a capable, articulate, and influential individual who profoundly affected the development of the religious movement with which she was associated."[2] I was transfixed.

In a display of both the depths of my nerdiness and the unbounded nature of my jubilation, I sighed deeply upon encountering the lengthy "selected bibliography." There was more to be read. So much more. In sheer delight and exuberance, I practically skipped to the car. For nearly a decade, I had, like the widow of Zarephath (1 Kings 17:8–16), survived by parsing crumbs, lovingly savoring every tidbit of female-based historical Church knowledge, fearful that faith-killing starvation was imminent.[3]

Reading works like *Mormon Enigma* and conducting research has made me aware that many Latter-day Saint women have struggled to reconcile their relationship with patriarchy and their understandings of themselves as daughters of heavenly parents. I have found within

2. Linda King Newell and Valeen Tippetts Avery, *Mormon Enigma: Emma Hale Smith* (Urbana: University of Illinois Press, 1994), xix.

3. I am aware that my renewed faith in divine equity occurred because of a book that has been sharply criticized by many Church members for its representations of polygamy and its centering of Emma Smith as a protagonist within the Restoration. I also know that the women who wrote it experienced pain and loss because of its publication. Like the missionaries who knocked on my door fifteen years earlier, I owe Linda King Newell and Valeen Tippetts Avery unpayable debts. Their scholarship was the catalyst for intense professional and spiritual growth.

their examples solidarity and survival strategies for navigating faith and frustration, testimony and trials, exclusion and eternal perspective.

Take the example of the fierce debates leading up to the American declaration of war in May 1898 that play a role in my dissertation on Latter-day Saint women and the Spanish- and Philippine-American Wars. It seems that leading men and women in the Church were diametrically opposed to war. President Wilford Woodruff preached from the pulpit in General Conference that "war is one of the troubles that belong to the generations in which we live. It will come to pass, and no power beneath the heavens can stay it."[4] The statement, when considered within its historical context, proclaimed the impending war to be inevitable, but the women of the Relief Society who attended the "ladies semi-monthly meeting" held in the fourteenth ward were uneasy. For many of them, the likelihood of war and its predetermined nature did not, in their opinion, justify Latter-day Saint acceptance or support of it. In the April 2, 1898, meeting, Mary Isabella Horne, president of the Salt Lake Relief Society, declared, "It is not the mission of the Latter-day Saints to shed blood."[5] Julia C. Howe, a board member of Deseret Hospital, encouraged her fellow sisters to "pray for peace rather than war." Returned missionary Armeda Young "spoke of teaching our children to be peace-makers, instead of the reverse." Clara C. Cannon, a general Primary presidency member, refused to believe that war was the only option and went so far as to bear a testimony that "our sons would not be called upon for active service" if the Saints remained faithful.[6] In the *Woman's Exponent*, the leading women of the Church continued to advocate for a peaceful resolution to the "Cuban Question."

But on April 28, 1898, when the First Presidency announced its official support of the war and Latter-day Saint male enlistment commenced, female pacifist sentiment disappeared from the published accounts of testimony meetings. That summer, in the place of explicit

4. *Report of the Semi-Annual Conference of the Church of Jesus Christ of Latter-day Saints*, April 7, 1898 (Salt Lake City, UT: The Church of Jesus Christ of Latter-day Saints), 32.

5. "Ladies Semi-Monthly Meeting," *Woman's Exponent* 26, no. 23 (May 1, 1898).

6. Ibid.

Latter-day Saint opposition to the war with Spain, the *Woman's Exponent* printed the words of non-Mormon antiwar feminists[7] and the exploits of Red Cross workers now necessary to reduce the human carnage resulting from this "relic of barbarism in humanity."[8] When Latter-day Saint women were featured in editorials or poetry about the war, they vocalized support for the troops while condemning war in general as a poor mechanism for resolution of international disputes.[9] The pivot to anti-Spanish-American War rhetoric by nonmembers, the generalization of their protest, and support of Utah troops allowed Latter-day Saint women to sidestep a confrontation with male leaders while continuing to advocate for pacifism. These shifts were rewarded with broad-based support for the statewide pacifism campaigns initiated by members of the Relief Society, Primary, and Young Women General Presidencies once Utah's soldiers began their journey home from the Philippines in May 1899.[10]

What did I take away from this case study? First, intelligent, progressive, and civically-minded women utilized a gender-segregated testimony meeting to formulate and vocalize a position on a highly charged political issue. Writing this essay amidst a pandemic and widespread protests against racism within the policing system of the

7. "Mrs. Henrotin's Letter," *Woman's Exponent* 26, no. 23 (May 1, 1898); "The War a Minor Question," *Woman's Exponent* 26, no. 24 (May 15 to 26, 1898); "Women's Council of War," *Woman's Exponent* 26, no. 24 (May 15 to 26, 1898); and "Anna Garlin Spencer on the War," *Woman's Exponent* 26, no. 24 (May 15 to 26).

8. "Clara Barton in Tampa Florida," *Woman's Exponent* 26, no. 23 (May 1, 1898); "Things of Interest," *Woman's Exponent* 21, no. 1 & 2 (June 1 & 15, 1898); "The Red Cross," *Woman's Exponent* 27, no. 3 & 4 (July 1 & 15, 1898); "Women's Work in War," *Woman's Exponent* 27, no. 5 (August 1, 1898); "The Red Cross," *Woman's Exponent* 27, no. 6 (August 15, 1898); and "Madame Mountford's Letter," *Woman's Exponent* 21, no. 1 & 2 (June 1 & 15, 1898).

9. Many leading Latter-day Saint women like Emmeline B. Wells, Dr. Ellis Shipp, and Dr. Margaret Roberts had male relatives who enlisted. They were conflicted in how they could best support their pacifist beliefs while ensuring their "boys" were properly cared for. "Utah Volunteers," *Woman's Exponent* 26, no. 24 (May 15 to 26, 1898); "Utah Volunteers," *Woman's Exponent* 27, no. 3 & 4 (July 1 & 15, 1898); "Thoughts About the War," *Woman's Exponent* 27, no. 3 & 4 (July 1 & 15, 1898); and "Ladies Semi-Monthly Meeting," *Woman's Exponent* 27, no. 3 & 4 (July 1 & 15, 1898).

10. Leonard J. Arrington, "Modern Lysistratas: Mormon Women in the International Peace Movement, 1899–1939," *Journal of Mormon History* 15 (1989): 88–104.

United States, I cannot help but see the potential for female organizations to be laboratories of social justice. It is clear that, as historical actors in an imperial moment and subject to the imperfections of mortality, these women frequently sacrificed racial and class inclusivity in favor of immediate gains for White, middle-class women; theirs was a flawed feminist articulation.[11] It did, however, exist and operate within Church organizations, publications, and rhetoric as a viable thread of Latter-day Saint female participation.

There is a sinew, a tenacious tether, that connects Latter-day Saint women today with their foremothers, stretching back the generations to Mother Eve and beyond her to the divine Mother of us all. Why we as women must work so hard to uncover the legacy of involvement in the Restoration remains a mystery. Yet within the excavation process, I have found both mortal purpose and spiritual fulfillment. My delight in these discoveries has led to an affinity not only with the dead but also with my living sisters in Christ. The desire to share this "good news" has encouraged me to replace aggressive questioning with compassionate inquiry. Accusations of inequity are reframed as female-centric lessons and talks. Through such approachable advocacy, I have engaged with many Latter-day Saint women thirsty for spiritual oases filled with female wells of knowledge. My work as a historian has not reconciled every concern I have as a feminist Latter-day Saint. However, I have come to see a consciousness of the persistent and creative faithfulness of earlier generations of Latter-day Saint women as essential to my apprenticeship as a follower of Christ. It is through reading and writing their histories that I believe I can be a dedicated, if at times discomforted, disciple.

11. Many Latter-day Saint women employed both racist and classist arguments in their opposition to American colonization in the Pacific. Using the rhetoric of imperial civilizers, they felt that missionary efforts and not violence should be utilized to raise "barbarians" from their degraded state. "Officer's Meeting," *Woman's Exponent* 27 (August 1, 1898): 21. The *Woman's Exponent* reprinted the articles of non-Latter-day Saint suffragists that expressed resentment of the potential for Filipino men, as citizens of a newly incorporated American territory, to obtain the franchise before what they considered to be better educated and more civically-minded White American women. "Letter from Miss Anthony," *Woman's Exponent* 27 (September 15, 1898): 41.

Warts and All

JENNY HALE PULSIPHER

Jenny Hale Pulsipher was born in the city (Los Angeles) and raised on the farm (Huntsville, Utah). She is a professor of history at Brigham Young University and the author of "Subjects unto the Same King": Indians, English, and the Contest for Authority in Colonial New England *(University of Pennsylvania 2005), which was named a Choice Magazine Outstanding Academic Title for 2006, and* Swindler Sachem: The American Indian who Sold His Birthright, Dropped Out of Harvard, and Conned the King of England *(Yale University Press 2018), which won the Norris and Carol Hundley Award for the best book on any historical subject from the American Historical Association–Pacific Coast Branch. She loves reading, scuba diving, hiking, knitting, and theater. She and her husband have four grown children and five grandchildren. They live in Salt Lake City.*

❖

I AM WHITE—some might even say blindingly white—based on my appearance, religion, and position of privilege. I was born to upper-middle-class, college-educated parents. The economic support and experienced guidance they provided for me, as well as their DNA, gave me an enormous advantage in securing my own economic and social status. However, I have both Native American and African ancestors. In some eras of history, the fact that I have non-White ancestors would have defined me as non-White. That is not the case today, and I would never claim that my ancestry qualifies me to speak for Indigenous or Black people. My own lived experience has not exposed me to the prejudice, discrimination, and oppression that some of my ancestors suffered or that brown and Black people suffer today. Nevertheless, I do think it is worth mentioning, if only to remind people that race is a social construct. It is not defined only by who your ancestors are. It is also shaped by what you look like; how, where, and when you were raised; who you socialize with; how much money you have; and what the laws say about who belongs to a particular racial category and what restrictions or benefits go along with it. In other words, race has a constantly shifting definition based on surface appearances and cultural perceptions, reinforced by laws, policies, and procedures of those who wield power in society.

Despite my Whiteness, issues of race and ethnicity have always loomed large for me, pushing me to explore them in both my personal life and my scholarship. Reconciling the demands of scholarship with my personal experiences and religious beliefs has led me to embrace a model of the past that recognizes the good and the bad—warts and all—in the people I study. I only recently learned a few details about my African ancestry, but my Shoshone ancestors have been part of my personal and family identity for as long as I can remember. Membership in The Church of Jesus Christ of Latter-day Saints runs just as deep in my Shoshone line as in most other ancestral lines in my family. My fourth-great-grandmother Sally, a Shoshone woman, was baptized into the Church in 1855 at Fort Supply, now Wyoming, two decades before the Northwestern Shoshone converted almost en masse. My parents and grandparents used to tell me stories about "Sally of the Shoshone," who was taken into servitude in St. Louis as a young girl. She ran away by swimming to an island in the Mississippi River, met and married a French trapper, and returned to her Native kin in the West.

I closely identified with this part of my family history from a very young age. Before I even knew the words *cultural* and *appropriation*, I had a Native American costume of faux deerskin with fringes, complete with yarn braids to go under my headband. I wore it to my ward Primary's Pioneer Day party when I was six years old. However cringeworthy that costume may appear today, it was a conscious effort—probably spearheaded by my dad—to make our Primary parade represent those who were already in the Mountain West as well as those who arrived in 1847, to show that our own family history was Indigenous as well as pioneer.

In the absence of lived experience, my Indigenous ancestry does not qualify me to act or speak on behalf of the Indigenous community. However, it is the source of my lifelong interest in Native American culture and history, including my own family's history. As I grew up, I discovered contradictions in various family accounts of my Shoshone grandmother's life. I wanted to learn more and unravel the messy tale that had come down to me. Eventually, that desire inspired my decision to study Native American history in graduate school, and it informs my present work as a historian of Indigenous people.

As a historian, I have been trained to see nuances in people. I try not to view them as all one thing or another—villain or victim, saint or sinner—but to recognize the complex, ever-shifting mix of good and bad that characterizes every human being. In the present cultural and political moment in the United States, nuance is a tricky position to take. The horrifying scene of a White policeman kneeling on the neck of a Black man—George Floyd—as he gasped his life away has been seared into our collective consciousness. The enforced isolation of the COVID-19 pandemic has given us space for introspection, and this seems to have allowed more Americans, finally, to take seriously the plague of systemic and individual racism made manifest in this and other incidents of violence against Black people. The traumatic aftermath of that event was not a time for nuance but for solidarity, for mourning with those who mourn. It was not a time to insist that all lives matter but to listen and respond to the stories of pain and prejudice that underlie the Black Lives Matter movement.

Nuance will come later, and hopefully so will reconciliation. While my historical training teaches me that people are never wholly good or bad, my belief in the gospel of Jesus Christ teaches me that all flawed and sinful people are redeemable. That gives me hope because I am a flawed and sinful person. I want to be able to repent and change as an individual. The atonement of Christ opens that possibility to every child of God, past and present. For that reason, I have hope in social reconciliation as well, in the possibility that the society I live in can repent, seek forgiveness, repair wrongs, and change, becoming more reflective, compassionate, and accepting of people who have suffered exclusion, discrimination, and violence. Recognizing past and present wrongs is the first step to reconciliation.

I believe that the reconciliation we seek as individuals and as societies is furthered by seeing people as complex individuals capable of change, not just in our social interactions but also in the histories we write. Heroes and villains are caricatures, not real people, and they have very little to teach the real, flawed people of the present. If we are to learn from the past, we need to be able to see ourselves in it. This is a controversial position to take, particularly within the field of Native American history. Indigenous people have been caricatured in history, made to appear uncivilized and doomed to vanish under the march of "superior" White civilization. After several centuries of negative or paternalistic representations of Indigenous people, it is not surprising that many historians choose to turn the tables, recasting White settlers in the role of villains and Native people as heroes, or for Native people to resent writers who point out flaws in Indigenous people of the past. It requires great sensitivity to push for nuance without causing offense. I am not easily offended, and I tend—insensitively—to assume other people are the same. I think I erred in naming my most recent book *Swindler Sachem: The American Indian Who Sold His Birthright, Dropped Out of Harvard, and Conned the King of England*.[1] Some people were so put off by the title that they would not read the nuanced argument of the book.

As I wrote that book, I wrestled with how to depict John Wompas,

1. Jenny Hale Pulsipher, *Swindler Sachem: The American Indian Who Sold His Birthright, Dropped Out of Harvard, and Conned the King of England* (New Haven and London: Yale University Press, 2018).

a Native American man who betrayed his own people, selling their land to English settlers without their permission and for his sole benefit. His own kin washed their hands of him, claiming his actions were driven only by selfishness and lust. He deserved their condemnation; while Indigenous choices were constrained by the dominant English power structure, they were not eliminated. But as I uncovered more and more about his life in obscure court cases, land deeds, and brief mentions in contemporary accounts, I came to see that he was not just the sum of his bad deeds. He was highly intelligent, witty, and determined. He had a sense of honor, insisting on paying his debts. Indeed, that sense of honor may have been what inspired a change of heart toward the end of his life as he came to the realization that his land sales, justifiable on some levels, had deeply wounded and undermined the sovereignty of his Native kin and friends. My analysis of his last years led me to conclude that he used his education and bicultural knowledge to attempt to repair the damage he had done, writing his will in a way that protected a significant portion of the Nipmuc homeland. Some of that homeland remains in Nipmuc hands to the present day—the only parcel of land in the state of Massachusetts that has never left Native ownership. While I still consider John Wompas deeply flawed, I believe that he had consciously begun the process of change.

All of us know such people—in our work, in our personal lives, in our family histories. My belief in the gospel and my training as a historian impel me to be slow to judge them, to try to understand them—not excuse them—within the context of their unique cultural expectations, beliefs, and personal challenges. My current research has brought me into the realm of family and Church history, where I have encountered people like my fourth-great-grandfather William Taylor Dennis. Like John Wompas, Dennis brought great suffering on his kin, friends, and others. He held men and women in slavery in Pontotoc County, Mississippi. After joining the Church in 1850, he loaded his family and goods in four enormous wagons driven by enslaved men and headed to Salt Lake City, arriving in 1854. He was pigheaded, refusing to take advice from anyone. Worse, he betrayed his family, abandoning his first wife (my fourth-great-grandmother) and all their children. He was abusive to his second wife, who divorced him; he committed adultery, fathering a child with an unmarried woman in Utah Valley, and was excommunicated from the Church. I have to look harder to find good in him than I did with John Wompas because Dennis had power within his community and society that Wompas did not have, and he abused that power. But his search for truth led him to join the Church and, after many years outside it, to be rebaptized near the end of his life. This suggests that he, too, was trying to change.[2]

As I have dug more deeply into the histories of my Native American ancestors within the context of the Church's racial policies and attitudes, I've repeatedly encountered another person who is easy to vilify —Brigham Young. He's everywhere in nineteenth-century Utah Territory records, ecclesiastical and otherwise. Among his many statements about Native people are some that sound exceptionally racist to modern ears and have caused deep pain to Indigenous people. That said, I see a clear difference between Brigham Young's actions and those of other nineteenth-century settler colonists. As I've read hundreds of his letters to people throughout the territory, I've been struck by the consistency with which he urged peaceful interaction with Native Americans, condemned violence, and defended Native rights to land. These actions were not the norm for settler colonists, and they undoubtedly contributed to better relations than would have prevailed without his continual admonitions. During a time when many of his contemporaries began to view Native people as irredeemably incapable of civilization or salvation, he proclaimed them to be children of Israel and spiritual equals. There was never a time when he or any other Church leader denied Indigenous people priesthood ordinances. But Brigham Young's attitudes and policies toward Black people were no better than those of his contemporaries, and they had stark implications for Black people's access to ordinances of salvation. Like

2. Tonya Reiter, "Redd Slave Histories: Family, Race, and Sex in Pioneer Utah," *Utah Historical Quarterly* 85, no. 2 (Spring 2017): 108–26, at 117; and Junction Ward Record, pp. 48–49, Film 26044, FHL. I thank Carl Carter for providing me with a copy of this record.

other nineteenth-century people within and outside of the Church, he saw them as "cursed" descendants of Cain and Ham, and thereby, he thought they should be cut off from receiving temple and priesthood blessings—a mistaken and racist perspective the Church now unequivocally disavows.[3] Those views and the policies arising from them had and continue to have profoundly painful consequences for Black members of the Church.

A few years ago, as I was researching Sally's daughter, my third-great-grandmother Adelaide Exervier, I learned something surprising about her and her Latter-day Saint missionary husband, James Morehead Brown. They were sealed for eternity in the Endowment House in Salt Lake City in 1857, but later, their sealing and endowments were cancelled, possibly on suspicion of African ancestry. The cancellation was temporary. After eight years cut off from the blessings of the temple, Adelaide and James seemed to have convinced Church officials that their ancestry was White and Native American—both of which were allowed full access to priesthood ordinances. In 1865, they were reendowed and resealed. While I don't have personal writings from Adelaide or James, I can't help but imagine how painful this exclusion must have been for them. It came to an end, yes, but the pain must have lingered. And if their exclusion was known in the community, it could have led to long-lasting suspicion and social ostracism. In fact, there is evidence that that was the case for some of their descendants.

I grieve for the pain that policy inflicted on Adelaide, on James, and on so many others. I don't understand why Brigham Young made such an abrupt turn between 1847, when he avowed that some of the "best Elders" in the Church were Black priesthood holders, and 1852, when he denied that anyone with Black ancestry could engage in priesthood ordinances.[4] I find the policy Brigham Young instituted and the

3. "Race and the Priesthood," Gospel Topics, https://www.churchofjesuschrist.org/study/manual/gospel-topics-essays/race-and-the-priesthood?lang=eng.

4. W. Paul Reeve, "Making Sense of the Church's History on Race," *Faith Matters*, June 30, 2020, https://faithmatters.org/making-sense-of-the-churchs-history-on-race/?fbclid=IwAR3G2jTkUAh2bfgeSYF-kNnA8i3ZMoa6msF-1FdwkcvFV8-6M73MNn7NY-s; see also W. Paul

attitudes he expressed about Black people contrary to the scriptures and teachings of the gospel. However, I don't believe he should be judged solely on those attitudes and actions any more than should William Dennis, who was guilty of some terrible things. Thankfully, I have never borne the burden of believing that Church leaders or family members, past or present, are perfect. I know some people have felt morally compelled to break with the Church because of its racist record. Perhaps they hope to find another institutional home that is less tainted. I wish them well, but I have no illusions that there are purer institutions elsewhere. I know that leaders and followers in the Church are fallible, but I choose to stay in what I consider my spiritual home, the place where I learned to seek and gain revelation for my life, where I consistently feel God's love, and where I nurture and am nurtured by my fellow fallible Saints.

I love the Church, and sometimes I feel protective of it. I think I understand those who believe dredging up past wrongs does little good, that we should put the past behind us. But as I write of Sally and Adelaide Exervier, of William Dennis, of Brigham Young, I choose to depict them as the whole humans they were—flawed, sinning, and sinned against, but also striving and capable of redemption. I hope they would do the same for me. I have come to believe that hearing the stories of individuals who sinned and fell short, of the suffering they caused as well as the good they did, is a necessary step toward the reconciliation we seek individually, in the Church, and in the world.

Reeve, *Religion of a Different Color: Race and the Mormon Struggle for Whiteness* (New York: Oxford University Press, 2015).

PART FOUR

The wars and the perplexities of the nations, and the judgments which are on the land

(Doctrine & Covenants 88:79)

Dynamics of human struggle and conflict can drive us to either hate or love in greater abundance. Which will we choose?

Civil laws reflect our collective responses to conflict over time.

Becoming Mormon

MARION BISHOP

Marion Bishop is an emergency medicine physician (MD, University of Utah), who practices in northern Utah and Wyoming. Prior to attending medical school, she earned a PhD in English from New York University and taught college English for eleven years. She writes and speaks regularly about the intersection of medicine and the humanities. Her writing has appeared in the Journal of the American Medical Association, Dialogue, *and multiple book collections on topics ranging from the practice of medicine to mothering. She is a frequent guest on television and radio programs, as well as a speaker to student and other groups. She is a single parent to two children. A blog and more of her writing is available at marioncbishop.com.*

I BECAME A PHYSICIAN because of Mormon—not the Book of Mormon or "Mormons"—but *Mormon*, the Nephite military leader, prophet, and scholar who led armies in battle while compiling the entire historical record of his people into a book of scripture still read today. That guy. He is the reason I went to medical school.

But I'm getting ahead of myself. Mormon is the reason I first earned a PhD in English too.

As a little girl, I had big dreams but was not sure how to make them come true. I grew up in a rural community in northern Utah as a bookish, nerdy child in a devout, determined Latter-day Saint family. Scripture study and academics were encouraged, but so were physical labor and all sorts of hard work. I carried a book with me to feed and water horses, and I read outdoors all summer long.

I also had four brothers. They were charismatic, larger-than-life boys who rode horses and motorcycles, commanded large groups of friends, and led expeditions through the neighborhood, looking for adventure. They hunted for deer with my dad in the fall and could build just about anything with a hammer and nails.

My father was an old-fashioned, general practice doctor who delivered babies, performed appendectomies, and made house calls. For many years, my mother, an artist and textile designer, performed the formidable task of keeping the house running well enough to support the sprawling activities that sprang from it. When I entered high school, she started a successful business that she ran from our home until she and my father retired.

In this world of my childhood, men's lives were the heroic ones, lived out in the open for everyone to see, while women's lives were more private and interior. This idea was layered on, morning after morning, reading the Book of Mormon before school—and I was not sure where my own aspirations fit. I did not doubt that my brothers, like Nephi, could hunt for game, build ships, or even slay Laban. I also felt pretty certain that they could have joined Moroni, outwitting their enemies and living long enough to bury the plates in the Hill Cumorah.

But what was a—book-loving, introspective—girl to do? My parents reminded me that there were women in the Book of Mormon too—wives and daughters who did courageous things that simply were not written about. But this answer seemed insufficient to me, and I was lonely for a Book of Mormon hero of my own—even if it had to be a man.

It took me a while, but eventually, I found Mormon. He was not a woman, but with his sober mind and immersion in books, he felt like me. I admired his wartime leadership but was even more fascinated by the life of his mind. That he had wrapped his brain around the thousand-year history of his people and then condensed it into the book I read every morning before breakfast seemed like the most heroic —and nearly impossible—task of all.

Growing up in this religious culture full of men and their stories, holding fast to the idea of Mormon not just as a soldier but also a scholar, steadied me and helped me believe that an introverted girl like me had worth. It also gave me permission to pursue academics and to grow a rich, internal life of my own.

As I moved through school, I leaned into the idea that studying and learning could be righteous endeavors. I studied English in college, earned a PhD in English from New York University, and spent ten years teaching English at the college level. Some of my East Coast, Ivy League–educated classmates saw me as a curious Western specimen, a survivor of a rural upbringing and conservative religious culture. Some considered it their job to interrogate or remove the Latter-day Saint from me. In a job interview for a teaching fellowship, someone once asked me if I had been successful "because of or in spite of being a Mormon woman."

But I saw my rural childhood and religious roots as contiguous with my academic pursuits. For anyone who doubted me, I shared stories about how I had been raised and offered exhibit A: Mormon—a literary prophet so central to our religious doctrine that our most sacred text was named after him.

My doctoral dissertation was a study of women's journals and diaries and included an exploration of the diary of a Latter-day Saint woman, Mary Perkes. Drawing on Mormon's example, it was my own, small effort at telling my story—and the story of my own people—through a record someone had already set down.

But as I finished my dissertation, something interesting was happening. The immersion in the life of the mind, and saturation with language and literature and stories that graduate school represented, created in me a desire to be more of a participant in the world than an observer. Writing a dissertation, teaching college English, and going toe-to-toe with other academics had also given me confidence and courage. I was ready to do the next thing—and I wanted it to be big and messy and to take place outside my office or library carrel.

I had been following Mormon-the-scholar for enough years and through enough stories that I had grown from a nerdy girl into a capable and more self-possessed adult. I was curious to see what I could do with the rest of my life. Since Mormon's life had been shaped by two very different occupations, his story continued to call to me. Only this time, rather than Mormon-the-scholar, it was Mormon-the-soldier who got my attention.

But that does not mean I was eager to go to war. Rather, Mormon's soldiering—particularly as an often reluctant military leader—spoke to me as an act of service. Over time, this example, together with memories of my father's old-fashioned doctoring, grew into a desire to go to medical school. Although soldiers killed and doctors healed, both occupations represented a visceral, immediate engagement in the experience of being human—and a willingness to take risks and join others on behalf of a greater good. After years sitting in dusty libraries, the fact that both jobs involved blood and guts was part of the appeal.

Nevertheless, training to become a doctor was hard for me. I had spent my twenties living in the world of ideas—luxuriating in conversations with smart people and learning to love the solitary but satisfying work of writing. Medical school was a four-year boot camp in rote memorization and extroversion. I crammed facts without time to consider their truth and spent waking hours surrounded by classmates and patients.

I survived by walking the dog late at night and continuing to write, keeping a journal and even occasionally submitting pieces for publication. Whenever I was not at the hospital, I lived a secret, stealthy life of a former assistant English professor, reading about everything from linguistic theory to current events, turning to words and ideas for comfort against the daily onslaught of human drama and physiology that is the practice of medicine. Perhaps like what Mormon did when not in battle, I found that this precious solitary time sustained me in the near unending pace of learning to be a doctor.

When it came time to pick a specialty, I chose emergency medicine. I liked the chaos of trauma and illness that comprised a day in the emergency room (ER), as well as the fact that I saw people from all walks of life. But I also probably wanted to prove that someone as bookish and introverted as me could be a player on the stressful, life-and-death landscape that is emergency medicine. Mormon had turned from books to battle. Could I do my own version of that too?

Residency turned up the speed on an already fast pace, and I found myself being asked to work harder, with less sleep, than I ever had before. Writing and solitary hours on days off continued to save me. I also began to see ways that my work in the ER was enriching my time alone.

Near the end of my residency, I published a personal essay, "Life Math," in the *Journal of the American Medical Association*.[1] It drew on my experience in the emergency room as well as the example of Anne Bradstreet—a mother and the first published poet in America—to explore the way an active external life can feed and even fuel the life of the mind. As I put in chest tubes and completed intubations, comforted trauma victims and titrated medications, I was discovering that the paradigm of Mormon as a soldier who retreated to be a scholar before returning to the battlefield was beginning to shape and bring meaning to my life too.

Since finishing residency, I have continued to practice medicine in the same way. For the first ten years of my career, I was a solo doctor working in an emergency room in rural Wyoming. Going to work there felt like returning to my childhood but in a different role. Instead of being the little girl watching the world move around me, I was in charge. The hospital had an enormous catchment area, and sometimes the trauma, disease, and pestilence that landed in the ambulance bay felt biblical—or at least larger than life.

However, working there, I came to realize that disease and misfortune are not larger than life. Rather, they are the most reliable and fun-

1. Marion Bishop, "Life Math," *Journal of the American Medical Association* 298, no. 3 (July 18, 2007): 266–68, doi:10.1001/jama.298.3.266.

damental components of life. Mormon-the-soldier had guided me to the wide-open, windswept Wyoming plateau. Working with a team of remarkable nurses and hospital staff, I had the priceless opportunity to immerse myself in the blood and guts, the grief and celebration of human experience—and also to try and do some good.

Reading and writing and walking the dog after all those long shifts and then returning to the ER, I found myself wondering if this was the way Mormon lived—if the contemplative life sustained him for battle or if the battle motivated and gave direction to the compilation of a book that was his other life's work. Or both. I also wondered if this is what God intended and what all those early mornings reading scripture were about: that risk and service undertaken on behalf of others—and a chance to contemplate what it all means—are their own reward.

Despite the years-long role Mormon has played in my life, I would be lying if I did not confess that sometimes I wonder if he was even real. When my testimony feels lush and full, I am confident Mormon walked the earth I am living on now. In dark moments, I have sometimes wondered.

But Mormon has transformed me. As I have grown older, I have concluded that however it came to me, Mormon's story has inspired me, guided me, and served as a template for shaping my life. I am better, and different, because of him.

Put another way, Moroni 10:4 states that God "manifest[s] the truth" of the Book of Mormon through the "power of the Holy Ghost." Across the course of my life, the truthfulness of the Book of Mormon has been made known to me through a burning in my bosom and comfort in times of trial. But I have also come to know the sacredness of the book in the way following Mormon's words and example has been "manifest" in me and through me. I am proud of my accomplishments but know that much of my life would have been impossible without what the power of the Holy Ghost has helped me create.

I started this essay in the early months of 2020 and ended it in 2022, when the pandemic had not completely subsided. What began as an homage to one of the central figures in Church scripture—and in my life—now feels more like a meditation on how to live and what I have learned about that from Mormon.

Part of what I mean is that when the pandemic came, the practice of medicine and COVID-19 pressed me into service in a way I had never imagined. For all of my following of Mormon's example and finding analogies between him as a soldier and me as a doctor, I never envisioned that practicing medicine would cause me to risk my health—or my life. But with the advent of the coronavirus, emergency departments have become the center of a fight over an invisible and sometimes lethal enemy. In the world of the pandemic, healthcare workers are heroes, and the ER is referred to as the front line.

I am uncomfortable with these labels. But I also realize that the scale and scope of my life have grown larger than I ever imagined. The little girl who dreamed of a meaningful life while studying scripture around the breakfast table became an academic who in turn evolved into a doctor who now leans back on the scriptures and stories that sustained her as a child. An interior life and role that sometimes felt confining grew fruitful enough to explode into the next thing and then the next.

Sitting with my books and my stethoscope, I would like to take credit for it all, but I cannot. Some of the credit belongs to Mormon and far more to God. I simply leaned in. I had no idea what God had in store for me or how following this path would shape who I am.

So these days, as I struggle to stay afloat in the sea of sick and dying patients that fill my emergency room, I lean on Mormon's example even more than ever. I read newspapers and write snippets of essays between treating patients. I pray. Then I see the next patient that comes through the door.

I hope to remain worthy of the next transformation and the next way that following Mormon's words might be made manifest in me.

The Relationship Between My Study of Law and My Faith

ESOHE FRANCES IKPONMWEN

Honorable Justice Esohe Frances Ikponmwen, emeritus chief judge, Edo State, obtained her degree in civil law from the University of Nigeria, Nsuka, Enugu State in Nigeria. Beginning in 1979, she practiced law in the then Bendel State attorney general's office as a public prosecutor. At the creation of Edo State, she was appointed as chief magistrate, a post she held from 1992 to 1999, when she was elevated to the High Court bench as judge. In 2017, she was appointed chief judge of Edo State and retired in 2019 at the age of sixty-five. The book "Holding Unto the Law": A Testimonial of Hon Justice Esohe Frances Ikponmwen, *by Basil Momodu (2017), summarizes many of her cases. She is a fellow of the Commonwealth Judicial Education Institute, the Nigerian Institute of Chartered Arbitrators, and the Institute of Chartered Mediators and Conciliators and is a Paul Harris Fellow of Rotary International. She served as stake Relief Society president in two stakes and currently is the area organization adviser for the Benin City Coordinating Council, West Africa office of the Church. She is married and blessed with children and grandchildren; she enjoys traveling, dancing, and teaching the gospel.*

MY JOURNEY to becoming a lawyer began with the seed sown in my heart years ago by my late father, Mr. Anthony Uwuigbe Okuonghae (April 16, 1913–June 24, 1989). He used to speak glowingly of the lawyers he encountered daily (as a health superintendent) prosecuting sanitation offenders in court. I feel gratitude always to my father for his guidance and light of direction, which prepared me for law as a course of study in college, thus fulfilling Proverbs 22:6: "Train up a child in the way he should go: and when he is old, he will not depart from it."

I recall that in my first year at the University of Nigeria in 1974, I went with my roommate to the faculty officer to ask for a transfer from the law department to the English department as we thought that if we qualified as lawyers, we would be superior to our husbands, or they might feel inferior given our cultural background. Female lawyers were not visible in our society then. If the faculty officer had not been well trained to handle cases like ours, I would have dropped out of the journey. He counseled us on the merits of the study of law and suggested that we could be law teachers if we were more comfortable being teachers, a profession more common among women then. Or we could be company secretaries, another choice for women as a career. In short, this God-sent faculty officer talked me out of leaving the study of law, and I am so indebted to him. This experience taught me a lesson in building our faith to be strong and in remaining focused.

On July 7, 1979, I was enrolled in the Supreme Court of Nigeria as a solicitor and advocate. I was part of the compulsory National Youth Service Corps as a legal aid counsel and a counsel in the Ministry of Justice, office of the attorney general of the state of Bendel, from 1979 to 1980. I served as state counsel in that ministry from 1980 to 1992, rising to be a principal state counsel. At that stage in my life, I would consider myself a passive Christian: a churchgoer not quite convicted by the Holy Spirit, though a baptized Anglican. I was raised at home by goodly parents who were not really religious and were not churchgoers. However, both my parents returned to church before their passing. They have been sealed in the temple and are safely home together beyond the veil. They instilled in us, their nine children, virtues of goodness, honesty, charity, and education. The training in the boarding school I attended also inculcated the essence of being God-fearing and disciplined.

All these qualities helped me in my practice as a state counsel. I made hard work and honesty my work values. These virtues paid off as I later was appointed a chief magistrate (1992–1999), High Court judge (1999–2017), and chief judge of Edo State (2017–2019). On the bench, my faith in the gospel of Jesus Christ helped me exceedingly. In 2002, when the anti-corruption courts were set up, I was singled out to be one of the pioneer judges and remained so till I was appointed chief judge. I believe integrity and honesty are both products of faith in Jesus Christ.

Faith and study of law

The study and practice of law often opens areas of conflict with one's religious faith, as well as some meeting points. Let me briefly highlight just a few of these obvious areas of conflict or contradictions. I find that my view is guided by the words of Alma in the Book of Mormon where it states, "The people who were of the Church of God … were … distinguished for their zeal towards God, and also towards men; for they were perfectly honest and upright in all things; and they were firm in the faith of Christ, even unto the end" (Alma 27:27). In the light of this scripture, as a judicial official charged with upholding the law, the Christian/godly requirement of honesty in my dealings also applies. In this regard, there should absolutely be no conflict: faith and the study of law mostly align. The principle of honesty is a fundamental and necessary ingredient in the administration of justice. In my view, when there are conflicts between law and religion, it is the principles of honesty and integrity that ought to point one to the path of justice.

I would like to look at three core issues: divorce, gender discrimination, and morality with respect to the law and lawyers.

Divorce

Most religious faiths seek to discourage divorce as a solution to an ailing marriage. For instance, the Holy Bible states emphatically that

> from the beginning of the creation God made them male and female. For this cause shall a man leave his father and mother, and cleave to his wife; and they twain shall be one flesh: so then they are no more twain, but one flesh. What therefore God hath joined together, let not man put asunder. (Mark 10:6–9)

To many, this clearly outlaws divorce between people of the Christian faith. Rebuking those who favored a pro-divorce interpretation of the scriptures, Jesus described this exception: "Moses because of the hardness of your hearts suffered you to put away your wives: but from the beginning it was not so. And I say unto you, Whosoever shall put away his wife, except it be for fornication, and shall marry another, committeth adultery" (Matthew 19:8–9).

In Nigeria, however, the study and practice of family law clearly provides for divorce under the law and expands the frontiers of reasons or grounds for divorce far beyond immorality. For instance, for statutory marriages, section 15(1) of the Matrimonial Causes Act provides that either party in a marriage may petition for divorce upon the grounds that the marriage has broken down irretrievably. Nigerian courts have interpreted this section as establishing the irretrievable breakdown of a marriage as the sole grounds for divorce. Omo JCA (as he then was) succinctly stated the legal position in *Harriman v. Harriman* (1989)5NWLR (pt.119)6CA:

> There is only one ground for the dissolution of marriage under the Matrimonial Causes Act, to wit, that the marriage has broken down irretrievably. Vide S. 15(1) of the Act. The subparagraphs of subsection 2 thereof, eight of them, (a) to (h),

> are only various species of breakdown or to put it differently, a petitioner who satisfies the court on any one or more of these facts, would be entitled to a finding that the marriage has broken down and consequently be entitled to a decree dissolving same.

A lawyer or a judge of faith is immediately at a crossroad when presented with a brief or asked to decide a case seeking dissolution of marriage on grounds other than immorality. However, in my practice, I always followed the provisions of the law, being of the view that we must follow the law since respect for the government and its laws is a scriptural principle taught by Jesus Christ when he told the Pharisees, "Render therefore unto Caesar the things which are Caesar's; and unto God the things that are God's" (Matthew 22:21).

Gender discrimination

The relationship between my study and practice of law and the dictate of my faith is also very evident in the area of gender relationship, as represented in discrimination against women. In this area, it is safe to conclude that most religions of the world tend to discriminate against women. Certain admonitions of the apostle Paul seem to denigrate women and inflame the passion of pro-discrimination advocates. For example, in 1 Corinthians 14:34–35, Paul expressly forbade women from speaking in church and required them to be submissive. According to him, women should remain silent in the churches. They were not allowed to speak but must be in submission as the law said. If they wanted to inquire about something, they should ask their own husbands at home, for it was disgraceful for a woman to speak in the church.

The above biblical admonition is clearly in conflict and finds no place in national or international law. In this regard, the Constitution of the Federal Republic of Nigeria, 1999, provides against discrimination, *inter alia*, on grounds of sex. This provision has been given international flavor in some international legal instruments such as the Convention on the Elimination of All Forms of Discrimination against Women (CEDAW) 1981 and the Africa Charter on Human and Peoples' Rights on the Rights of Women in Africa 1981. I must hasten to say that in The Church of Jesus Christ of Latter-day Saints, discriminatory practices are not allowed, as all can speak in church under the priesthood authority. This is one factor that endeared me to the Church.

It is therefore going to be absurd in the present day reality for any customary law (a practice in Nigeria) to discriminate against any gender as this would be an affront to the Almighty God. In this regard, I would like to echo the words of Eso, justice of the Supreme Court of Nigeria, in the case of *Thomas & Sons v. Olufoye* (1986) INSCC 336 that "the reasoning in religion is one of God—which passeth all Jurisprudence." Our Lord Jesus Christ died to set us free, and we are free indeed, male and female.

Morality, the law, and lawyers

A popular but erroneous perception held by some is that morality and lawyers are two sharply distinct entities. Lawyers are therefore seen by some as professionals who lack morals and who are prepared to do anything just to win a case. Dismissively, lawyers are said to be liars and cannot therefore be taken seriously in a religious sense. However, my study of the law has clearly shown that the above perception and stereotype is grossly inaccurate and misleading. The intertwine between the lawyer and moral values is underscored by the *Rules of Professional Conduct in the Legal Profession*, rule 24:

> Service or advice rendered or given that not only accords with the letter of the law but also embraces moral principle cannot be too highly commended. He must also observe and advise his client to observe the statute law, save that until a statute has been construed and interpreted by competent adjudication, he is free and is entitled to advise as to its validity and as to what he conscientiously believes to be its just meaning and extent.

> Above all, a lawyer finds his highest honour in a deserved reputation for fidelity to private trust and to public duty, as an honest man and as a patriotic and loyal citizen.

This rule is necessary because, in a typical third-world country like ours where poverty and illiteracy are prevalent, there are instances when ignorant and illiterate litigants may be taken advantage of by dishonest lawyers who do not give sound legal advice because they want monetary benefits by filing cases unnecessarily in courts.

As an advocate and magistrate, my mind was open to new ideas. I questioned a lot of things, and I had a lot of questions left unanswered. I was seeking truth and wanted to know a better way to serve God. When my brother was converted in August 1989, I learned of the Book of Mormon. I was skeptical initially, but with my learning, I was inquisitive about the new teaching of Christ. It was easy for me to ask pertinent and relevant questions that the missionaries of the Church answered creditably to my satisfaction, and I was converted in 1994.

After I joined The Church of Jesus Christ of Latter-day Saints and was truly born again, as it were, I found that I appreciated more my role as a trained lawyer and, at that time, a chief magistrate grade 1, a lower court judge. I saw how the Holy Spirit can assist one in the dispensation of justice. I often experienced the still small voice directing me on what to do and where to look for solutions within the law when trying to crack knotty cases. I may be led to a relevant legal authority, usually after a prayer to God for help. Faith-based principles of honesty, integrity, and hard work are helpful in times when societal influences of corrupt practices, poor remuneration, and work environment would otherwise have tempted one to compromise legal standards. Corrupt practices can indeed fuel negative perceptions of lawyers. Hence gospel values by discerning lawyers should be used in supporting the law. Otherwise, Galatians 6:8—which states, "He that soweth to his flesh shall of the flesh reap corruption; but he that soweth to the Spirit shall of the Spirit reap life everlasting"—would be the repercussion.

Another principle of note is charity, which applies very well to the law, especially the idea that "charity never faileth" (1 Corinthians 13:8). Usually when a defendant (the accused) is found guilty and convicted, the court calls on the defendant's counsel to make a statement in mitigating the sentence to be passed by the court. This statement by the lawyer is called an allocutus—it seeks for mercy from the court for the convict. When defendants are brought from correctional facilities, at times hungry and with no shirts on (conditions are now better), I used to provide money from my personal resources for court officials to get basic necessities for such hungry and unkempt prisoners brought to court.

In deciding cases, we find that judges refer to biblical examples. The law and religion are separate, but at times, they intertwine. In the following cases, for example, the judges obviously make references to biblical injunctions.

In the case of *Societe Ban caire (Nig) Ltd v. De LLuch* (2005) All FWLR (pt 242) 429, Pats Acholonu, justice of the Supreme Court of Nigeria, referenced Lord Atkin of House of Lords, England, in the locus classicus of *Donoghue v. Stevenson* (1932) A C p562 thus: "The lawyer's question [is], 'Who, then is my neighbor?' … The answer seems to be persons who are so closely and directly affected by my act that I ought reasonably to have them in contemplation as being so affected when I am directing my mind to the acts or omissions which are called to question." (This is in reference to Matthew 22:37–39 and Luke 10:27–37.) Similarly, in *State v. Anohue* (1983) INCR p85, Honorable Justice Achi-kanu, in sentencing the accused, refused to apply the godly virtue of mercy, stating as follows: "Our hearts are not closed against mercy, but mercy would be meaningless if abused by giving it in thoughtless measure to a heartless animal."

Finally, by faith, I am able to cause changes in customary practices that are unconstitutional. I speak truth to the powers that be without fear or favor. My faith makes me understand that everything good is right; I am able to do the right thing no matter whose ox is gored. In the case of *Osaro Obaze v. Governor Edo State & Ors* {Suit B/46/OS/15}, I ruled against my state government that illegally removed a local government chairman from office. This was not difficult because it was the right thing to do. There were good and bad repercussions. I was perceived as anti-government and was posted out of the station, but this added to my reputation of being incorruptible, fearless, and a judge that stood for truth and righteousness.

Conclusion

In this paper, I have sought to examine the relationship between my faith and my study of law. In doing so, I have highlighted the influence one has had on the other, especially as it relates to the vital importance of my faith as a guide in my study and application of the law. I have also underscored areas of conflict and agreement. In all of these, a combination of my faith and study of law has acted as my bulwark against all forms of injustice and oppression. Consequently, I find myself in agreement with a quote often attributed to Mark Twain: "The two most important days in your life are the day you are born and the day you find out why." I am happy that I was born of goodly parents into this world and that when I was called to the Nigerian Bar to practice law, I found the reason why I was born.

"The Great Check"

Reflections on Disaster and Faith

LISA GROW

Lisa Grow was born and raised in Utah. She studied chemistry at the University of Utah and then followed in her dad's footsteps by going to law school. Lisa was the first woman (and the first person in fifteen years) to graduate summa cum laude from Harvard Law School. After clerking for US Supreme Court Justice Anthony Kennedy, she taught in the Temple/Tsinghua University master's in law program in Beijing and then at Stanford Law School. Lisa is now the Howard W. Hunter Professor of Law at BYU Law School, where she teaches disaster law, constitutional law, and torts. Her research centers on the intersection of law and disasters, and she is a coauthor of the definitive disaster law textbook Disaster Law and Policy. *She enjoys traveling, hiking, and being outside with her three amazing children.*

❖

I STUDY BROKEN THINGS. Of course, that's not the way I would present my research at an academic conference. I would say, instead, that I study the legal and policy frameworks for disaster mitigation, response, and recovery. But at heart, I think about the events that can break us—that can shatter the earth, ravage cities, destroy lives, and devastate communities—and the ways that individuals and communities can mitigate and prepare for, and then heal from and rebuild after, those catastrophic events.

Clearly, disasters aren't the only source of brokenness. Much that is broken in our lives and in our communities is chronic rather than catastrophic. Yet because the impacts of disaster almost always fall most heavily on the most vulnerable among us, disasters force us to confront the brokenness of our everyday world.

Disasters illuminate how racism, poverty, and inequity shape so much of the human experience and cause so much suffering, both during catastrophe and "normal" times. When Hurricane Katrina devastated New Orleans in 2005, poor, Black neighborhoods clustered on marginal land around neglected levees suffered the most; the storm's victims were disproportionately poor, elderly, and Black. Hurricane Maria, which ravaged Puerto Rico in 2017, exposed how poverty and chronic neglect had left Puerto Rico's people and aging infrastructure exceedingly vulnerable. The meager, listless federal response to what some estimate was the deadliest disaster on US soil in a century underscored the many ways Puerto Ricans have so often been treated as second-class citizens. The same inequitable patterns of death and suffering were also on display during the COVID-19 pandemic: racial minorities and the poor have suffered both significantly higher death rates and greater economic hardship.[1]

Where is God amidst all of this brokenness? Historically, people believed that natural disasters were divine punishment for human disobedience. And, certainly, the scriptures suggest that God sometimes speaks to us through disasters—that he calls to us through the voice of earthquakes, thunder, tempests, droughts, and other natural events (see Doctrine and Covenants 43:25).

1. This essay was written in November 2020, in the midst of the COVID-19 pandemic, and reflects the concerns of that time in the present tense even as it seeks to grapple with more enduring questions and issues. For a more in-depth discussion of the disparate effects of disasters on vulnerable populations during the pandemic and other disasters, see Lisa Grow et al., *Disaster Vulnerability*, 63 B.C.L. Rev. 957 (2022), https://lawdigitalcommons.bc.edu/cgi/viewcontent.cgi?article=4055&context=bclr.

More often, though, I believe that natural disasters, like so much else that causes human suffering, are a manifestation of a fallen world. Like death, disability, and disease, disaster is an inherent part of this mortal realm, not an expression of divine displeasure. 1 Kings 19 recounts how the prophet Elijah was confronted with "a great and strong wind" that "rent the mountains" and broke the rocks in pieces (1 Kings 19:11). But, the scripture explains, "the Lord was not in the wind." And "after the wind [came] an earthquake; but the Lord was not in the earthquake: And after the earthquake a fire; but the Lord was not in the fire: and after the fire a still small voice" (1 Kings 19:11–12).

Like Elijah, I find that God is not in the wind or the earthquake or the fire. Instead, I hear God in the "still small voice" that moves neighbors to come to each other's aid, communities to rally and come together, and strangers across the world to donate to relieve suffering. I witness God in the resilience of the human spirit. In disaster's aftermath, God is in the human kindness and the healing, the compassion and the courage to begin again.

Indeed, those who study disasters have found that, contrary to most people's expectations, disasters often bring out the best in individuals and communities. In the chaos of disaster, we often expect looting, disorder, and even violence. What we usually find, instead, is cooperation, collaboration, and community. Most people who are saved in the aftermath of disasters are rescued by fellow citizens and neighbors who pull together to organize response efforts, coordinate distribution of needed resources, and support each other.

Sometimes, dire predictions about post-disaster human behavior can distort and hinder disaster response efforts. After Hurricane Katrina, for example, there were widespread reports of looting and violence, most of which were later retracted because they were false or exaggerated. That perception of disaster-induced chaos and antisocial conduct diverted resources from search-and-rescue to anti-looting patrols, delayed the receipt of critical aid and supplies, led to restrictions on movement that hampered evacuation (and, later, delayed residents' return home), and likely contributed to vigilantism and police violence against people trying to evacuate. One focus of my scholarly writing has been urging legal reforms that make it more likely that we will respond to disasters as problems requiring humanitarian responses rather than law enforcement interventions.

Perhaps as a result of my understanding that individuals and communities usually come together to respond to disasters, I have been disappointed in the divisive response to the COVID-19 pandemic in many communities in the United States.[2] Our communities have not come together in the spirit of compassion and healing as much as I would have expected and hoped. The numbers tell the stark tale of this failure: the United States has access to some of the world's most cutting-edge medical infrastructure and technologies, but as of April 2022, its number of COVID-19 deaths per 100,000 people was 299.33, lagging far behind much less privileged nations, including Colombia (277.42) and Mexico (253.35), and paling in comparison to other wealthy nations, such as Germany (156.36) and Japan (22.38).[3] This failure is not just a national failure; it is also a local failure that has played out in many communities where large numbers of Latter-day Saints live. Despite our ethic of collaborative service and loyalty to prophetic counsel, in many of our communities, some Latter-day Saints responded with derision to the First Presidency's call to "limit the spread of these viruses" by using face masks and "immunizing a very high percentage of the population."[4]

2. These statistics from the Pew Research Center show how Americans' experience of and response to the pandemic reflected partisan political divides. Bradley Jones, "The Changing Political Geography of COVID-19 Over the Last Two Years," Pew Research Center, March 3, 2022, https://www.pewresearch.org/politics/2022/03/03/the-changing-political-geography-of-covid-19-over-the-last-two-years/.

3. Regional, national, and worldwide COVID-19 statistics can be found at the Johns Hopkins University website. "Mortality Analyses," Johns Hopkins University, https://coronavirus.jhu.edu/data/mortality.

4. "The First Presidency Urges Latter-day Saints to Wear Face Masks When Needed and Get Vaccinated Against COVID-19," Church Newsroom, August 12, 2021, https://newsroom.churchofjesuschrist.org/article/first-presidency-message-covid-19-august-2021; in Utah, where Latter-day Saints comprise a majority of the population, the Utah state

Maybe I can be forgiven of my disappointment in the response of such Latter-day Saints. After all, we are supposed to be particularly good at responding to disaster: we're the people filling sandbags, the Helping Hands in the yellow shirts mucking out people's basements after the hurricane. However, during the pandemic, many of us living in the Church's geographic heart fell prey to the same wrenching polarization and partisanship that has infected so many communities throughout the country. Despite apostolic teachings that "wearing a face covering is a sign of Christlike love for our brothers and sisters" and exhorting us to have special consideration for "the vulnerable and disadvantaged in our societies" who were especially affected by the pandemic, some Latter-day Saints did not take this counsel to heart.[5] Instead, they mocked mask-wearers and derided basic public health measures, including health measures enacted within meetinghouses and temples as official Church policy, as sinister infringements on one's "freedom" to do as one pleases. To me, that narrow focus on "freedom" neglects our understanding of freedom as a principle of agency governed by eternal laws and animated by our commitment to make choices in service of a cause larger than ourselves.

The lawyerly, academic side of me can posit some of the reasons this failure may be occurring. Studies show that people are generally terrible at processing information about risk,[6] yet the pandemic has

---

coronavirus dashboard showed that as of April 3, 2022, only 61.6% of Utahns were fully vaccinated against COVID-19. https://coronavirus-dashboard.utah.gov/vaccines.html. In response to President Russell M. Nelson's January 19, 2021, post on social media declaring, "My professional and ecclesiastical experiences convince me that vaccinations administered by competent medical professionals protect health and preserve life. Receiving the vaccine today was part of our personal efforts to be good global citizens in helping to eliminate COVID-19 from the world," over 100,000 people following the prophet's post responded positively (with a "like," "love," or "care" symbol), but 527 of those following his page responded negatively with a symbol that indicated they found this message "infuriating," "saddening," or "laughable."

5. "Masks a sign of 'Christlike love' during pandemic, apostle says," *Deseret News*, December 7, 2020. https://www.deseret.com/faith/2020/12/7/22158497/mormon-lds-church-masks-covid-19-coronavirus-christlike-love-pandemic-apostle-renlund.

6. See, for example, "Evaluating and Responding to Risk," in Daniel A. Farber, James

required everyone, every day, to weigh the risk of a thousand otherwise routine activities and to decide how best to reasonably manage those risks. A flood of misinformation and disinformation about the origin, reality, and lethality of COVID-19, including the proliferation of conspiracy theories, has also distorted some people's risk perceptions.[7]

Perhaps more importantly, most disaster events are relatively short-lived, and it is presumably easier to sustain a feeling of individual and community sacrifice and selflessness for days or weeks than for many, many months, particularly when there is no clear end in sight. Similarly, most disaster response is collective work that draws us out of our comfort zones and individual silos to engage with each other—that builds community spirit and solidarity by bringing us together to help our neighbors. Managing this pandemic has required instead that we physically distance ourselves, that we engage with each other less, that we retreat into the relative safety of our homes. Perhaps it is not surprising that a disaster response that isolates, that pushes us inward rather than drawing us out, undermines—at least to some degree—our community ties and our willingness to sacrifice for others.

Moreover, a large body of research demonstrates that partisan identity is ascendant—that, for many, partisan identity has eclipsed other aspects of identity, including religious identity, and has become a (if not the) primary way that people define and align themselves. That

---

Ming Chen, Robert R. M. Verchick, and Lisa Grow Sun, *Disaster Law and Policy*, 3rd ed. (Boston: Aspen Publishing, 2015), 283–329.

7. See Ed Pertwee, Clarissa Simas, and Heidi J. Larson, "An Epidemic of Uncertainty: Rumors, Conspiracy Theories and Vaccine Hesitancy," *Nature Medicine* 28 (March 2022): 456–59, https://doi.org/10.1038/s41591-022-01728-z. The update on "Seeking Information from Reliable Sources" to the *General Handbook of Instructions* in December 2020 reflects Church leadership's response to the proliferation of conspiracy theories and misinformation during the pandemic. The updated *Handbook* reads, "Seek out and share only credible, reliable, and factual sources of information. Avoid sources that are speculative or founded on rumor." https://newsroom.churchofjesuschrist.org/article/general-handbook-update-december-2020.

research demonstrates that our political beliefs can even influence the way we process information: we tend (subconsciously) to credit information that reinforces our political priors and discount information that contradicts those preexisting beliefs.[8] Given the powerful pull of partisanship, it isn't surprising that political leaders successfully politicized public health measures in the run-up to one of the most contentious elections in recent memory.

Nonetheless, despite my academic understanding of the ways that this pandemic makes community-oriented response more difficult, I have struggled to be kind in my judgments of others. At times, my disappointment has deepened into despair, and—perhaps even more troubling—my resolve to do the right thing has sometimes hardened into self-righteousness. After reading several articles that described the pandemic as "The Great Pause"—a chance to reflect on our busy lives, to reassess our priorities, to rebalance our schedules to align with our values, and to renew our commitment to what matters most—I commented cynically to a family member that many people didn't seem to be learning much from this chance for reflection.

A few days later, my family was reading together in Alma 15 and came across Alma's description of church members experiencing "a great check." My son, who served a Mandarin-speaking mission in Paris, France, noted that the French version of this verse rendered the phrase as a "great stop" and the Mandarin version as a "great turning point or change." Like us, the people of Alma had experienced a "great check," but—in contrast to me—they "were checked as to the pride of their hearts," "humble[d] themselves before God," and drew closer to him (Alma 15:17). I realized with sudden clarity that I wasn't learning much from my chance for reflection either—certainly, I wasn't becoming more Christlike in my views of others.

8. For a fuller explanation of the studies demonstrating how our partisan commitments influence our processing of information, see RonNell Andersen Jones and Lisa Grow Sun, *Freedom of the Press in Post-Truthism America*, 98 Wash. U. L. Rev. 419 (2020), https://papers.ssrn.com/sol3/papers.cfm?abstract__id=3588625.

I wish I could say that my sudden clarity produced an equally sudden change of heart, one that completely eliminated my inclination to judge others uncharitably and that helped me chart a clear path for advocating for my convictions with love. However, it did instill in me the desire to do better, to seek once again for that change of heart, to sing anew "the song of redeeming love." Instead of focusing so much on the brokenness of others, I recognized again my own brokenness and how much I need the healing power of the Savior in my life.

I have thought often in the last few months since that day of an experience I had in college when I was studying at BYU's Jerusalem Center. One beautiful fall day, I visited the limestone ruins of the traditional site of the Pool of Bethesda, where Christ healed a man who had been waiting and hoping for that healing for close to forty years. That day, the question that Christ asked that man—"Wilt thou be made whole?"[9]—penetrated my heart. I realized that Christ was asking me, every day, "Wilt thou be made whole?"

Implicit in this question is a promise that, when I am ready, Christ can and will make me whole. As I contemplated Christ's question, wondering what might be holding me back, I reread the story in Alma 22 of Aaron teaching King Lamoni's father. King Lamoni's father first promises to give up all that he possesses and even forsake his kingdom to know God and to experience that great joy, but he quickly realizes what he needs to offer instead: "I will give away all my sins to know thee" (Alma 22:18).

For many years after this experience, I thought of giving away our sins as the price that we needed to pay to come to know God. More recently, however, my perspective has deepened. To be healed, we must lay our sins on the altar, including our pride and our attachment to our own stories about who we are, who we should be, and what our lives should be like. We must offer a broken heart and a contrite spirit, but giving away our sins isn't merely the price we pay to know God;

9. John 5:6.

instead, that process is *how* we come to know him. We can't really give away all of our sins and weaknesses on our own; it takes his help, his power, his grace to heal and transform us. We come to know Christ as we test out his promises, and we experience his power to redeem us by changing our hearts.

While I have not always been good at humbling myself and turning my life over to God, I have found that, when I do, those promises are realized in my life. I have found the words of President Ezra Taft Benson to be true: "Men and women who turn their lives over to God will discover that he can make a lot more out of their lives than they can. He will deepen their joys, expand their vision, quicken their minds, strengthen their muscles, lift their spirits, multiply their blessings, increase their opportunities, comfort their souls, raise up friends, and pour out peace."[10]

It is a good thing that God is patient with us because this is a lesson I have had to learn over and over again and that I am still learning today. God isn't with us just in our triumphs, our moments of kindness, and our new beginnings. He is with us in our failings, our moments of weakness, and our well-traveled dead ends, inviting us to make our identity as children of heavenly parents our central identity and to access his power to become our best selves. He stands ready to redeem our brokenness, to heal our hearts, and to make our weakness strength.

And it is because, not in spite of, that healing power that God expects us to do his work here—to help address and heal brokenness wherever we find it, emulating his effort to bind up the brokenhearted, lift up the hands that hang down, and strengthen the feeble knees. While there is much injustice and suffering in this fallen world that only Christ can heal and redeem, we are nonetheless called to do what we can, called to be our brothers' and sisters' keeper and to be our Savior's hands.

10. Ezra Taft Benson, "Jesus Christ—Gifts and Expectations," BYU devotional, December 10, 1974, https://speeches.byu.edu/talks/ezra-taft-benson/jesus-christ-gifts-expectations/.

One day, this pandemic will end, but many other long-term challenges will remain, including war, climate change, disease, poverty, racism, and other forms of oppression. Indeed, the pandemic's disproportionate effects on vulnerable individuals and communities have underscored how powerful and entrenched structural racism, poverty, and inequity are in America and societies around the world. All of these challenges will require sustained, long-term collective and individual action to solve.

How can we muster that kind of sustained commitment and energy for addressing these critical problems? Law certainly has a role to play in all of these arenas: it can check our worst impulses and express our highest aspirations, encouraging and—yes—sometimes even compelling us to act with greater regard for others. Law can also be an important part of our collective conversation about societal norms and values: it is shaped by those norms and values, and, over time, shapes them as well. Generally, law reflects our commitments and values more than it generates and drives them.

I certainly don't have all the answers, but I am convinced that relieving human suffering and building Zion, where there will be no poor among us and where all will be fully welcome and embraced, will require us to make our identity as children of heavenly parents—as members of the family of God—our primary identity. That identity grounds us in who we are and who we can be, both individually and collectively. It reminds me that, while this work is deeply personal, the work of building Zion is also a family affair, so we can strengthen and lift each other when we get discouraged and falter. Most fundamentally, it reminds me that we will have to cast aside our fear, our pride, our prejudices, the false traditions of our fathers, and everything else that separates us from God and from our brothers and sisters.

The Great Check has given us time to reflect—to reexamine ourselves and the state of our hearts—but thankfully, it needn't take a catastrophe to spur this introspection; we are invited to engage in this reflection each week as we renew our covenants. That continuous reflection and recommitment is critical because finding the sustained motivation to do the work ahead will require us to give our hearts over to God not just once but every day so that he can teach us anew how to sing the song of redeeming love.

Our Inescapable Connectedness

MICHALYN STEELE

> In a real sense all life is inter-related. All men are caught in an inescapable network of mutuality, tied in a single garment of destiny. Whatever affects one directly, affects all indirectly. I can never be what I ought to be until you are what you ought to be, and you can never be what you ought to be until I am what I ought to be. This is the inter-related structure of reality.[1]
>
> —Rev. Martin Luther King Jr.

Michalyn Steele is a member of the Seneca Nation of Indians[2] from the Cattaraugus Reservation in western New York state. She earned a BA and an MA in humanities from BYU before working in Washington, DC, for several years at the United States Senate. She graduated from the Georgetown University Law Center in 2001 and began at a small DC firm specializing in representing Indian tribes. In 2004, she joined the United States Department of Justice as a trial attorney in the Civil Rights Division,

1. Martin Luther King Jr., "The Man Who Was a Fool," in *Strength to Love* (Boston: Beacon Press, 1981), 68.

2. In this essay, the use of *American Indian* to refer to Indigenous people reflects the terminology used in the federal statutes and legal cases of the United States. It is also sometimes used colloquially among Indigenous people, though *Indigenous* or *First Nations* is a preferred collective term when not using the specific tribal nation of affiliation.

specializing in enforcement of the Fair Housing Act. In 2009, Michalyn began work as a counselor to the assistant secretary of the Interior for Indian Affairs, Larry Echo Hawk. In 2012, Michalyn began her academic career at BYU Law School where she is currently the Marion G. Romney Professor of Law and the associate dean for faculty and curriculum. Michalyn loves serving and teaching Relief Society in her branch, which meets at the Utah County Jail.

ONE METRIC for measuring the health of our democratic ideals and aspirations is the story of Indigenous peoples in America and their struggle to retain their cultures and identities in the face of unrelenting pressure to assimilate. Felix Cohen, one of the founders of the field of federal Indian law, warned in 1953 that "the Indian plays much the same role in our American society that the Jews played in Germany. Like the miner's canary, the Indian marks the shift from fresh air to poison gas in our political atmosphere; and our treatment of Indians, even more than our treatment of other minorities, reflects the rise and fall in our democratic faith."[3] Because I believe in the aspirations of America's founding principles, I am interested in the story of America as told through the voices of those for whom its lofty promises have fallen short: the dispossessed and the vulnerable. In their stories, we see the remarkable resilience of culture and identity and the yearning for freedom. We see the determination of the human spirit's dignity inherent in each of our heavenly parents' children whether or not law or society respect that enduring dignity.

My great-grandmother Florence Huff lost her first husband and their two children to the flu pandemic of the early twentieth century.

3. Felix Cohen, *The Erosion of Indian Rights, 1950–1953: A Case Study in Bureaucracy*, 62 Yale L.J. 348, 390 (1953); "Getting a Bead on Felix Cohen's 'Miner's Canary,'" https://indiancountrytoday.com/archive/getting-a-bead-on-felix-cohen-s-miners-canary-NFPFJijcfk6Qt2coKh8eMw.

During the same era, my great-grandfather William Parker lost his wife and several children when the wagon he was driving was hit by a train. He survived, as did one of his sons. My grandmother told me the story of how this son, her half-brother, was rescued when he was thrown into the air by the impact of the crash and the conductor of the train caught him by the leg.

The shattered lives of Florence Huff and William Parker merged following these tragedies; out of life's darkness, they forged hope and faith into light. They were members of the Seneca Nation of Indians living on the tribe's reservations in western New York. Both lives marred by incalculable pain, they met and married, building new life from the broken pieces. In the trials they overcame and the lives they built, I see a courageous pattern that has played out in the lives of many people who have chosen to move forward in hope even as personal and political circumstances have combined to make the path of hope difficult.

Florence and William had six children together. Their lives tell the story and map the challenges of the nation's history, especially among America's Indigenous peoples during the decades they lived. One son, Kenny, joined the Marines at age sixteen and was killed at Iwo Jima.[4] Their daughter, my grandmother, Norma Parker Seneca, was sent as a young girl to a Quaker boarding school. Like all the Native students, she was prohibited from speaking the Seneca language and punished when, forgetting herself, she exclaimed in excitement in her native tongue. She was trained in the rudiments of domestic service and Quaker piety. Like so many of the approximately 100,000 Native

4. American Indians and Alaska Natives have traditionally served in the military at disproportionate rates to their population. For example, in World War II, from a population of around 350,000, some 44,000 American Indians and Alaska Natives served. See the Department of Veterans Affairs, "American Indian and Alaska Native Servicemembers and Veterans," September 2012, https://www.va.gov/TRIBALGOVERNMENT/docs/AIAN__Report__FINAL__v2__7.pdf. In "A 'Warrior Tradition': Why Native Americans continue fighting for the same government that tried to wipe them out," *Military Times*, November 19, 2019, https://www.militarytimes.com/off-duty/military-culture/2019/11/15/a-warrior-tradition-why-native-americans-continue-fighting-for-the-same-government-that-tried-to-wipe-them-out/; J. D. Simkins concludes, "To this day, American Indians serve in the armed forces at a higher rate than any other demographic."

children of the era separated from their families, they were institutionalized and schooled by those who believed that to "save the man," you had to "kill the Indian."[5]

The goal of this federal policy—the forcible assimilation of American Indian people into the dominant society's culture, religion, and language—has consequences that continue to reverberate through Native families and communities today. Though as Americans we may never fully count the cost or even own the loss, I am convinced that those elements of Indigenous culture lost to this destructive process leave humanity bereft of some priceless cultural knowledge, to say nothing of the incalculable waste of individual potential. Despite those wounds to tribal identity and culture, much of the precious wisdom of Indigenous traditions remains; many truths preserved by them endure.

As a Seneca woman, a disciple of Jesus Christ, a descendant of Mormon pioneers, an attorney, and an academic, many identities meet in me. I am at the confluence of many stories and the heir of many traditions. I have navigated the paradoxes and complexities of identity and history in my personal and professional life. But we are all many things at one time. Whatever our complex histories and the diversity of many societies and cultures across the world, as children of heavenly parents, we aspire to harmonize those diverse parts into a cohesive whole that draws strength from its constituencies so that we may each flourish together.

My work as an academic studying federal Indian law and as an attorney working in civil rights has required that I scrutinize the ideals and aspirations of sacred truth, secular laws, and societal norms in ways that often reveal how we have fallen short of those aspirations and ideals as nations, societies, and individuals. Our struggle to live out the ideals of equality and dignity, both as communities and as

5. Captain Richard Henry Pratt founded the Carlisle Industrial Indian School in Carlisle, Pennsylvania, in 1879 with this philosophy, which was adopted at other schools around the United States. See *Official Report of the Nineteenth Annual Conference of Charities and Correction* (1892), 46–59. Reprinted in Richard H. Pratt, "The Advantages of Mingling Indians with Whites," *Americanizing the American Indians: Writings by the "Friends of the Indian" 1880–1900* (Cambridge, MA: Harvard University Press, 1973), 260–71.

individuals, yields complex and nuanced stories revealing moments of both the triumph of human dignity and the despair of human cruelty. My personal and professional endeavors are rooted in a tremendous faith in the merit of striving for the ideals of democratic equality, which values the differences, contributions, and—most of all—the dignity of all God's children.

Dr. Martin Luther King Jr. described the fundamental interconnectedness of the human family as an "inescapable network of mutuality" and said that we are all "tied in a single garment of destiny." In leading the movement for a society that drew upon the gifts of all in a more robust equality, Dr. King argued that a more just society blesses all and that an unjust society limits all.[6] As we are better able to perceive and realize our interconnectedness, we may heal the wounds of division and escape the bondage of racism to build a more welcoming future.

In establishing the reign of the judges, King Mosiah envisioned a system of laws that would foster equality among the people of Nephi and would rid the society of inequality. He expressed his "desire that this *inequality* should be no more in this land ... but I desire that this land be a land of liberty, and every man may enjoy his rights and privileges alike" (Mosiah 29:32, emphasis added). Like Dr. King and like King Mosiah, I believe that we must strive for laws and a culture that foster opportunity for each individual to fulfill both earthly and divine potential. I also believe that we can do better than we have done to live out our ideals.

I have learned a great deal in my study and practice of civil rights law and federal Indian law from those who have been excluded from society's full acceptance and who have, through their sacrifices and strivings, helped the United States to do and be better: to repent and to "make real the promise of democracy" for all, as Dr. King envisioned.[7]

6. Our experiences with the COVID-19 pandemic and the inequalities it has exacerbated certainly underscore the truth of this idea.

7. Martin Luther King Jr., "I Have a Dream," in *A Testament of Hope: The Essential Writings and Speeches of Martin Luther King, Jr.*, ed. James Melvin Washington (New York: HarperSanFrancisco, 1986), 218.

For example, John Lewis and Amelia Boynton Robinson marched with others in Selma, Alabama, in 1965. As they crossed the Edmund Pettus Bridge, they were beaten and bloodied, but their courageous footsteps marked the path for passage of the Voting Rights Act of 1965, making access to the ballot—the right that is protective of all other rights—more equitable for all. So too the Freedom Riders, joined by a young White woman, Joan Trumpauer Mulholland, who more than self her country loved as she faced the vitriol of mobs. Their work has invested the constitutional ideals of equal protection and due process with more fulsome protection and meaning for all of us.[8]

As a student of federal Indian law, I have been interested in the question of how tribes have survived the legal, political, and cultural onslaughts of settler colonialism. Even as it continues to unfold, I am interested in what that story has to teach those of us who will listen about democracy and diversity, resilience and survival. I believe the preservation and survival of the Native American people is a story replete with failures of law and policy, even when well-intentioned, that have led to untold suffering. But it is also a story of miraculous resilience and of a country working to redress its failures through more just laws and policies as it grows more tolerant of diversity and indigeneity.

How has it been that, with the full legal, cultural, and political might of the United States intent on erasing indigeneity and on laying claim to the lands and resources of tribal homelands, the tribes have survived as unique cultural and political entities? What can we learn about cohesion and resilience from that story? And what does the story of America's evolution toward a more inclusive society, more tolerant of tribal self-determination, tell us about how to live out America's ideals and aspirations more meaningfully?

In a real sense, my faith helps me to see the hand of the Lord in

8. For more context about the struggles for the Voting Rights Act, see John Lewis and Michael D'Orso, *Walking with the Wind: A Memoir of the Movement* (New York: Simon & Schuster, 2015); Bryan Stevenson, *Just Mercy: A Story of Justice and Redemption* (New York: Random House, 2014); and Isabel Wilkerson, *Caste: The Origins of Our Discontents* (New York: Random House, 2020).

these stories, protecting and preserving the Native American people and culture from eradication. I do not claim to know who the descendants of Lehi are in modern times, but I find meaning for American Indians in the story of Joseph who was sold into Egypt. After Joseph was sold into slavery, betrayed by his brothers, he became an instrument in the hands of the Lord to help save the house of Israel by advising Pharaoh to preserve grain against the coming famine. When the house of Israel—Joseph's family—were starving from the famine, they came to Egypt seeking relief. Joseph forgave his brothers and provided the means for them to survive the famine.

Lehi and his family, descendants of this same Joseph, preserved the record that would become the Book of Mormon: Another Testament of Jesus Christ. In a time of spiritual famine, the Book of Mormon is spiritual manna, inviting all to come and feast on the plain and precious truths of the gospel of Jesus Christ and to rejoice in the testimony of his Resurrection. The introduction to the Book of Mormon tells us that the descendants of Lehi "are among the ancestors of the American Indians." Indeed, the Lord promised Lehi that some remnant of his posterity would be preserved to inherit the land of promise. It may be that we see the Lord's promise fulfilled as the Indigenous peoples of the world not only endure but prosper as peoples with much to contribute—wisdom and truth—stored up against the significant challenges of our day, just as Joseph stored up grain anciently to preserve the house of Israel.

The seven generations principle from Seneca tradition is an idea similar to values found among many tribes and has potential to make a profound contribution. The principle stems from the Iroquois Constitution, organizing the six tribes of the Haudenosaunee (or Iroquois) Confederacy in a political and cultural alliance. Delegates to the deliberative governing councils were required to consider the consequences of their decisions on the next seven generations. They were to ensure the enduring wisdom of their choices for those who would bear the consequences or reap the benefits in the long term, as opposed to the temptation for leaders to make expedient or self-interested choices. Self-interest and short-term thinking diminish the ability of leaders to build enduring institutions or to act on lasting principles of altruism and public service. The seven generations principle, if adopted more broadly, would temper the partisan battles of the moment that detract from the cohesion of our polity.

In seeking to take the long view of the American story, and indeed, of the story of human dignity in multicultural societies, my professional and personal endeavors overlap in profound ways. The ideals of human dignity, of liberty, and of equality are worth working for in law, in our communities, and in our interpersonal relations. Dr. King's profound letter from the Birmingham Jail, where he was held in connection with his peaceful demonstrations for equality and dignity, notes that "human progress never rolls in on wheels of inevitability."[9] Instead, human progress happens due to what he called "the tireless efforts" of those "willing to be co-workers with God."[10] It is my conviction that we can be those "co-workers with God" in our professional and personal lives as we strengthen the bonds of love and kinship among his children, proclaim peace, and advocate for the vulnerable among us.

When missionaries from The Church of Jesus Christ of Latter-day Saints came to the Cattaraugus Reservation of the Seneca Indians in the 1940s, one of the people who embraced their message was Florence Huff Parker. She told me that in reading the Book of Mormon, she found the peace and healing she had been seeking since her first family's passing in the early twentieth century's pandemic. She was baptized as a member of the Church and hoped that her husband, who she called Willie, would embrace the faith with her. She prepared Sunday clothes for him each week in the hope that he would come with her to church meetings. A decade later, after the invitation of one particular missionary, he at last donned the Sunday clothes and came to church. He was baptized in January 1958 and ordained a deacon at nearly eighty years old. He died the following January, leaving Florence

9. Martin Luther King Jr., "Letter from Birmingham City Jail," in *A Testament of Hope*, 296.
10. Ibid.

widowed again for almost forty years. She died on her 105th birthday in 1997, her life almost touching three centuries. I was blessed to know her well. I often found her reading her large print Book of Mormon with a magnifying glass in her room. As her eyes dimmed, her faith continued to burn bright.

Florence and William's faith and resilience have been a blessing to all who have followed. Despite the significant heartbreak in their lives, they chose faith, hope, and optimism. They pressed forward. From them, as well as from my studies of the excluded and the vulnerable, I am able to see the arc of the moral universe bending toward justice because of the significant efforts of those who choose to make the moral universe more just. I see the urgency of doing my part personally and professionally, seeking the privilege of being a coworker with God by working toward more just laws and a more just society for the next seven generations, and advocating for and tending to the poor, the vulnerable, and the excluded as the Savior modeled.

PART FIVE

A knowledge also of countries and of kingdoms— that ye may be prepared in all things when I shall send you again to magnify the calling whereunto I have called you

(Doctrine and Covenants 88:79–80)

Journeys away from home take us out of our comfort zones, mother tongues, and spheres of influence, showing us truths of being we never could have imagined.

Recognizing the dignity of difference in others helps us develop the divine discernment of our Mother and Father in Heaven.

The Pillars of My Faith

Tautua, Alofa, Fa'aaloalo

O le faleo'o ma ona pou
(The house is held up by its pillars)

TANYA WENDT SAMU

Tanya Wendt Samu was born and raised in Apia, Samoa. She is Samoan through her father and Māori (Ngāti Kahungunu) through her mother. Before her career in academia, Tanya's experiences included teaching and leadership in geography and social studies within secondary schools in Samoa and New Zealand and writing social studies and geography textbooks. She is a senior lecturer in the Education and Social Work Department at the University of Auckland, Aotearoa New Zealand. Tanya is also a consultant in national curriculum and teacher development. Her university has supported her involvement with education projects in places such as Samoa, Nauru, Kyrgyzstan, and Myanmar. Tanya is married to Nathan, and they have three children and three grandchildren.

❖

I AM A SAMOAN WOMAN with Māori heritage. I am in my mid-fifties. I migrated to New Zealand almost thirty years ago from Samoa. Before I turned twenty-one, I had experiences living in Hawaii and New York (with my family) and studying in the United Kingdom and New Zealand. I currently hold a senior academic position in a large university in Aotearoa New Zealand. My work sometimes takes me overseas for conferences (United States, Australia, Fiji, Tonga, Samoa) and to work on projects (for example, in Samoa, Kyrgyzstan, Nauru, Myanmar). I teach, research, and consult. My field is education, within which I have two separate specialties: curriculum development and Pacific/Pasifika education.

When I was invited to contribute to this special publication, I was asked, "How does your scholarship or professional learning influence your faith?" A good question. A big question, actually. However, I decided that, for me, it is the other way around—the question is more about how my faith in God and in his Son, Jesus Christ, has informed my efforts with education and learning, both personally and professionally. I believe certain pillars in terms of my faith hold up my work in education. These same pillars hold up my efforts in other significant spheres of my life—spheres in which I am wife, mother, grandmother, daughter, aunt, older sister, cousin, niece, trustee on the school board, and Sunday School teacher.

The pillars of my faith are like *poutu*, or the central posts, that hold up a traditional Samoan *fale tele*, or meeting house (see Figure 1). The *fale tele* is carefully constructed and centrally located in service to a particular clan and community. In constructing the traditional *fale tele*, the *poutu* are set in place first. The rest of the building, particularly the vaulted circular roof, is built on and around the *poutu*. Shorter posts are installed at the rim or outer edge of the building, but the *poutu* provide the structural integrity. For me, the core values of *tautua*, *alofa*, and *fa'aaloalo*[1] are the

1. *Tautua* refers to the Samoan concept of service. *Alofa* refers to love. *Fa'aaloalo* refers to respect.

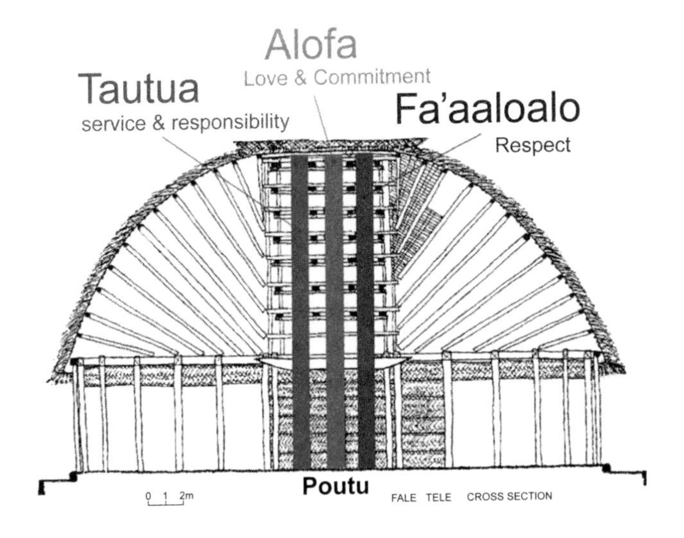

Figure 1. Pillars: *Tautua*, *Alofa*, and *Fa'aaloalo*[2]

poutu that give my work (both personal and professional) its purpose, holding it together and holding it up.

These values are so integral to who and what I am today as a Samoan woman of faith, daughter of God, sister-disciple of Christ, and member of his restored Church. I know and understand these values as cultural values, which I observed in action and experienced via my family growing up. Please note this poem, "My Own Shade of Brown," by Tai Mulitalo (2001), written when she was a young fine arts student.

God-bronzed
gene-baked
trap me not in cliché
but set me free my friend
judge me not and let me be
my own shade of brown

2. V. Podmore, T.W. Samu, and Aoga Faasamoa, *O le tama ma lana a'oga, O le tama ma lona fa'asinomaga: Nurturing positive identity in children*, final research report for the Ministry of Education (Wellington, NZ: 2006).

Samoan women? We are not identical; we are not all the same. Nevertheless, we do have commonalities in *how* we live by faith within the cultures we inhabit.

The *whakapapa* of my faith[3]

Like Nephi, I was born of goodly parents. They, in turn, were raised in families led by God-respecting parents and grandparents. My mother, a third-generation member of The Church of Jesus Christ of Latter-day Saints, grew up in a small town in Aotearoa New Zealand that did not even have a branch. Their family was visited on occasion by the missionaries or district Church leaders. When they came, my grandmother put out the very best in terms of food, crockery, and table linen. To her, these visits were sacred opportunities for gospel teaching and connection. When the Church secondary school, the Church College of New Zealand (CCNZ), was built, she sent her youngest children (my mother and her younger brother) away to attend as boarders. This meant full immersion in a gospel-living community of predominantly Māori students with predominantly American teachers, alongside the recently constructed temple.

After attending CCNZ, my mother trained as a primary school teacher. She met my father, a scholarship student from Samoa who was studying agricultural science.[4] Much to her mother's dismay, they married. He was from neither of the two main ethnic groups in New Zealand: neither European nor Māori. My father was not even a member of the Church. He had politely taken missionary discussions when he lived in New Zealand (as a courtesy to my grandmother) but was not interested. The ultimate disappointment for her was that they left to live in faraway Samoa after their wedding.

However, it was my father's grandmother and family matriarch, Mamā, a wise and wizened woman in her nineties, who persuaded him

3. *Whakapapa* is Māori for "genealogy."

4. Samoa is now the official name for what used to be called Western Samoa.

otherwise in terms of the Church. At the time, our little family lived in a small house in the family compound behind the police station in Apia. The main family home was a large white two-story homestead where my father's father, wife, children, and other relations lived. A large oval *fale* was situated beside the homestead. This was Mamā's house. It was centered on the property in such a way that she could sit or lie and watch the comings and goings of everyone that lived in that compound. And nothing escaped her notice.

She soon noticed what her oldest grandson and his wife did on Sundays. She observed how my mother would get herself and me (baby) ready, call a taxi and go to church (that "Mormon" one). She watched my father get himself ready and go in a different direction—to play golf with his friends. She called him over and told him in no uncertain terms that his duty as a husband and father was to be with his family at church on Sundays. Not golf. If he wasn't going to attend their family church, he may as well attend that other church.

I credit my father's grandmother, Mele Wendt Tuaopepe, for my father's conversion to the gospel. I credit my grandmother, Kuini Wikitoria Te Hinewai Johnson (*nee Matenga*), for the gospel in my mother's life. I credit my great-grandfather (Kuini's father), Kaki Tui Matenga, for joining the Church. Their lives exemplify the nature of their discipleship of *Iehu Karaiti* / *Iesu Keriso* / Jesus Christ, and his Father, the one true *Atua* / God.

Learning (and living) *tautua*

I was almost five when we (my parents, myself, and my younger brother) went to live in Hawaii while Dad studied at the University of Hawai'i–Mānoa. We lived in three different places in Honolulu, and each time, Mum made sure we found the nearest ward and attended regularly. After Dad graduated, we returned to Samoa but not for long. We travelled back to the United States but this time to the east side so Dad could study for his doctorate at Cornell University in upstate New York. It was the early 1970s—the daddies going to school and the mummies raising children in married student housing, creatively trying to make ends meet through bake sales and under-the-table house cleaning.

Again, Mum made sure we went to church, this time a stunningly mono-cultural congregation. We were the only family of color. We went on several Church history tourism road trips—the Sacred Grove, Joseph Smith's family home—oh, and the Hill Cumorah Pageant. I remember how a young missionary who looked like us came bounding up to my mother and me in excitement, thinking he had found relations. We got excited too, thinking the same thing. Turns out, he was Native American.

My parents were explicit about the purpose of these moves away from home. They taught us that the purpose of higher education was to serve our people. When I was older, I understood their decisions to be the enactment of *tautua*, an underlying principle of the *fa'a Samoa* or Samoan way. *Tautua* is not simply the rendering of material goods and time in service to people in need. *Tautua*, given humbly, over time leads to respect, social prestige, and even greater responsibility and status, as expressed in the Samoan proverb *O le auala I le malo o le tautua*, or "The road to power/authority is service." Due to its relational nature, *tautua* involves certain incremental rights and obligations. This means that recipients of *tautua* have a duty to give back in terms of support and assistance when the opportunity arises.

There were two other important influences on my understanding of *tautua*, particularly in relation to schooling and education. My grandfather, who cut short his own education to support his parents and siblings, delivered fiery sermons to his grandchildren about succeeding in education for the "honor and glory" of our family. I developed my own personal testimony when I was quite young, and so I came to believe that serving my family and country naturally melded together and became a way to express my faith—after all, "faith, if it hath not works, is dead" (James 2:17).

Experiencing *alofa* as the love of and for God

Other formative experiences enabled the gospel to take root deep in my heart. I was eleven when I had an accident that resulted in my being in intensive care at Moto'otua Hospital in Apia. It was not a dramatic accident. I was playing on top of a bunk bed in the middle of the day (goofing off, according to Mum) and fell off backwards onto a concrete floor, my elbow taking the full weight. It shattered. I never told anyone, but on the way down (the fall felt like it was in slow motion), I received the impression to "just fall"; otherwise, I would break my neck. So I listened. I fell, like a rag doll, and resisted the instinct to twist and turn on the way down.

Nights in the hospital were hard though. I was a preteen in an acute ward of adults, in physical pain but reluctant to ask for painkillers because it meant a painful (old-school) injection in the backside. Unable to sleep, I found companionship with the geckos on the ceiling and simple prayer-conversations with my Heavenly Father. A year later, I was having corrective surgery for my elbow at Shriners Children's Hospital in Honolulu. The Honolulu Tabernacle was right next door.[5] I knew that chapel and its gardens well—it was the first ward we attended when we lived in Hawaii, and Dad worked there as a part-time gardener to afford Christmas presents for us.

My mother had to return to Samoa after my operation due to airline regulations pertaining to her pregnancy. One night, in the midst of post-op pain, I literally had a come-to-Jesus moment. I silently cried out into the darkness of homesickness and loneliness for him, my Older Brother. I heard a voice confirm that he was—and then experienced a blanket of peace and quiet comfort. After I said my prayers each night, I looked outside the window to watch the light at the top of the Tabernacle's tower until I drifted into sleep. It personified my Older Brother, watching over me.

I was fourteen, and in our English-speaking ward in Apia, there

5. The Honolulu Hawaii Stake Tabernacle is a Latter-day Saint meeting space that was completed in 1941.

were growing numbers of youth like myself and my brother who did not attend the Church secondary school, Church College of Western Samoa (CCWS). We attended either government schools or other mission schools, so early-morning seminary was established. I believed in President Spencer W. Kimball's promise to the youth, that if we were obedient and made the commitment to study the scriptures, we would be blessed in our efforts to study and do well at school. I also believed completely in the doctrine that we are responsible for gaining as much knowledge in this life as possible.[6] I was earnest about school and doing well. I was earnest about being an obedient daughter of God.

My father was dead set against seminary; he could not see the point. Sunday School and the youth program, he felt, were enough. By this time, I had several younger siblings. There was a newborn, two toddlers, and an introverted eight-year-old. My brother and I, as the oldest, were expected to be hands-on with their care. Our being at seminary first thing in the morning meant leaving Dad and Mum to deal with those little kids without our help. But I insisted. He relented, albeit begrudgingly. Then something inspired happened. Dad was called as the seminary teacher. The course of study was the Old Testament. It did not take long before Dad remembered that, as a child, his own parents sent him to pastors' school (after-school Bible study), and he knew the Bible like the back of his hand because of it. He was our seminary teacher long enough to be converted to its value before being released due to the overseas business trips his work as a university professor required.

I needed seminary. I was hungry for that learning. I was also not a particularly quick learner when it came to schoolwork. I struggled. I learned that I had to work hard and to do it prayerfully in order to do well with both academic and religious studies. At that point in my life, I learned that if I invested time studying the gospel with my head and heart, he, God, would open my mind, and I would see the beauty of his gospel. I learned that if I did this in tandem with schoolwork, even

6. Doctrine & Covenants 88.

if it seemed like sheer drudgery, initial glimmers of insight would be followed by an avalanche of light and knowledge.

I credit my efforts with seminary and my prayerful, methodical approach to secular study for the academic achievements that followed. When I was sixteen, I received the second-highest exam results in the whole country. I had the highest marks in two subjects. When I was seventeen, I was selected by the government scholarship committee for a prestigious scholarship to an international senior secondary school in Wales. Before I left home, I received my patriarchal blessing. I learned God had blessed my efforts in education and would continue to do so in accordance with the righteous desires of my heart. Education, mine and that of others, was to be a part of my mission in life.

Fa'aaloalo and relationships

The third pillar of my faith is respect. Respect for God, for my elders, for the past, present, and future. In the *fa'a Samoa* as I know it, relational space between myself and another person regardless of their status is not empty, impersonal space. To be in relationship brings inherent responsibilities to actively respect and nurture. This is known as *teu le Vā*. I cannot think of any traditional practice in the *fa'a Samoa* that does not require gifting of time, food, valued material goods, and an associated presentation protocol accompanied by oratory. These are tangible expressions and actions for that relational space. I learned via my own extended family that significant events like weddings, funerals, and title bestowals were opportunities to show respect, meet obligations, nurture relationships (especially kinship ones), and support one another.

Here is an example. At the age of twenty-two, I was a university student in New Zealand and planning to get married in the Apia Samoa Temple. My father's sisters in the United States asked my mother if they could make the wedding dress. I mailed them my measurements and a photo of the plain, simple gown I liked. Just a few days before the wedding, my aunts arrived with a long-sleeved, Cinderella, satin dress, resplendent with drop pearls, crystals, and sequins, which fit perfectly. My aunts loved me, but the dress was not about me. Rather, it was a tangible measure of the depth of their respect for my parents, particularly my father (their elder brother and *matai*, the high chief of the extended family), and what my parents had done for them and the *aiga*, the extended family, over the years. They honored obligations and provided support by ensuring that the bride was bedazzling—in this instance, literally.

For me, *fa'aaloalo* involves a duty of care, respect, obligation, responsibility. These happen to be values and beliefs that inform my understanding of what is required of me as a daughter of God and a sister-disciple of Christ. *Fa'aaloalo* influences my approach to relationships, including those within non-Samoan contexts and settings. I recognize that I think, feel, and act with a more Samoan mindset.

My faith and work today

I was almost twenty-five, and my first real job was as a secondary school teacher in Samoa. My colleagues and I shared many of the same spiritual and cultural beliefs and values, which informed the nature of our professional, work-based interactions. But when I migrated with my husband and young children to live in New Zealand, I found myself working in schools and then within a university where the majority of colleagues and students did not identify as Samoan, or Pacific, or Māori. So how did my faith influence my work in far more secular, culturally different contexts and settings? Especially now, within the university where I currently work?

I am part of a faculty of education and social work in which many of us were teachers and social workers before moving into the academy to be teacher and social work educators, academics, and scholars. When I began to work here, I was blessed to be part of a group of predominantly Pacific-heritage women who, in addition to their roles as academic staff, held leadership roles within their extended families and church communities; were the main breadwinners in their homes; and held roles such as wives, mothers, aunts, and grandmothers.

We see our positions as callings to serve our Pacific communities. We are contributing to the development of teachers, social workers, and counselors who will work with Pacific peoples. As Pacific women scholars, researchers, and academic practitioners, we purposefully turn to and draw on our respective cultural heritages and spiritual pillars to navigate the inherent tensions and challenges of working within an institution that can at times be very mono-cultural and biased.

My place to stand

My pillars are service, love, and respect (through a Samoan lens). I am confident that my metaphoric *fale tele* (still a work in progress) represents, first, the purpose of my scholarship and learning and, second, a meeting house within which the capacity and capability of Pacific peoples is enhanced and developed. But please note—there's a name for the site on which a *fale tele* is built. It's the *tulaga fale*, or the "place to stand." My standing place is composed of my family (past, present, and future) and my Heavenly Father and my Savior Jesus Christ (and what they have meant to me at different stages of my life). I credit The Church of Jesus Christ of Latter-day Saints for the gospel of *Iesu Karaiti* that has shaped my family and enabled me to know the one true *Atua* for myself and for the simple, straightforward truths that will anchor me and mine in these challenging times.

Embracing New Identities

A Conversion Journey from Beijing

CONNIE XIAOHUA ZHANG

Connie Xiaohua Zhang was born and raised in Beijing, China. She earned her BA in economics from Beijing University and MBA from Harvard Business School. She is the founder and CEO of Riley River Consultants, established in 2009. She helps North American green technology companies and medical device companies develop business in China. She is a renowned speaker and instructor who teaches about networking and marriage relationships across multiple key Chinese social media platforms. She is the author of Network Up (2019) *and* How to Raise Socially Intelligent Children (2020). *She teaches online courses and gives talks to broad audiences in China about networking. She also holds a real estate license from the state of Texas, where she manages a broad portfolio of real estate. She enjoys international travel with her husband and two sons and oil painting in her leisure time.*

I GREW UP IN BEIJING, CHINA, in a typical atheist family. My father was a leader working in the Beijing government, and my mother was a sixth-grade Chinese teacher. My parents taught me good values, such as integrity in our actions, a strong work ethic, respect for others, and equality among all people regardless of their profession or background. I went to Beijing University for my undergraduate degree in economics and then worked in multinational companies.

I met my husband at work. He grew up in Shanghai and, in 1996, was working for GE Aircraft Engines in Cincinnati. Through a phone interview, he hired me, a college senior, as his intern. We worked together for six months over the phone and the internet. After graduation, I joined LG Electronics in Beijing, and he went on to a different rotation in his company. We lost contact for over a year, and then he found me again through another GE college's connection. A few months after we got reconnected, we met in Beijing for the first time in person. It was Christmas, and we quickly fell in love with each other. Soon enough, I found out that he was a member of the Church (though he was not very active then). It was the first time I had heard of the Church. After seventeen months of a long-distance relationship, we decided to get married. To be together as a married couple, I needed to move to the US to start a new life. Obtaining a graduate degree became a natural choice for me to build a solid foundation to obtain future employment in the US. I applied to the MBA program at Harvard Business School and got in.

During my second year, I met Professor Clayton Christensen. He was very vocal about his beliefs in class and was very involved with the students. He and his wife, Christine, hosted a fireside for all Church members at the business school one Sunday, and my husband and I went as well. After listening to his and his wife's talks, I walked up to Professor Christensen and asked if I could hear more about his beliefs. He punched his fist into his palm and said, "You made my day." He invited my husband and me to learn the gospel at his house every week. It was at his house where I learned to pray and where I felt the Spirit. It always felt holy and special in his house; then when we drove away and went on with our day-to-day life, I would struggle to feel the Spirit. I could not help but wonder if God existed or not. After eight months of study and thirteen missionary elders, I was finally baptized on the day after my graduation commencement. The way I see it is this: right after graduating from a top business school, I entered a school of faith as a new student.

After graduating from Harvard, I stayed in America, except for a period of three years living in Hong Kong. During the past eighteen years, I have worked in both large and small companies and established my own consulting business.

In my life, my faith has played an extremely important function. After a true conversion to the Lord, all the actions I took and all the decisions I made were influenced by my faith, one way or another. For example, my primary work was in the area of sales. In the business world, sales are always related to trading and transactions. Because of this relationship to profit, it's very likely that conflicts of interest will arise. But, as I see it, the significance of whether or not I sell a particular project is not as important as whether, in our interactions, the customer and I have established a positive, constructive relationship. China has a saying: "Even when buying and selling are not successful, righteousness should still be there." The righteousness referred to is that of Confucian "benevolence and righteousness," but in my mind, this righteousness is the loving-kindness and righteousness of Heavenly Father. It has to do with the truth of the gospel. Before each client meeting, I always say a prayer to Heavenly Father. I ask, "Father, please bless me that I can build a constructive relationship with this person. I would like to be an instrument in thy hand to do thy work for thee. Please have the Holy Spirit be with me so this person can see the light and have interest in knowing the truth and light of the gospel of Jesus Christ."

The person I was before my baptism would respond to a conflict with someone at work or at home in a black-and-white or win-or-lose way, which tended to generate resentment. Now that I have been baptized and possess the doctrines of the gospel, I respond with prayer, asking for Heavenly Father's help to let me understand the other person's position and to deal with our differences in a loving way. Under the influence of the Holy Spirit, I changed into a person who had more wisdom in the eyes of other people. My business unfolded more smoothly, and my family became more harmonious.

In May 2016, my mother became ill and passed away. She had worked as an elementary school teacher. Quite a few of her students, many of whom had reached their fifties, came to pay their respects. I thought, *When I am lying on my deathbed, what will I leave behind in this world? Sales performance? Or accumulated wealth?* I'm afraid that neither of these will remain. I hope what I will leave the world will be a positive and truthful influence on every single person around me. If I can achieve this, I believe that my life has its worth. Since that time, I have eagerly sought to find opportunities and to take actions to help others. This sort of thinking does not only come from my mother's funeral but reflects the influence of my professor, Clayton Christensen.

In searching for the purpose and worth of my life, in November 2016, I started to use my free time after work to write on the microblog site WeChat under the name "Connie USA Channel." Very quickly, a few essays were picked up by some big media sites and were read by hundreds of thousands of people. In July 2017, I started to teach an online course on networking. I hoped to use networking techniques I learned at Harvard Business School and had picked up through working in America to help students in China. In March 2019, I published my first book in China, titled *Network Up*. A year later, tens of thousands of people had read it, and over a million people had listened to my lectures and talks on numerous subjects. Before writing or speaking, I would always kneel down and say a prayer to Heavenly Father.

The words of my prayer were as follows: "Dear Heavenly Father, I'm so grateful for the opportunity thou hast provided for me to speak to or write for these audiences. I'm so grateful for Jesus Christ and for the gospel. I ask thy blessing to have the Holy Spirit be with me, so I can loosen up my tongue to speak the words thou wouldst have me speak. Let the messages I would share with them benefit their lives and also generate sincere interest in their hearts to know the truth and light of the gospel of Jesus Christ."

Living in the US for over twenty years and not speaking much

Chinese has definitely caused my Chinese language capability to deteriorate significantly. When I started my writing journey, my father joked about my writing being like a running account, no focus, just plain stuff. I didn't have confidence in delivering content through writing or speaking. Actually, many, many times, either before writing something or before speaking in front of people, I was not sure what on earth I was going to write or say; I felt inadequate being in that role and felt emptiness in my head. Especially when I faced the camera, knowing that there were 800,000 people actually watching me, my heart raced and almost jumped out of my chest.

Once again, I turned to Heavenly Father and prayed. After praying, the words and the language bubbled up like water from a fountain and gushed out like a running spring. In writing an essay or giving a lecture, I always share with the audience the wisdom I have received from the gospel. In China, missionary preaching is against the constitution, and speaking on religious topics is not encouraged. But I use the more subtle approach of using quotes and explanations to share gospel messages with my readers and listening audience. People perhaps do not know who Jesus Christ and President Nelson are, but they can listen to their words in my messages.

For example, I have taught parents how to have Family Home Evening regularly to build connections with their children in my *Raising Socially Intelligent Children* podcast series. When the Hollywood movie *Coco* was on air in China, I wrote an article with the title "Remember Me," referring to genealogy studies. In the article, I used Elder Gong's family record as an example and quoted Professor Christensen's words from his book *How Will You Measure Your Life?* I also quoted from Matthew 6, "For where your treasure is, there will your heart be also," and David O. McKay's words, "No other success can compensate for failure in the home."[1] I was not trying to preach a message explicitly about Jesus Christ or God, which could cause trouble in China, but

1. David O. McKay, in the Conference Report, April 1935, p. 116, quoting from J.E. McCulloch, *Home: The Savior of Civilization* (Southern co-operative league, 1924), 42; https://www.churchofjesuschrist.org/study/manual/teachings-david-o-mckay/chapter-16?lang=eng.

to share core truths of human life. In this subtle approach of sharing, I believe that the messages themselves can register in people's hearts.

Often enough, when I look back on what I've written or when I listen to my recorded talks, I think, *Is that really me writing or speaking?* I do not dare to believe it because the way I organized my thoughts and the words I chose to deploy were of a caliber that was way beyond my ability.

For example, in my "Remember Me" article, I asked the question, How much do I know about my ancestors? I continued by talking about the visit I paid to the Shanghai Public Library Genealogy Center where I found Elder Gong's genealogy records. Comparing the genealogy efforts done in the US (also mentioning www.familysearch.org in the article) and my regret that my family has no records in China led me to the second question: How do I recognize my ancestors when I pass the veil of death? I went on to talk about how I organized the family history on my mother's side. I wrote about the history of my grandmother and grandfather with the hope that we can pass on their legacies to our descendants. I also mentioned how I am going to memorialize my mother by writing about her and assemble a memoir for her by gathering stories from relatives and her colleagues and students.

In the last part of the article, I posed another question: What can we leave for our descendants? How will we be remembered as a good father, mother, spouse, friend, mentor, etc. versus being remembered by the worldly successes people try to pursue? I invited readers to ponder on President McKay's quote regarding worldly and family success and said, "Worldly wealth will disappear. The most popular movie or song today will be irrelevant next year. But family is eternal. Let's open the softest part of our heart, in the beginning of this new year, to our family. Let spouses, parents, and children work together, cultivate this intimate relationship with each other, to strengthen our families." This article was read and shared by 100,000 people in China. Every time I read my own writings, I know that I have received the Holy Ghost's gift and revelation because I am doing the Lord's work.

God's revelation is something that we cannot understand or predict. Although networking is a core skill that I studied in American workplaces and life, I never thought that one day, by means of these skills, I would be sharing wisdom with others and be called a "networking expert" in China. At the time my networking book came out, I was called to be the Relief Society president of my ward in Minnetonka, and around that same time, President Nelson changed our visiting teaching program to ministering. In those days of serving in that calling, I felt love coming from my Heavenly Father to me and to all the sisters I served. The preparation and the business insights that he had given me could now be used in my calling.

When I received the calling and was just starting to understand the responsibilities of the Relief Society president, I had a real panic attack one day. One of my sons was sick, the other had not done his homework, and my husband was on one of his weekly work trips to New York. That evening, I sat in the corner of my bedroom feeling utterly defeated. I did not feel up to the task of this calling that demanded so much time and energy on top of work and looking after my family. I gave my husband a call and pleaded, "Why don't you quit your job now and just stay at home with the kids, so I can fulfill my calling?" But he had just started at a new company and naturally didn't want to quit.

Then my thirteen-year-old son came over and said, "Mom, you should pray to Heavenly Father because 'the Lord giveth no commandments unto the children of men, save he shall prepare a way for them that they may accomplish the thing which he commandeth them'" (1 Nephi 3:7). My son's words gave me inspiration. I prayed to Heavenly Father and asked him to give me strength and faith. Immediately, my mind calmed down. I felt strength to face the potential challenges of this calling. My experiences thereafter confirmed that the promises Heavenly Father makes to the children of humankind are true.

As a first-generation immigrant from China, I was very different from the sisters in the ward in terms of skin color, age, cultural background, and socioeconomic background. I was not a typical Relief Society president, who in my mind would be White, born and raised in the Church, in her late forties to fifties, a stay-at-home mom or an empty nester, very experienced with life, very knowledgeable in the scriptures, seasoned, compassionate, calm, and, most of all, one who knows everybody in the Church, etc. (You might laugh about this stereotype of the Relief Society president.) For my part, I had just moved to this ward a few months earlier and didn't know many people. I was a convert, a Chinese American, with a full-time job and managing two young children. I felt very junior in gospel knowledge and definitely not seasoned. How could I get to know the sisters and be their friend? Being a good Relief Society president was a big challenge for me.

But my learning and practice in networking skills helped me tremendously. As I illustrated in my book *Network Up*, when we try to network with people or make friends with strangers, focusing on differences will not get us anywhere.[2] Instead, we need to focus on common traits to build connections with people. Isn't this also true regarding serving others? Besides finding common traits or common interests, there are three fundamental principles in networking that can be applied to serving others.

First, let curiosity lead the way. Have a curious heart about people. This does not mean gossiping about other people's lives. Rather, try to understand who they really are, their true passions and interests, their desires and struggles, and their happiness and sorrow. When we have an open mind and let curiosity lead the way, it is much easier for us to get to know others in a deeper way. Because in our heart, everyone desires to be seen by others. If we try to truly understand who they are, the sisters will start to feel seen and appreciated much more.

Second, be sincere and warm. Doesn't this sound easy? When we fulfill a calling, we should be sincere as we serve others. Our ultimate motive is to do the Lord's work and not to drive our own agenda. However, the sincerity needs to be felt by the sisters. Sometimes a person has a sincere heart, but the action she takes might be perceived as selfish or aggressive or dominating. So how to project warmth to

2. Connie Zhang, *Network Up* (Beijing: CITIC Publishing, 2019).

sisters and have them feel the love and light from Heavenly Father is critical. Both our body language and our verbal language are equally important.

Third, seek opportunities to help others or create value for others. This networking principle applies perfectly to serving in a calling. Start a day with prayers to Heavenly Father and ask his guidance on how to best minister to others or teach his children under your stewardship. Reach out. Sometimes it might be a phone call to a sister who needs emotional support. Sometimes it might be a visit to a sick brother who needs a warm plate of food. Other times, it might be some patient guidance to a young child who needs to learn how to deal with unkindness in school. When we match our resources to other people's needs, we are creating value for others.

As Relief Society president, my role was to help the sisters with their spiritual and temporal needs and to draw them closer to Jesus Christ. We had lots of sisters suffering from financial distress, facing physical and mental health challenges, experiencing turmoil in their marriage relationships, etc. Knowing how to best help them in their individual situations involved constant prayers to Heavenly Father. I prayed for guidance every morning to identify what I could do, whom I could help, and how I could serve them better. From serving as Relief Society president, I gradually learned that I cannot personally meet every single need because that is not what the Lord would do. I need to be mindful in my efforts to help the sisters be self-reliant and make sure that, through my actions, they feel Heavenly Father's love.

I tried to use these networking skills with love, allowing myself to be led by a curious heart, sincerely trying to understand the sisters and "zoom in" on them. As I worked to learn about their personal traits, interests, passions, successes, and struggles, I was able to bring warmth to them and constantly try to help them. In this way, our hearts drew closer together.

I visited every sister's house and got to know them in their own living environment. Looking for points in common with them helped us make connections. For example, we both were mothers, we liked to read books, we were sensitive to literature and language, we both painted and appreciated art, and so on. I would ask them what their passion was. I would try to understand who they really were behind their labels of wife, mother, etc. One after another, I saw the image of a cherished daughter of Heavenly Father. All of us might've faced challenges that were similar or different, but we were all trying diligently to live the life of a Latter-day Saint.

In Chinese, the word that we use for ministering can be broken down into *shi* 施 and *zhu* 助. *Shi* is giving, and *zhu* is helping. At the core of ministering is love. It is a process of becoming instruments in the hands of Heavenly Father and going to spread his love to every person. The more we serve people, the more we love them. If we only visit a sister but do not really love and understand her and do not become a friend to her, then this visit is just our going through the motions. If we do not become their friends, how can they open their hearts to us? How can we know the help we give them is really the help they need?

The experience and wisdom I gained from serving and ministering to sisters further helped me develop my theories of networking. It gave me lots of real-life examples to enrich my theories. For example, I wrote an article called "They Don't Really Need Your Kind Advice," which addressed a situation where a ministering sister would give advice to another sister, but the advice was not actually what she needed. The same principles apply to social networking experiences as well. I wrote about how to find out people's true needs and help accordingly. I shared my findings in "How to Create Value for Other People" with an audience of a million Chinese.

If you ask me—as a career woman, a wife, and a mother—what the relationship is between my life experiences and my spiritual growth, I would say that we often count our blessings from Heavenly Father when we live a happy and successful life. However, the challenges and adversities in life are gifts from our Heavenly Father as well. I grew much stronger as a person and in faith when I endured these challenges and adversities. I know in my deep heart that I am a precious daughter of our Heavenly Father and that he has a plan for me. All I need to do is follow his plan and hearken to the counseling voice of the Holy Spirit. Because of my faith in Heavenly Father and Jesus Christ, I can put myself completely in God's hands and allow the Holy Spirit to lead and guide me, to be an instrument in God's hands, to be a vessel, to carry God's light into every corner of the world, especially nurturing the sons and daughters of China on the earth.

“For Such a Time as This”

Faith and Female Exegesis[1]

ARIEL CLARK SILVER

Ariel Clark Silver grew up in northern Virginia, where she trained as a classical ballet dancer. She is the author of The Book of Esther and the Typology of Female Transfiguration in American Literature *(Rowman & Littlefield 2018) and a contributor to* Esther in America *(Maggid 2020). Her work on Margaret Fuller and May Alcott was recently published in* The Forgotten Alcott *(Routledge 2022). She writes on women, literature, and religion in nineteenth-century American culture. Like her mother and mother-in-law, she holds a PhD. Like her grandmother and great-grandmother, she is the mother of five daughters and one son. She currently serves as president-elect of the Hawthorne Society.*

As a scholar, I spend most of my time thinking and writing about how the lives of women in nineteenth-century America are conceived and understood in literature, art, and culture. I

1. Esther 4:14.

investigate the profound parallel changes that transpired for women and society with the advent of modern life, from the end of the eighteenth century to the beginning of the twentieth. The global movement towards modernity required a reconsideration of women as fully human beings, capable of independent insight, autonomous action, and self-integrity. The philosophical foundations had been articulated during the Enlightenment, but few thinkers applied these principles to women. Would they be granted authority and accountability as beings who could receive an education, vote, hold property, and control their own destiny? Many reform efforts were needed for women to be granted social status above that of property, to be represented in and protected by law, and to be respected as beings whose thoughts were distinct from those of fathers, brothers, husbands, or sons.

This search for female rights and responsibilities led many writers to invoke ancient scriptural types such as Eve, Hagar, Miriam, and Esther to articulate the scope of female agency and action in this unprecedented and irreversible shift away from social structures that had governed life for centuries, if not millennia. What emerged was a more complex and compelling view of female engagement. I first read the remarkable stories of these biblical women as a high school student in Church seminary classes and marveled at their courage, insight, and conviction. It was significant for me to find female stories in holy writ; I felt like an explorer who had stumbled upon the riches of an undiscovered country. Their narratives redeemed the Old Testament for me, even at that age, and I rejoiced in the respect our theology extended to these and other females. Inside the landscape of creation, destruction, and deliverance, scattering and gathering, the soil teemed with the seeds of a different set of promises made to women: a fortunate fall, personal visitation, a vow to the rejected, power to lead and direct, and a keen sense of mission, even in the midst of oppression.

My initial encounter with these female biblical figures was built on a foundation given to me by my father, who transformed dinner table conversations into a more careful study of scripture than I encountered in my Sunday School classes. That theological education then extended beyond the dinner table, often far into the evening. In those exchanges, I thought of the story by Nobel Prize–winning author Isaac Bashevis Singer where a girl named Yentl reads and discusses the Torah with her father under the cover of night.[2] Above all else, my father taught me to value my own insight and my own voice. As much as he loved to hold forth and was certain of his own answers, he resisted the urge to reply to my questions. He wanted me to look at the text again and then again. He wanted me to see the revelatory spaces that existed in and between words. He wanted me to see the doctrinal difference a comma, dash, or period could make. He wanted me to believe that the word was God. As I tried to refine my understanding, primarily by reading the word in all its wondrous forms, I found myself dancing across the page. I had been a dancer all my life, but now, my mind was also dancing. My curiosity became insatiable as I pursued the edict to study all things in heaven and on earth and to seek "knowledge upon knowledge" and "revelation upon revelation" (Doctrine and Covenants 42:61).

Soon I was seventeen and serious about my future. I asked for a patriarchal blessing. I specifically wanted to know if I should pursue a professional life as a dancer or seek further education. I received a beautiful piece of personal revelation, but on the face of it, I could not have been more disappointed. There was really no mention of a career of any kind; instead, the blessing was centered on the promises of motherhood. My own mother, who acquired a PhD while raising six children, worked full-time, and I was deeply involved in the care of my three younger siblings, whom I adored. But at that moment in my life, becoming a mother was the last thing I wanted to dwell on or discuss. Tucked into the crevices of that document, like prayers shoved into the Western Wall, were a few caveats to which I clung, among them the encouragement to "lay up in store by study."

2. Isaac Bashevis Singer, *Yentl the Yeshiva Boy* (New York: Farrar, Straus and Giroux, 1983).

The desire for further enlightenment proved irresistible. When I arrived at Smith College, I thought I would major in English but decided instead to study religion and biblical literature. In one course, I became convinced that the structure of scripture could teach me to read texts closely. What I had studied informally at home for many years I could now pursue in a more formal way at school. And I did not have to cut my hair like Yentl in Singer's story. When her father dies in the story, Yentl removes her beautiful long locks and flees to the city to continue her Torah studies dressed as a young man.

As I pursued my academic studies in religion, I also continued to dance. My dance training had begun when I was very young, but at twelve, everything changed. A friend confided to me that real dance came out of the Eastern Orthodox tradition, not the Western Roman one. She sent me to Oleg Tupine and Tania Rousseau, émigrés from Russia who traveled the globe with the Ballet Russe de Monte Carlo. When I approached the studios of Virginia Ballet, they were inauspicious; the dance academy was located on the first floor of a three-story suburban office building.

Then I opened the door. I saw Tania first: she was four foot ten, ninety pounds, gold bangles from her wrist to her elbow, honey hair curled at the crown of her head, tiara still intact. Her eyes were like fire, her body like moving flames. She seemed fierce and wise and gentle and stern all at once. She indicated a place for me at the barre. By the time class was over, I was drenched in sweat but strangely energized. I trained in the Vaganova Method with Oleg and Tania for six years, six days a week.

At Smith, one of my favorite classes was in African dance forms, taught by the renowned African American dancer and choreographer Pearl Primus. She encouraged me to conduct ethnographic field research on dance forms in West Africa as she had done earlier in her career.

With a grant from the Dana Foundation and support from the Parsons School of Design, I traveled to Côte d'Ivoire the summer after my sophomore year of college, living among the Baoulé and Senufo peoples in the interior of the country. It was a tremendous privilege to be invited into the communal life of these Indigenous cultures, accompanied by interpreters and guides who knew their languages and art practices intimately. I was granted the opportunity to observe and study ritual dance cycles with carved and painted wooden masks and full-body costumes made of cloth and raffia that were integral to Indigenous spiritual understanding and social order. Beyond what I was learning, what I felt amazed me even more: the beautiful red soil was vibrant and alive. I had come from a place where the planet was covered in asphalt and concrete; whatever Mother Earth wanted to say had been smothered over for several centuries.

Now I was immersed in cultures where important stories were conveyed both verbally and visually. Dance and literature were no longer two distinct modes of expression; both were engaged to tell tales of the life of the mind, spirit, and body. Women I met wondered aloud why, at age nineteen, I was not already married with three children. If only I had followed my patriarchal blessing more promptly! They offered to help, wrapping me in a beautifully patterned textile inscribed with this parable: *Notre richesse est dans nos enfants* (our wealth is in our children).

Indeed, the Baoulé and Senufo women I met in the interior of the country lived lives that spanned generations and spheres: they shaved their heads and mourned the passing of their fathers, brothers, husbands, and sons; they worked hard from dawn to dusk, carrying water, building fires, and cooking food; and they perpetuated life on earth. Their experiences of engaging spiritually with life and death gave me a renewed appreciation for all the women who creatively perform work and contribute insight while holding families together over time.

The opportunity I was afforded to live and work among the Baoulé and Senufo confirmed my conviction that both the body and the spirit are essential to any real religious understanding. Knowledge and revelation are conveyed through both. As luck would have it, my summer in Côte d'Ivoire followed the first formal Latter-day Saint missionary efforts in the country. In both Abidjan and Bouaké, I met many of the first leaders and members of the Church as they worked to establish and proclaim the restored gospel of Christ. My desire to be a part of that effort led to a mission call a year and a half later. I held out hope that all truth could be circumscribed into one great whole. I yearned to return to Côte d'Ivoire, but greater wisdom than my own prevailed, and I was called to France. I found that, as is the case in most Latter-day Saint communities in Europe, local branches and wards were extremely diverse, including many Ivorians, along with many Romanians, Iranians, and Algerians. I had a companion whose family came from Islamic Morocco. My experience as a missionary worked me over, from the inside out, and this is how I knew: for the first time in my life, my spirit carried my body rather than the reverse. I felt as though I had entered the rich vein of our religion. As I sought to nourish others by rejoicing in the power of Christ and his plan of salvation, my whole soul felt nourished. I felt full of joy.

After serving in France, I returned to graduate from Smith in 1993. I choreographed a senior dance thesis entitled *Chorea Sancta*, but already, I felt the absence of the mantle I had worn as a missionary. There was no other role in the Church that matched it for a woman trained like Yentl who spent her waking hours thinking about how to bind all truth together. At that point, making sense of my religious culture seemed to require a theological deep dive. My inclination was substantiated when my religion professor strongly encouraged me to pursue a PhD in the field of biblical literature. I began by applying to a graduate program at the University of Chicago Divinity School. Luminary Church scholars such as Sidney B. Sperry had attended Swift Hall in the early twentieth century, but I was perhaps the first Latter-day Saint woman to study there.

Now I began to reckon with the Hebrew Bible on its own terms, from eminent Jewish and Christian thinkers who helped me to understand these records in the light of a history thousands of years in the making. I completed my master's degree feeling deeply enlightened; I now had an insatiable thirst to better understand how scripture elucidated the human experience. But I could not envision a professional path as a Latter-day Saint woman with an advanced degree in religion. This too was a tremendous reckoning because, despite my education at a women's college, I was still a student trained in a religious academic world conceived by and for men, in and out of the Church. Like Yentl, I had somehow slipped in, but I did not think I would be permitted to pass further. I had not cut my hair, and now they could tell.

Then there was the matter of motherhood: the importance of perpetuating life and selflessly plowing gifts into the next generation. One quiet evening in the Regenstein Library, the power of that patriarchal blessing returned. I had already learned that knowledge and revelation came through both the body and the mind. Remembering myself wrapped in textiles proclaiming that wealth comes in the form of children, I finished my thesis and got married. Just after the birth of our first child, I started teaching literature classes to high school students. That opportunity was instrumental. As a student of exegesis, I knew the shape of commentary on scriptural text, but here, in novels and short stories, biblical narratives were being deeply reconceived and reconfigured to enrich and illuminate our understanding of the urtexts on which they were built. I could not imagine more exciting theological ground. At that point, I was positively delighted to exchange the study of ancient Greek for stories that seemed to have the capacity to give endless insight. When we moved to California, I began a doctoral program in English at Claremont Graduate University with two young children and finished twelve years later with six. Each child is a remarkable treasure, and I will always be grateful that I chose them first. But like Yentl, I wanted and needed more.

Approaching a dissertation topic, I realized that I had not yet really wrestled with the questions that had first compelled me toward an advanced education. I had almost forgotten about the women from the Hebrew Bible and their encounters with the divine, but I remembered my ballet teacher Tania, the women in Côte d'Ivoire, and my own mother. I had myself become a mother even as I was continuing to "lay up in store by study." Only now did I have any real appreciation for the incredible texture and complexity of their temporal and spiritual lives.

Then those scriptural women returned to my mind with tremendous force. I began to see them dancing all over the pages of nineteenth-century American literature. Writers like Hawthorne, Stowe, Melville, Alcott, Twain, and Adams, deeply versed in the Bible, engaged the figures of Eve, Hagar, Miriam, and Esther to create female figures of salvation who demonstrate remarkable development and devotion to the redemption of others.

I gravitated toward Esther and, at one spectacular juncture in my research, felt a clear prompt to carefully read and reconsider a late romance by Hawthorne, *The Marble Faun*, which features a female artist named Miriam Schaefer. The inclusion of this text transformed my project in profound ways. These literary women, like their female types in scripture, are surprisingly multi-faceted and capable of very meaningful insight and action. They assert the importance of female agency and authority even when they are oppressed, constrained, and outcast, and they cultivate their own relation with the divine. I began to see more clearly the significance of these sacred female figures even as they created the dynamic contours of the female protagonist in American letters.

After decades of studying and writing about American authors who have employed Hebraic women characters in their fiction to claim gifts of procreation, prophecy, and power in places that did not seem full of promise, I wonder what more Eve, Hagar, Miriam, and Esther may have to say to us now. Can we see in Eve a sense of spiritual agency that enriches our understanding of divine engagement? Can we see in Hagar and her son Ishmael the capacity of a covenant that extends to bless those we have placed at the margins? Can we see in Miriam a model that could complement the work her brothers Aaron and Moses had been set apart to perform? Can we see in Esther the strength to transform ominous threats and existential difficulties into opportunities through the Lord to prevail, to save ourselves and others, through fasting, supplication, and carefully inspired solutions? These scriptural women were all called upon to imagine and create a multi-faceted female capable of carrying modern society through so many unimaginable challenges. Can we follow the model of these biblical matriarchs and those who wrote about them to help us claim the full measure of our creation and circumscribe all truth—including the truths of female spiritual capacity and authority—into one great whole?

A Journey into the Sacred

KEAKAOKAWAI VARNER HEMI

> [She] who invades the domain of knowledge must approach it as Moses came to the burning bush; [she] stands on holy ground; [she] would acquire things sacred.... We must come to this quest of truth—in all regions of human knowledge whatsoever, not only in reverence, but with a spirit of worship.[1]

Keakaokawai "Keaka" Varner Hemi is the first assistant vice chancellor Pacific appointed by the University of Waikato. Keaka is Kānaka Maoli, Kanaka Ōiwi (Native Hawaiian), and part of Na 'Ohana o Kalama of Lāiē, O'ahu, Hawai'i through her mother and Cherokee from Northwest Arkansas through her father. She earned a bachelor of laws (hons) and PhD from Te Piringa–Faculty of Law, University of Waikato, where she later taught legal theory, Indigenous rights, and human rights and was associate dean undergraduate. Her research interests include Indigenous education, equality and nondiscrimination, and learner success. She is the chair of Universities New Zealand's Komiti Pasifika and a member of the New Zealand Ministry of Education's NCEA Pacific Peoples Review Panel. Her

1. J. Reuben Clark Jr., "Charge to President Howard S. McDonald," *Improvement Era* (January 1946): 15; quoted and cited in Dallin H. Oaks and Kristen M. Oaks, "Learning and Latter-day Saints," *Ensign* (April 2009): 22.

recent publications include "Reclaiming Hawaiian Sovereignty" in the Palgrave Handbook of Ethnicity *(Springer 2019) and "Māori Education Through a Human Rights Lens: Learners and Educators as Everyone, No-one, Someone, Complex, and Indigenous Rightsholders" in* Waking the Taniwha: Māori Governance in the 21st Century *(Thomson Reuters 2021). Keaka loves family history, creating stuff, and staying active, but her greatest joy is being with her family, especially her five* moʻopuna *(grandchildren).*

I AM THE DESCENDANT of Makaopiopio, a Kānaka Maoli (Native Hawaiian) woman who became a member of The Church of Jesus Christ of Latter-day Saints in the Kingdom of Hawaiʻi in 1862 and a Christian even earlier. In our family history, Makaopiopio stands as a nearly legendary ancestral figure, one who followed her faith first from Waimea on the Big Island of Hawaiʻi to the settlement of Lāʻiē on the North Shore of Oʻahu and then to the settlement of Iosepa, once located south of modern-day Tooele, west of Salt Lake City, Utah. Her pioneer life was one of sacrifice and "mov[ing] forward" long before she crossed oceans, mountains, and deserts as a widow in her sixties to follow her faith and to make covenants and receive blessings in a temple in a foreign land.[2] After further sacrifices, including nursing a dying daughter through Hansen's disease (commonly called leprosy), she also succumbed to the painful disease and was the first person buried at the little cemetery in Iosepa, in the dry, windswept bowl of Skull Valley, a world away from the green hills of Waimea and the waves and trade winds of Lāʻiē.

Journeys into the sacred are a familiar concept in many religions. Multiple faiths remember Adam and Eve leaving the Garden of Eden,

2. Napua Baker and Nalani Fonoimoana, quoted in Marianne Monson, *Frontier Grit: The Unlikely True Stories of Daring Pioneer Women* (Salt Lake City, UT: Shadow Mountain, 2016), 190.

the travels of Abraham, Isaac, and Jacob—and their families—to, from, and across covenant landscapes, and their ascensions up sacred mountains. Many are familiar with Moses, the exodus of the children of Israel into the wilderness, and, finally, their arrival in the promised land. New Testament roads to Jericho and Damascus and apostolic missions traversing the Roman Empire by land and sea are turning points and testing grounds for Christians. Members of The Church of Jesus Christ of Latter-day Saints remember the journeyings of the prophet Lehi's family through their own wilderness to another promised land in the Americas as recorded in the Book of Mormon. We also look back with awe to nineteenth-century pioneers like Makaopiopio whose sacrifices, endurance, and movement across historical and geographical space are less memorialized in physical monuments than in the spiritual heritage paths they have left for their descendants to follow.

While it does not entail the physical hardships experienced by some of our ancestors, a legal education bears some similarities to a pioneer's journey as it entails challenge, promise, and movement across time and the almost geographic spaces of a person's soul. This is true for many women and especially for women of faith. It certainly was true for me.

The path

Education changes lives, opens doors, and organically multiplies opportunity and equity. Fundamental rights, including the right to vote, are virtually meaningless without the ability to read and write. Education equips individuals for citizenship and effective participation in society, for the tangibles and intangibles of participation and substantive equality.[3] Education has logarithmic impact. When a woman gains an education, families, communities, and generations benefit. The children of an educated woman are more likely to be healthy, survive past their fifth birthday, be educated themselves, and to live above

3. Brown v. Board of Education of Topeka, Kansas, 347 US 483 (1954), 492–95.

poverty.[4] Education is so vital to the exercise of other rights that it has been equated with the right to life in some jurisdictions.[5]

A legal education allows women unique opportunities to develop their thinking and capacity to help others. Such an education potentially "teaches the policies and principles that undergird the social compacts we agree to as a society and which lawyers are uniquely charged with understanding and protecting while advocating for successful, just outcomes."[6] Principles include basic rule of law, democracy, and equal protection before the law. "Social compacts" include constitutions and the fundamental civil and political rights, liberties, and freedoms which they commonly protect. Lawyers have the unique ability to stand between individuals or groups and the state—or other actors with more power and more resources—to defend, champion, advocate, and mediate for those who cannot speak for themselves. Beyond high-flying, comedic, or hired-gun caricatures of lawyers on television, real lawyers increasingly represent women, children, the elderly, those with disabilities, minorities, refugees, and the poor. Increasingly, lawyers must also protect religious rights.

A legal education takes one far beyond the practice of law, however. It creates advocates and problem solvers and teaches values and qualities of leadership.[7] The study of law "emphasizes and develops ... analysis, advocacy, precision in communication, [and] problem-solving" skills, which are universally important.[8] Law graduates are more employable because the legal job market is broad, including work

4. UNICEF, *The State of the World's Children 2007: Women and children—the double dividend of gender equality* (New York: UNICEF, 2007), 5; and UNESCO, *Education Counts: Towards the Millennium Development Goals* (Paris: UNESCO, 2010), http://unesdoc.unesco.org/images/0019/001902/190214e.pdf.

5. *Unni Krishnan v. State of Andhra Pradesh* 1993 AIR 217, 1993 SCR (1) 594, 1993 SCC (1) 645, JT 1993 (1) 474, 1993 SCALE (1) 290.

6. James Lupo, "Measure of Legal Education's Value Extends Far Beyond Big Law," *National Law Journal & Legal Times* 38, no. 4 (2015): 39–40.

7. Ibid.

8. David Epstein, "Judging the Pros and Cons of Law School," *Richmond Times Dispatch*, February 6, 2011, http://WW2.timesdispatch.com/news/2011/feb/06/TDCOMM03-judging the-pros-and-cons-of-law-school-ar-822018/.

in law firms, public sector work, business, health care, intellectual property, and environmental law, among others.[9] Given these features and others, law is a highly transferable education.

And yet, despite all these benefits, studying law can be daunting, especially when one's path is not ideal, as in my case.

The journey

I began my legal education in my early thirties, with a husband, three daughters under the age of ten, a mortgage, and a small business. As I enrolled in classes, purchased my textbooks, and took my student ID photo, I felt old. As I bought school supplies for my children and then myself—for the first time in over a decade—I knew I was an impostor. I worried about my children's well-being, despite wonderful support from my husband and an amazing mother-in-law. Between lectures, endless reading, and a continuous flow of assignments, I did not know where I would find the time to be a good student or even to be a student. The first week, I received a parking ticket and had to rush out of class when my three-year-old went to the emergency room. She recovered soon after, but it was not a promising start to the journey.

As I kept moving forward, however, I felt my faith grow as well as my love of the law. Given the challenges, I prayed more—and listened more after praying—than I ever had before. In doing so, I gained a sure sense that the Lord was guiding my path. Often, I knew what the right thing was even if I did not know how it would be accomplished. I learned that if I did my best, was organized, and prioritized my family and the Lord, everything would work out. As I tried to do what was right, the Lord expanded late nights, early mornings, and small pockets of time. He multiplied limited budgets, energy, strength, and knowledge. On many occasions, I was able to recall things that I had only read briefly at crucial moments. Despite more emergencies, work, school events, coaching sports, church responsibilities, and

9. Cynthia E Nance, "The Value of a Law Degree," *Iowa Law Review* 96 (2011): 1629–48, at 1641–44.

being a wife and a mother, I completed my degree with first class honors. The math and physics should not have added up, but somehow, it did.

I grew to love much of what I was learning. In torts and contract law, I could see the basic components and mechanics of law and why things are the way they are for good and ill. In legal theory, I discovered law's potential to help people but also to create injustice in fields such as human rights and constitutional law. Indigenous law was like coming home. I felt close to my ancestors but also saw more clearly the injustice they faced. While principles such as equality and nondiscrimination were consistent with my knowledge that each of us is a beloved child of our Heavenly Father endowed with various rights and freedoms, the injustices were not.

Later, inspired by a singular moment at a family reunion in Hawaii when an injustice brought the power of law home to me, I completed a PhD in law. Our son was born during my PhD, and life brought new challenges. Once again, I felt my relationship with our Heavenly Father grow closer as I learned more fully to listen for his will and then do it. Ultimately, my PhD was one of the hardest things I have ever done, but I came to know without a doubt that God will answer prayers and smooth paths. Both degrees have opened doors for me, including having a job where I am constantly learning and growing as a person and am working with a diverse group of stakeholders to achieve better outcomes for students who are not experiencing all the blessings of education. I get to work on the injustices. Teaching and researching on the right to education, human and Indigenous rights, constitutional law, and legal theory continue to challenge my thinking and strengthen my testimony.

Sister travelers

Along the way, I have also been blessed to witness the pioneer journeys of other women. As a law student, my closest friends were other mothers, including a small group of young single mothers. When we began our degrees, many of them were in their early twenties with tough roads behind them. They were focused, organized, hardworking, and passionate about making a difference in the world. They approached law with the maturity and deep knowledge that comes from experience and significant adversity. All of them ultimately earned their degrees with honors, and most continue to practice law.

Later, as a teacher, I received an inquiry one day from a senior leader about how late a particular mooting competition would go. I later learned that one of the competitors was on parole. I thought of all the times this slightly mature student had been one of the first to arrive in my large jurisprudence lecture and sit at the front, of the smile that she always wore on a weathered face, of her diligence, and of the high marks she was achieving. I was humbled both by her example and the redemptive power of legal education. We ensured that she finished on time.

As an associate dean, I often saw students in my office that were in serious circumstances. A student who had been missing my class came to see me one day for options with a late assignment. She did not make excuses but did eventually share her extreme circumstances of a fatherless family, a mother struggling with many challenges, and younger siblings in state care after their mother had assaulted them and my student. In her final year, working two jobs with long commutes, the slim young woman in front of me visibly carried the fate of her family on her shoulders. Her ability to endure and press on would determine what came next for the family that she was trying to hold together almost single-handedly.

As Pacific women and fellow Christians, we shared our faith that day. I was humbled that she knew that God listened to her prayers and kept her going. When I said that I knew that she was a daughter of God, she already knew that too. I later had the opportunity to stand on a stage and acknowledge her excellence in and out of the classroom through an award. We were both trying not to cry, but we did anyway. She has now completed her degree.

Promised land and sacred charge

In many religions, promised lands are sites where covenants and associated blessings are fulfilled. They are the goal of the faithful and the ultimate destination at the conclusion of a journey into the sacred. The completion of a law degree is certainly an accomplishment and the reaching of a destination, but it is not the raison d'être of the journey nor a promised land. It may open logarithmic opportunities to women and their families, but on its own, a legal education is not the pioneer's legacy or the prophet's Sinai. Rather, what we *do* with a legal education is an ongoing journey into the sacred.

With a degree and professional qualifications, lawyers take on a sacred charge. The late Boyd K. Packer, former president of the Quorum of the Twelve Apostles, once warned against the pitfalls of practicing law in a "morally mixed-up world,"[10] but then said,

> I wonder if you who are now lawyers or you who are students of the law know how much you are needed as defenders of the faith. Be willing to give of your time and of your means and your expertise to the building up of the Church and the kingdom of God and the establishment of Zion, which we are under covenant to do—not just to the Church as an institution, but to members and ordinary people who need your professional protection.[11]

President Packer also implied that lawyers of faith are a "line of defense" against many evils in the world and warned that one day we will stand accountable for what we have done as lawyers and judges.[12] I have sensed that sacred charge many times when someone at church or a friend in distress has asked for help in a legal matter. It has been

10. Boyd K. Packer, "On the Shoulders of Giants," BYU J. Reuben Clark Law Society devotional, February 2004; published in *Life in the Law: Service & Integrity*, ed. Scott W. Cameron, Galen L. Fletcher, and Jane H. Wise (Provo, UT: J. Reuben Clark Law Society, 2009), 225–38, at 233.

11. Packer, "On the Shoulders of Giants," 236.

12. Ibid.

said, "Knowledge is power ... but it is power only when it is put into service."[13] I have witnessed tears dried, burdens eased, and hearts reassured when a lawyer shared and applied knowledge they possessed.

Our opportunity to serve others through law is greater than ever. We live in a time when the villages of Galilee and the crowded streets of Jerusalem are so much larger, where beggars do not cry for alms from the hems of our garments on the side of a cobbled street but from statistics and numbers too unfair and unjust to be believed at times. An ever-larger portion of humanity suffers not from the shame of leprosy but from poverty, political marginalization, poor health, lack of access to education, and even chronic stress across multiple areas of well-being. The COVID-19 pandemic has merely highlighted and magnified existing disparities, gaps, and inequities that are seemingly drawn to and accumulate around particular groups, including women.

My journey and those of the women who have touched my life and helped to build my faith are not over. Pioneer legacies are yet to be written. And there is much work still to be done in the world. But each one of their stories so far has strengthened my faith in God and my trust that he is a loving, kind, and gracious father to his children. I believe that, one day, these women will be remembered by their children and others for the way they have moved across historic space and created change in their families and communities.

As a postscript, two of my daughters are now studying law, including our middle daughter, who is named for Makaopiopio. She is a young mother, pressing forward to make a better life for her little family. She is also courageous, bothered by injustice, and eager to make the world a better place. She follows in her grandmother's footsteps as she keeps moving forward toward greater challenges and blessings, ever relying on the Lord. I know that Makaopiopio would be proud.

13. Stephen L Richards, *Where Is Wisdom?* (Salt Lake City, UT: Deseret Book Company, 1955), 408.

Afterword

ROSALYNDE FRANDSEN WELCH

Rosalynde Frandsen Welch was raised in Southern California and earned a BA and a PhD in English from Brigham Young University and the University of California San Diego. She is a senior research fellow at the Neal A. Maxwell Institute for Religious Scholarship at BYU, where she writes on Latter-day Saint scripture, theology, and literature. She is the author of Ether: a brief theological introduction *and the editor of* Are We Not All Beggars?: Reading Mosiah 4. *She loves hiking, gardening, and making music with children. She lives in Provo, Utah, with her family.*

I INHERITED from my father a penchant for books. I read them, yes, but mostly, I just like to live with them. I'm happiest surrounded by stacks of books, read or unread; my normally clutter-averse eye sees them as comforting, essential ballast to any space. As new books arrive, I stand them on my desk, awaiting their turn to be read. Inevitably, the new books fill the available desk space, and I must lay the next books horizontally across the top of the stack. With new linear space now available, it's only natural to stack a second story of books upright. Thus it was that I discovered a hidden power of books: beyond their ability to contain and convey stories, information, and ideas—beyond, that is, what they *mean*—books make very serviceable bookshelves.

Look around your room: I'd wager that books and other printed materials are quietly performing all sorts of duties beyond conveying meaning. As rectangular weights, books press flowers and smooth wrinkled paper. As stackable blocks, they support tracks for toy cars and serve as doll furniture. Arrayed in a color-spectrum formation, they add decorative interest to a room. Stacked beneath a laptop, they elevate a computer screen. Tucked within a window frame, they hold the window ajar to the breeze. And in my book-cluttered study, books act above all as resting places for other books.

I want to imagine what this book, *Every Needful Thing*, might be capable of doing beyond its obvious role as a delivery vehicle for the ideas of two dozen accomplished scholars. For example, one can imagine copies being used as weights to balance the sensitive scales of ethnic, professional, family, and religious identity by which Teitter, DeLoach, and Armstrong calibrate their lives. Volumes might be stacked as the mighty *poutu* posts of service, love, and respect that support Samu's Samoan *fale tele* or used to anchor the tense, tough web of faith, gender, and science explored by Krakos. I like to imagine a mountain of *Every Needful Thing* arrayed as a bulwark against injustice and oppression in Ikponmwen's courtroom.

These images are fanciful, of course, not least because many readers will read *Every Needful Thing* as an e-book, not as a physical volume. But my question remains. What happens if we think for a moment about what this book can do rather than what it can mean?

To be sure, these essays are brimful of ideas, claims, experiences, and all manner of meaning that will richly reward their readers. This meaning deserves consideration and relish. But any attentive reader will have noted that the approaches represented herein are widely diverse and sometimes exist in tension with one another. Lubomirsky, with her mathematician's faith, sees a reality defined by logical patterns and governed by a God of perfectly rational truth; Bates and Tuminez, by contrast, discern a world in which the bad and good are intractably mixed, and faith is made more resilient by doubt and ambiguity. Or consider that each scholar of any cultural or racial identity inflected by encounter with Western colonialism contributes a perspective that is beautifully particular in its historical and personal contours, despite the fact that these identities are sometimes broadly likened to one another. The counterpoint between these voices reflects complex historical realities that can create tension between the two covers of a single book.

Such differences are natural in any collection of real voices, and they generate delight and intellectual spark. But they suggest to me that a harmonizing assessment of what this book means—the type of assessment one might try to provide in a book's afterword—won't work well. Instead, I want to think about what this book can do. Not as a physical object, as I fancifully imagined above, but as what literary scholars call a speech act. What action does *Every Needful Thing* perform beyond communicating the meaning of the essays in its pages? To answer this, we might set aside the essays for a moment and take up instead the humbler parts of the volume, those "extras" often overlooked as peripheral to a book's message.

Consider for instance the Table of Contents. This list of textual components, encompassing as it does a wide variety of academic and professional approaches, accomplishes more than guiding the reader through the book. It makes a wager about the nature of truth. Brigham Young taught that "our religion measures, weighs, and circumscribes all the wisdom in the world."[1] Indeed, the Latter-day Saint tradition holds that "all truth may be circumscribed into one great whole."[2] Notice the vigorous activity implied in these statements: to measure, weigh, and circumscribe truth is to actively grapple with it, to make decisions about which tools to use, which standards to consult, and where to begin and end. Truth is not served up pre-weighed and pre-circumscribed.

The Table of Contents in this volume is a kind of geometric compass

1. Brigham Young, *Discourses of Brigham Young*, selected by John A. Widtsoe (Salt Lake City, UT: Deseret Book, 1941), 2.

2. See D. Todd Christofferson, "Truth Endures," *Religious Educator* 19, no. 3 (2018): 1–13, https://rsc.byu.edu/vol-19-no-3-2018/truth-endures.

made for such circumscription: it works to draw a capacious circle encompassing things that are true. By taking in a variety of approaches not easily reconciled, the Table suggests that truth may be found in a diversity of approaches to faith and reason, in many voices and many places rather than in one. Perhaps, indeed, the truest thing about *Every Needful Thing* is the very attempt at circumscription itself. The ambition, energy, and love reflected in the variety of titles and approaches included in the Table is as powerful as the resulting essays themselves. No doubt this Table, like any, is provisional; other editors and authors will tackle other acts of circumscription, and those circles may give a different account of the kind of thing truth is. That is to be expected. The joint performance of this circle, inscribed by this Table of Contents, is no less courageous for being provisional.

Consider, too, the Contributors page. This page of biographical notes is a kind of surveyor's tool for mapping the borders of a young community. Documents have always served to charter new collective identities. Scripture gives definition to religious traditions, including our own, by inspiring fidelity in believers. Newspapers generate new national identities by creating a sense of belonging and involvement in readers.[3] Likewise, the Contributors page in *Every Needful Thing* traces a border that solidifies a new sense of community—in this case, a global community of Latter-day Saint scholars. Given the geographical and disciplinary distance between the scholars included, it is no small feat to trace an inclusive border of belonging bounded by academic credentials and religious commitment. The Contributors page is not a complete register of this community's members, to be sure. The border it surveys is not definitive but evocative, acting to evoke a new axis of fellow feeling among contributors and readers. If it succeeds, it can act as an additional cord to extend and stabilize the global tent of Zion.

It's worth noting, when considering this emerging global community of Latter-day Saint scholars, the contributions of people of color to this volume. Scholars hailing from Latin American nations, African

3. This is the seminal thesis of Benedict Anderson's *Imagined Communities: Reflections on the Origin and Spread of Nationalism* (London: Verso Books, 2006).

nations, Asian nations, Pacific nations, and from Black, Indigenous, and other communities of color within the United States pioneer new boundaries of a more inclusive, racially diverse circle of global belonging. These thinkers' presence is crucial to establish, in this emerging moment, a perimeter in which diverse racial experience is constitutive and central, not decorative or optional, to our sense of togetherness in faith and thought.

The Contributors page readily discloses another parameter of this community: all the contributors are women. The framing elements of the book do not vigorously foreground the gender of the contributing scholars though most of the essays consider the writer's gender as an essential part of her experience and identity. To highlight the voices of women scholars is plainly a central part of the book's work; to let the question of gender settle lightly on the volume is also an evident part of its work. That tension reflects a hope for a Latter-day Saint people in which female scholars—and all-women volumes—are as ready-to-mind as their male counterparts. A community whose men *and* women read the work of women scholars, not only because the writers are women but because they are essential voices in the community. The Contributors page hopes to invoke an expanding covenant fellowship where women are more present than ever as guides for the global Latter-day Saint experience.

Finally, consider the book's covers. These covers act as a kind of lighthouse to signal book readers of all kinds from around the globe. The thoughts in essays themselves might exist in many forms—as personal writings, letters, videos, social media posts, and so on. The only reason to put the essays between two covers is to offer them to readers of books, to a readership. Does such a readership exist? Will a global community of book readers, male and female of different nations and ethnicities and circumstances, open—or swipe—these covers? It is an act of tremendous faith and imagination to bring a book into the world, particularly when its readership is still cohering, as is the potential readership for a volume of global Latter-day Saint women scholars. But the very act of producing a book can signal to individual readers that they are part of a readership, and thus, a book can sometimes call into being its own interpretive community. Readerships, in turn, are powerful as their reading habits elicit new approaches, new communities, and indeed new authors who began as readers.

One way to assess *Every Needful Thing* and begin to frame its contribution, then, is to examine what it does. It takes a stab at drawing a new circle of truth around a unique assemblage of voices and ideas—indeed, the first assemblage of global Latter-day Saint scholarly voices examining the intersection of faith and reason of which I am aware. It sketches a radically enlarged border for the community of Latter-day Saint scholars and thinkers, borders which may generate belonging and membership across far-flung geographical distances. It subtly integrates its readers' mental image of scholarly conversation to include women as essential participants. And it imagines into being a readership for global women's scholarly voices and for cross-cultural Latter-day Saint exchange—that is, if it succeeds.

If you've read the essays in *Every Needful Thing*, you've been conscripted into its work. I hope you scribbled notes furiously in every margin, copied quotes to send to your friend, encountered a thought you'd never entertained before, and perhaps even recognized your own wrestle with faith, reason, and identity reflected in its pages. You will soon close the covers; now ask yourself what the book will go on to do. Go ahead, stack it under your laptop. May it raise your gaze to see beyond old borders. Prop it in a window frame. May it hold your mind ajar to allow "intelligence, or the light of truth," to stream in (Doctrine and Covenants 93:29). Set it on your nightstand and pile books on top. May it be a resting place for your faith, your voice, and the faithful voices of many more.

FROM THE EDITORS

Melissa Wei-Tsing Inouye

From almost any point of view, to be a professional academic is to be incredibly privileged: paid to travel, research, read books, write, teach, and lecture on a full-time basis. I remember sitting alone in my new office at the University of Auckland in June 2014, enjoying the assurance of peace and quiet for what felt like the first time in eight years, looking out at the ocean, envisioning my husband at home with the kids (and potty training the fourth and final kid, hee hee), and thinking, "This is amazing!" From a certain point of view, to be a cancer patient is to be incredibly underprivileged: hooked up to postsurgical tubes dripping liquid poo, jabbed and thumped and poisoned, fed into huge imaging machines like a pencil into a sharpener, feeling death swell under your ribs as you bend to pick up a sock.

In the wide void between these two kinds of experience we find the dimensionality of life—the encompassing oppositions of which Eve and Lehi spoke. I have been a good student, a bad student, a parent, a child, an athlete, a patient, a local, a foreigner, a woman in a patriarchal ecclesiastical system, a minor bureaucrat within the corporate Church, a member of a tiny American religious group, a member of a state's dominant cultural force, an authority, and a person of no account. I am grateful for the depth and breadth of experience in my life that causes me to carefully consider Jesus's promise, "The last shall be first, and the first last" (Matthew 20:16). I am grateful to Jesus for being born in a barn, conversing with foreigners, touching the unclean, teaching female disciples, and offending the local religious and political powerbrokers. I am grateful to the coauthors of this book, who pursue discipleship with their minds and hearts, and to my coeditor, a true fellow traveler.

Kate Holbrook

Gardening is a place of reconciliation for me: the garden focuses me entirely on the present, time among all of the life and beauty uplifts my spirit, and the work process is a spiritual practice. One thing that practice has taught me is that no matter how much I study the soil, water, and light needs of a plant before making it a comfortable place in the ground, I can never fully predict whether it will thrive. The more years that I work on this plot of land, the better I get at guessing, but every time I introduce some life to new ground, I'm aware of the many limits to what I can control. Despite my efforts, the plant might die. But then there are those varieties that find all they need where they're planted. Sometimes they even spread and do so in surprising ways. Why, last summer, did the Rozanne geranium grow a new plant across the lawn from its colony, in the wet, shady, root-filled place where nothing else wants to live? An order beyond my comprehension is at work; this spring it returned and grows larger.

When it comes to human lives rather than those of plants, relationship with God is the system that can lead us to the place and conditions in which we can flower. Crucial to my experience and understanding of life is the knowledge that when we reach toward God's light, God will meet us where we are and offer us the personal conditions for our flourishing. Through all of the soil and light conditions I have known, privilege and struggle, belonging and ostracism, I am grateful for the companionship of The Church of Jesus Christ of Latter-day Saints. I am grateful for the relationship with heavenly beings that commitment to this tradition fosters more abundantly than any I have seen. This collection is written by women who have reached toward God's light and, in partnership with that light, done concrete good in the world. I am grateful for them and for my inimitable coeditor, whose own light burns so bright.

A note from the series editors: Kate Holbrook died as this book went to press in 2022. This book is a monument to the vision and faith of Kate and Melissa. God bless them for their grace, wisdom, and confidence to pursue "every needful thing."

SUBJECT INDEX

SCRIPTURE INDEX

Old Testament

New Testament

Book of Mormon

Doctrine and Covenants

Pearl of Great Price